T0281839

Thanks to:
The Wizard of New Zealand, Ciaran MacCoinneach,
Bevan Freeman, Terry Freeman, James Driver, Victor Jekic,
Rebecca Lennie, Vanessa Tansey, and Lucette Hogg

For their help and encouragement

PRAGMATIC MAGICAL THINKING

PRAGMATIC MAGICAL THINKING
Real Magic Explained

Ari Freeman

AEON

First published in 2023 by
Aeon Books

British Library Cataloguing in Publication Data

A C.I.P. for this book is available from the British Library

ISBN-13: 978-1-80152-066-9

Typeset by Medlar Publishing Solutions Pvt Ltd, India

www.aeonbooks.co.uk

CONTENTS

CHAPTER 1

Introduction

For those of us raised in the modern Western world the term "magical thinking" can raise eyebrows. Associations with madness, superstition, and woolly thinking have created a gulf between those subjects we feel free to talk about, and those which are "spiritual", "magical", or "occult".

This belies the fact that all cultures have a concept of magic. I would argue that magic has, in the past, been a human universal. I would also argue that in the present magic is *still* a human universal, only that in certain cultures, especially here in the West, we have forgotten how to openly talk about it.

Every one of us descends from people who believed in and engaged with magic; be it good luck charms, blessings, curses, invocations, communication with spirits, or in other forms.

In this book I will explain why magic can be a practical approach to achieving real world results. The tools I will use to do so come from science, philosophy, history, and anthropology, and ought to appease the intellectually rigorous, while still being accessible to the lay person. My aim is to allow you to access magic without having to leave your scepticism at the door.

I intend this book to serve as a bridge to allow people of different worldviews, subcultures, and ethnic backgrounds to speak openly with each other about magic in ways that are fruitful and encourage understanding.

For this reason, the various chapters of this book are written from different points of view, with different tones. The purpose is to explore the subject of magic from many vantage points in a rigorous way which, to my knowledge, has never been attempted before.

This book should also serve as an entry point for those who have never had any direct experience with magic, or a proper understanding of it, to cross into an intellectual territory where they can begin to try magic out for themselves.

It is for the sceptic who wishes to understand why people do magic, and why they engage in varieties of magical thinking.

It is also for the already practising magicians, spiritualists, diviners, witches, and wizards who wish to be able to explain what they do to their "nonmagical" friends and family without being written off or easily dismissed.

It is time for magic to escape the boundary of the "new age" section in the bookstore or the little witch shop on the corner and take its rightful place as a serious and mainstream subject of conversation and inquiry.

Arguably the last time that magic underwent a serious update in terms of explanation was with the Chaos Magicians of the late 1970s and '80s, who aimed to simplify occult practice, keeping only that which produces real world results. This was a very important but small movement compared to the great spiritual uprising of the nineteenth century, which produced world-famous magicians such as Helena Blavatsky, Dion Fortune, Aleister Crowley, Rudolf Steiner, and societies such as The Golden Dawn, Theosophy, Thelema and Gerald Gardiner's Wicca, to name but a few.

Now that we are in the twenty-first century, we find our whole world culture is changing direction in what will undoubtedly be seen in the future as the beginning of a new age. The nineteenth- and twentieth-century dreams of a utopian future based on technological progress have waned and a new shift in values towards a sustainable future is replacing it. Behind this is the concept of the "information age". Unbridled access to science, online courses, online videos, lectures, and a great uncovering of the past due to the digitisation of old books has, amongst other things, brought about a new twenty-first-century spiritual and magical uprising, the likes of which we haven't seen since the mid 1800s.

Because of all these factors, we are due a new reframing of magic. One that will be more useful to us in our current age. That is the final purpose of this book. An introduction to a new approach to magic that will better serve us in the twenty-first century, and which will not only allow us better communication between the aforementioned groups, but also with our own cultural past and the stories of our ancestors.

I hope that you enjoy it.

Ari

CHAPTER 2

On attention

The universe is mind-bogglingly filled with information. You might even be forgiven for calling it infinite.

Through our pursuit of science, we have learned a few known unknowns. We know that our senses are imperfect and that our brains are often preoccupied with filling in the blanks. Even worse, some of the things that we perceive as reality are not at all what they appear once we measure them. One visual example is the colour magenta. Humans see magenta as a single colour, yet the study of optics shows us that it is actually a combination of blue and red light. These are two frequency bands that are at opposite ends of the visible colour spectrum. This means that the colour magenta does not manifest as a single concept anywhere outside our own heads. It's an optical illusion.

In a similar way, the colour yellow can be sensed either as a result of a single yellow band in the light spectrum, or by a combination of green and red frequencies, the way it is delivered to us on a computer or TV screen. The weird thing is that we have no way of telling, from our eyesight alone, which yellows are a red and green mixture, and which are a single colour.

Our sense of hearing is similarly limited. We also know that we can only hear a band of vibrations, roughly between 20–20,000hz, as discernible pitch. Equivalent to ten musical octaves. Below 20hz, pitch blurs into rhythm, and we start to feel it more than hear it. Most humans cannot hear above 20,000hz, and that threshold gets lower as we grow older and deafer. Any sounds above that can only be measured for us by machines. The more one explores the limits of our perception, the more one finds that our experience of the world differs drastically from what can be measured scientifically. Because of these limitations, we must consider our perceptions of the world to be only a mere fraction of all that is really going on in reality.

When I was a child, I often enjoyed looking through a cardboard tube because of the way it narrowed my vision to a small circle. This peephole worldview can be thought of as a small scale version our human perception in relation to a wider reality. As organisms, we have limits to our senses and limited cognitive processing power to make sense of the information we receive. Because of this, the universe doesn't reveal itself to us as a unified thing that we experience all at once. Instead we are forced to comprehend it at many different levels of understanding, depending on what we are trying to achieve. Some of these conceptions contradict each other, which is less than convenient. Physics tells us that light is either a particle or a wave, depending on how you test it. A table in our living room could be a place for setting down a coffee cup, an obstacle to avoid in the dark, or an imaginary play-fort for a child. The possibilities of our interactions with the physical world are endless, and the meaning of an object changes to us with its use. Reductionism would have us try to discover the "real" state of the table by zooming into its smallest parts. Yet, according to physics, the physical objects that appear to us to be solid are actually mostly empty space, separated particles held together by force fields. Some of these forces attract and some repel.

These interacting fundamental forces are all that gives matter its solid, liquid, or gaseous properties. Consider for a moment that the only thing that stops your body from becoming part of the table when you lean against it is the repulsion of polarised electrons at its surface. Without this repulsion, the world would behave like a big soup with no boundaries, like an endless, featureless ocean. Though it is fun to ponder, and grants us certain powers over chemistry, physics, and engineering, this scientific materialism doesn't appear to have much in common with the ways in which we subjectively experience the world.

Rather than directly interacting with particles and atoms, we mostly perceive the world in terms of concepts and relationships. If you were to choose a new table for your living room, would you first conduct scientific tests on the chemicals that it's made of? It's probably more likely that you would select a new table based on practical and aesthetic concerns. Does the table match the rug? Does it have drawers for storage? What impression would it provide visitors? Does it look refined or rustic, cheap or classy?

Reality tunnels

Timothy Leary, the famous 1960s psychonaut and controversial counterculture professor, coined the term "reality tunnels" for our various individual experiences of what we think is going on. These reality tunnels are not only affected by our senses, but also by our culture, ideologies, and education.

To understand something, you first have to pay attention to it.

The sum total of our attention is limited. Advertisers and marketing psychologists discuss the precious attention of their customers as "mindshare". This "mindshare" is a valuable resource.

Without the attention of their customer, the ability for companies to sell their products or services disappears.

Our individual conceptions of reality are highly susceptible to suggestion by others. This is where we become prone to the effects of magic. These suggestions have a constant effect on us. Consider the Baader-Meinhof phenomenon, or as I like to call it, "Red Toyota Corolla syndrome".

Red Toyota Corolla syndrome

Imagine yourself as a car owner. You come into the possession of a red Toyota Corolla. A reasonably common type of automobile. Chances are high that as you drive around in your new car suddenly other red Toyota Corollas will pop magically into your attention. Were these red Toyota Corollas always there in the background? Or have they popped into existence when you started to pay attention to them? Sometimes this effect can feel so uncanny that it is as if the universe rearranged itself in order to send you a special message. When these "special messages" are acted upon, they often create domino effects. The way you start paying attention to one thing will cause a change in what you notice about another. Sometimes a very positive or very negative shift in attention can bring about a self-fulfilling prophecy. If you are afraid of getting into fights with people, often opportunities to fight will present themselves. If you look at strangers you meet as potential new friends, you will often find your circle of friends increasing. These phenomena, often maligned by sceptics as "cognitive bias" or "magical thinking", can produce genuine benefits for the observer.

What's your personal red Toyota Corolla?

In our modern culture, many people seem to use large parts of their intelligence to come up with reasons why they are screwed. I often wonder how much potential could be harnessed if people were to look for opportunities rather than restrictions. If you only look for problems, that is certainly what you will find. Likewise, if you only factor in the positive, then you will easily be capsized by chaos. The real power comes with casting a wide net for what you want and learning to dodge the shit. I call this luck, and I regard luck as an attitude rather than a condition or a force. Put simply, if you aren't getting what you want, try changing your belief system.

Now, take a moment to look around you. How many objects and things that you can observe started as an idea in someone's mind? Chances are high that unless you currently reside in the middle of the farthest jungle, much of what is around you has been designed by other human beings. Are ideas real? They are certainly capable of manifesting real tangible change in our environment if we act upon them. Even false ideas, such as hallucinations, can produce real change.

Imagine a weird fellow who sometimes hallucinates fairies that only he can see. Many people would dismiss his ability as a useless side effect of madness, and would consider him cured if these hallucinations disappeared.

Now let's imagine that this fairy seer is also a fine artist who can paint his hallucinations with great beauty. What if his art fascinates certain people enough that they buy his paintings and he earns a living?

Suddenly, what from one perspective was a madness starts to look more like an enviable talent. We all probably have our favourite eccentrics. People whose unique view influences our imaginative world. We might not always want such people to be running the show, but life would be dull without them.

Perhaps a curious and adventurous fan of our artist might themselves try to obtain the ability to hallucinate fairies. Perhaps over time a lineage of people could produce a tradition of fairy seers.

> We create the world that we perceive, not because there is no reality outside our heads, but because we select and edit the reality we see to conform to our beliefs about what sort of world we live in. The man who believes that the resources of the world are infinite, for example, or that if something is good for you then the more of it the better, will not be able to see his errors, because he will not look for evidence of them. For a man to change the basic beliefs that determine his perception—his epistemological premises—he must first become aware that reality is not necessarily as he believes it to be. Sometimes the dissonance between reality and false beliefs reaches a point when it becomes impossible to avoid the awareness that the world no longer makes sense. Only then is it possible for the mind to consider radically different ideas and perceptions. (Bateson, 1972)

A truly adventurous individual can explore various reality tunnels for the different advantages that they offer. What you believe in determines what you notice, and what you notice determines the opportunities you have to act. Some people have cottoned on to the idea of altering their reality tunnel in order to gain opportunities in the world. I would term this type of individual, a magician.

CHAPTER 3

A definition of magic for our times

The word "magic" means different things to different people. To many, it's commonly used as a slur.

Magic: *The futile belief in impossible things.*

This definition serves as little more than a roadblock preventing further thought or discussion, and is only useful to signal which team one is on.

There is another common definition for magic that splits the world unhelpfully into believers and non-believers:

Magic: *The use of paranormal forces to create change in the physical world.*

This is the type of magic that one sees depicted in fantasy novels and films. The fireball that flies forth from the mage's hand to assault some evil monster. As the term "paranormal" creates many issues, I will be avoiding it. It's hard enough for us to define "normal", let alone "paranormal".

For the purposes of this book, I will be evaluating magic based on its pragmatic use. Therefore, neither of the previous definitions will do.

Instead, I have a definition I have adapted from occultist Dion Fortune, who wrote:

> Magick is the art of causing changes in consciousness in conformity with the Will.

I like this definition, except for the spelling of the word magick. While this was once a popular alternative spelling in older forms of English, spelling magick with a K is now usually used as an attempt to differentiate occult magick from stage magic. This differentiation was recommended by the infamous magician Aleister Crowley (1875–1947), who was trying to update a conception of magic for his contemporary audience. For my purposes, I require no such distinction between stage

Dion Fortune, 1890–1946.

magic and occult magic. The term "occult" means "hidden", and occult societies usually revel in secret knowledge that is hidden from the uninitiated. In the past perhaps they hid to avoid persecution from a highly religious society, but I feel, for the most part, that this danger has past. In the twenty-first century we live in an age of information after all, and entire libraries of occult books that were once hidden from the public eye are now searchable to read or download from the internet.

I'm not interested in keeping knowledge hidden away so the K has to go. I also wish to directly compare, traditional magic, stage magic, social magic, occult magic, and other magical forms, and consider them as parts of one interrelated subject.

For these reasons and more to come, the definition of magic used here will be: *The manipulation of perception in accordance with the will.*

This definition allows me to relate various magical traditions with other concepts that I consider magical such as, advertising, performance art, oratory, music, acting, and many other related manipulations of perception. If by this stage one is still squeamish with the use of the word "magic", then feel free to cross out every instance of the word that appears in this book and replace it with one's own word, as long as the definition remains the same. Concepts must matter more than the words we use to label them, otherwise we can become mired by semantics.

Magical thinking

I am reclaiming the term "magical thinking". The pejorative use of this term throws the baby out with the bathwater. By "magical thinking", I wish to address unconventional and altered states of perception, and how they might cause real change in the world. Even false ideas can sometimes have useful consequences.

The clear issue with magical thinking is that anything goes. Where does one draw the line between what is real and what is mere wishful thinking? Every one of us with integrity should be willing to admit that sometimes we are fooled. Not all models of reality are correct. Not all ideologies deliver on their promises. Some people make an art out of fooling themselves, and develop an extraordinary level of denial. Others are prone, due to disorders, or special abilities of the mind, brain, or body, to experiencing things that other people can't. The famous neuroscientist Oliver Sacks describes some fascinating instances of this among his brain-damaged patients in his book, *The Man Who Mistook His Wife for a Hat* (1985):

For not only did Dr P increasingly fail to see faces, but he saw faces when there were no faces to see: genially, Magoo-like, when in the street he might pat the heads of water hydrants and parking meters, taking them to be the heads of children; he would amiably address carved knobs on furniture and be astounded when they did not reply. (Sacks, 1985)

Pragmatism

I believe that the philosophy of pragmatism, as put forth by the American philosopher William James, can help us anchor magical thinking in reality and restore magic to a useful concept.

> Pragmatism is an approach to philosophy which holds that the truth or meaning of a statement is to be measured by its practical consequences.
>
> (Bruce Kuklick, from his introduction to
> William James's book *Pragmatism* (1907))

If a method delivers discernible results, then we can consider it useful and add it to our bag of tricks. If a method, no matter how tantalising, fails over and over, then we must ditch it, no matter how painful it is to let go.

Anything goes, as long as we keep what works, and throw away what doesn't.

The good thing about pragmatism is that results can be acknowledged whether or not they fit into a current model of the way we think the world should be. Many people confuse models for reality, and ignore useful data because it doesn't fit what we previously believed. The map is not the territory. This bias is unfortunately common in the modern science establishment, which is discussed in Paul Feyerabend's firebrand of a book, *Against Method* (1975):

> The consistency condition which demands that new hypotheses agree with accepted theories is unreasonable because it preserves the older theory, and not the better theory. Hypotheses contradicting well-confirmed theories give us evidence that cannot be

obtained in any other way. Proliferation of theories is beneficial for science, while uniformity impairs its critical power.

What's real? Things that work. What isn't? Things that don't work. It's beautifully simple. This is the pragmatic worldview. When one is able to let go of one's preconceptions and instead embrace pragmatism, the world starts to look like a series of opportunities to be attempted and pitfalls to avoid. I like to call this approach "luck as an attitude". A much more self-empowering option than fate.

Scientific thinking vs. pragmatic magical thinking

Now I hear a few of you protest. Ari! Why use the word magic at all? The entire world is scientifically explainable! Even if we don't have the knowledge right now, one day progress will lead us to the answer! After all didn't Arthur C. Clarke say that: "Any sufficiently advanced technology is indistinguishable from magic" (1962).

That's fair enough up to a point, but no matter how much you esteem science, and despite its beauty and usefulness, you must understand that it has clear limitations.

Hard science is concerned with achieving the most concrete and objective answers available. It's utilitarian. As much as is possible, subjective, emotional, and aesthetic responses must be removed from scientific data.

On the other hand, magic is almost entirely concerned with the subjective. Especially those subjective experiences that can be recreated over and over in another person, or shared by many people at the same time. I like to call this communicative space between minds, "intersubjectivity". Intersubjectivity is the realm of shared experience. The very concept of usefulness that underpins the utilitarianism of science is itself subjective. Useful to whom? In magic, something needs only to be useful to the magician.

Science affirms scientific reality through the repetition of results. It's very hard to scientifically test rare occurrences. However, rare yet meaningful events stick out to human beings as being subjectively more noteworthy than common events. Stories usually prefer to deal with the extraordinary than the mundane. Rare events often make a disproportionately large personal impact on us. Whereas, during the writing of scientific papers, inconvenient rare events are often removed by statistical trickery. The manipulation of people's perception in accordance with the will of the writer. Magic!

Science also builds and relies on models to formulate predictions. There is a bias towards information that can fit best into an existing model. Information that is a complete anomaly has to be put aside from the model, even if it is totally correct. Gravity is an example. We don't currently know why it works. The science is still being cooked up. Thankfully gravity is hard to ignore, so we know it is going on even if we don't know what causes it. Now and then this pressure towards only including information that agrees with established models causes valuable results to be overlooked. This is less of a problem in magic, where results are to be noted, discussed, and used regardless of whether we currently have an explanation. In magic, you can use it now and explain it later. If something works then you can use it, even if it shouldn't work. Indeed the magic I find most interesting is the stuff that we think shouldn't work, but does anyway.

Two phenomena, once considered magic, that we now have scientific evidence for, are: hypnotism, and the placebo effect.

I find the placebo effect particularly interesting as, when understood properly, one realises that it has an effect not only on sugar pills, but all medicine. Scientific testing methods are always looking for ways to be as objective as possible. The placebo effect, however, acts on the patient's subjective experiences through suggestion. Because of this, it can be very difficult to separate the magical placebo effect on a patient from the chemical and physical effects of a drug or treatment.

People often think that patients must be lied to in order for placebos to be a factor, but studies now show that placebo still works in some scientific tests even when the patient knows they are getting a sham drug. If you are interested in this, look up the talks of Dr Ted J. Kaptchuk, one of the world's leading experts on placebo (Kaptchuk, 2014).

Though scientists may wish for a convenient neutral baseline by which to conduct their experiments, placebos are always altering that baseline. Placebo is an unremovable factor in all medicine. Studies show that the very clothes and manner of the doctor, the colour of a pill, the name given to a drug, can all measurably affect the healing of a patient. These results perfectly fit my definition of magic.

Hypnotism is another scientifically proven, yet mysterious form of magic. Once considered the height of pseudo-scientific delusional thinking, or maligned as "parapsychology", hypnotism, or the power of suggestion through trance, has been shown over and over to produce powerful psychological and physiological results. Especially in its application in altering or retrieving memories, and its effectiveness as pain relief, including during surgeries where a patient cannot use anaesthetics.

Musical perception also acts in accordance with my definition of magic, and is poorly understood by science. We know that human beings can synchronise their actions together in rhythm, a phenomenon called "entrainment". This sync allows us to shift awareness from our individuality towards a type of collective consciousness, or feeling of oneness with the crowd. For example, during a dance event or a rock concert.

We don't know why music has this psychological effect. Even weirder is why we can find music so emotionally affecting, despite it bearing no direct relation to other emotional causes. How can a piece of music sound "lonely" when normally loneliness is a condition caused by a lack of social interaction? There seems to be no logic as to why the pattern recognition of sound should have evolved to sync with our emotions. Despite this, most of us have at some point been brought to tears by a piece of music.

Music is very often used as part of a magical ritual to shift consciousness, be it the Catholic mass, a heavy metal concert, or an Olympic opening ceremony.

On the other side of the picture from scientists are the occultists. Somewhere in between are the stage magicians. Scientists aim for objective and certain measurable results. Stage magicians aim to trick their audience into perceiving that which should be impossible. Occultists aim to control their own, or their target's, perceptions towards fulfilling their wilful intentions. In my mind, occultists, who accept magic as part of reality, are too ready to remove themselves from the company of stage magicians. Stage magic makes no bones about being a trick. I think the stage magicians are right. Magic is trickery. If only we were to add what science tells us to what stage magic shows us, we would realise that almost all of our perception is a trick. A trick that we are stuck with. Therefore occult magic and stage magic are not so different as many will claim.

CHAPTER 4

Useful fictions

An idea whose theoretical untruth or incorrectness, and therewith its falsity, is admitted, is not for that reason practically valueless and useless; for such an idea, in spite of its theoretical nullity, may have great practical importance.
—Hans Vaihinger, from *The Philosophy of "As If"* (1911)

We live in an uncertain world, without a unifying model to understand it all by. Our perceptions are limited. Our memories, identities, and predictions of the future are intrinsically tied to and constrained by narrative. Because of these factors, humans are prone to useful fictions.

Useful fictions are those rules, ethics, and pieces of common sense that generally produce good results, despite not actually being true in any absolute sense. Most people deal with useful fictions every day.

One such beloved useful fiction that most of us can agree on is: "All people are created equal." It's clear to most of us that this simple statement is not literally or practically true. Clearly, some people are smarter than others, some are stronger than others, some are in ill health, some are gifted, some are handicapped.

So, the sentiment is something more like, "We all agree that giving people the benefit of the doubt leads to a more fair society than prejudice does."

While people are not literally all created equal, it would be a very dangerous thing indeed to put any one person or any single ideology in charge of deciding who is more deserving of rights and who is rightfully prejudiced. This sentiment goes hand and hand with "Do not judge a book by its cover." We must leave space for people to exceed our expectations, or we will miss out on what they can have to offer.

Another useful fiction that all of us seem to hold dear, is the line-marking down the middle of roads. While driving cars or riding bicycles and other road vehicles, we treat these markings as if they are sacred barriers which must almost never be crossed, and even then, very carefully. While there is nothing actuality stopping one from driving anywhere along a road, on the left, the right, or down the middle, we all prefer the idea that oncoming cars keep to their side and we keep to ours. Many people become quite disturbed when they see others disobey these rules. Our safety depends on this agreed "barrier", even though the barrier in question is merely a marking that affects our behaviour, and not a physical obstacle. The mid-line on a road is a mark of faith.

This concept might at first appear trivial. It is important when judging a belief system that might seem absurd, to look not only at whether it is true, but whether it produces useful results. Often a shared ritual, such as team building exercises, a wedding, an initiation such as a christening or bar mitzvah, establishes one's membership in an institution. These shared rituals build trust in the way that a promise or an oath does. When one notices how many of these oaths and beliefs are in action around us, one begins to feel how big a role they play in holding together the very structure of society. Without trust, cooperation is impossible.

Another all-powerful example of a useful fiction is money. Money in truth is a faith-based institution of "trust tokens" maintained through the shifting of numbers to establish what is owed, what is borrowed, and what is earned. Units of money behave like individual trust spells that all combine to form powerful economies which affect our very survival.

When people lose faith in their currency, these trust spells collapse, and that type of money can no longer be traded for goods and services.

This economic and magical downturn can actually be measured as it happens, with a denomination of money buying a dozen eggs one week, and half a dozen the next. During 1922 in the Weimar Republic, the highest denomination of currency was a 50,000 mark bill. By the very next year, the highest denomination was a 100,000,000,000,000 mark bill! Stories are told in Germany about East Germans starting fires with paper money because it was worth less than scrap paper. This is what a loss of faith can look like.

50 trillion mark bill from the Weimar Republic, 1923
("Billionen" in 1920s German).

On bank notes there are many little combined spells that add to the persuasive power of that bill as a trade token. There are "law spells" written on money such as "this note is legal tender for ...", spells of spiritual authority such as the United States' "In God We Trust", or the picture of the Queen on notes from the British Commonwealth (she being tied to God through the magical concept of the divine right of kings). What exactly is a twenty dollar bill? It's twenty trust tokens, whose exact worth is in constant negotiation by the force of people's desire to buy goods and services, verses their desire to acquire more trust tokens.

A further example can be found in the cardinal directions. On the compass, and accordingly on modern maps, the general consensus is that north should be pointed upwards and south downwards. Most of us alive today accept this without question, yet it took quite a lot of negotiation historically for this to become the norm. Some medieval European maps put the east upwards, because that was the location of the Holy Land in relation to Christian mapmakers. Likewise, there have been south-up maps, such as that printed by the Official Wizard of New Zealand. There is in fact no reason for any particular compass direction to be at the top, other than convention. The convention of north-up is partly due to the popularity of the "mercator projection" map of the world, which takes its name from the Flemish geographer and cartographer, Gerardus Mercator. Perhaps it made sense to him to put Europe near the top of the map, for the sake of a European audience whose eye would more easily locate them at the top of a page?

We don't often question these useful fictions, and they are often mistakenly taken to be "real".

Now that I have given some examples of established useful fictions that operate in our world, we may ask how far this concept stretches. How many concepts, commonly held as fact become flimsy under investigation?

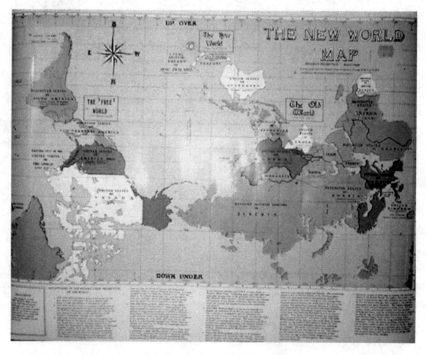

The Wizard of New Zealand's south-up map.

Hans Vaihinger, 1852–1933.

In his 1911 work *Die Philosophie des Als Ob* (The Philosophy of As If) the German philosopher Hans Vaihinger argued that human beings can never directly understand the underlying reality of the world. The best we can do is to construct systems of thought, metaphors, and other organising concepts, and then test their results. Atoms, protons, electrons, electro-magnetic waves, he argued, are in fact, useful fictions. They are not perfect units of reality. To Vaihinger, they are only concepts that we pretend exist in order to make observations. Many of these concepts, he pointed out, are not directly observed, but are merely very dependable assumptions based on data.

Since then, matters have only grown worse for anyone hoping to find certainty in physics. Atoms, an ancient Greek concept of the irreducible, are now known to be reducible. The parts of atoms, protons, electrons, and neutrons, are themselves reducible to quarks, which cannot themselves be directly measured, only deduced by mathematical models. At this point, our once certain physical world melts into spectres of probability. A short introductory lesson on quantum physics is all that is necessary to blow apart one's world of certainty.

Some of you may be departing or making excuses of headaches at this point. However, for those of you brave enough to face the underlying chaos below our paper-thin sheet of fictional certainty, I recommend this lecture by scientist Allen Buskirk (2010) explaining how useful fictions are very much an unavoidable part of scientific investigation:

A very common metaphor that scientists use, in explaining the stability of the natural world, is the atom, and this is the idea that there are stable, fundamental, indivisible particles, and because they never change, we can use them to explain why things stay the same over time, and because we can arrange them in different ways, we can explain how this does change over time. So this is a neat philosophical answer to some problems that bothered ancient Greek thinkers ... Atoms are a nice way of explaining what is going on, but we are nowhere near seeing them, or really characterising them ...

The efficacy of a useful fiction should always be measured by its results. That is, just because an idea is imaginary, doesn't mean that its effects aren't real. A pragmatic magician should always be looking for these results. The ways in which you frame the world determine the ways in which you can move and interact within that world.

If someone's stated beliefs seem strange at first, it is right to look for the practical outcomes of their beliefs before writing them off. Useful fictions are inescapable. We all rely on them. They also grant us a magical power. If you don't like the world you have, try reframing it. With enough creativity, skill, and confidence, you might just end up with a better world!

CHAPTER 5

A pragmatist's approach to scepticism

In my attempts to be a good sceptic, I've noticed a trend. Many people proudly identify as sceptics, but most of these people only ever engage sceptical methods in order debunk other people's claims.

I find this to be lopsided. A bias to always uphold the status quo. Somewhat ironically, these same people also often remark on the "wrong-headed" status quo ideas of the past. What's more, they frequently hero worship those historical intellectuals who were brave enough to say something different which we now hold to be true. If one is truly interested in the truth of a claim, then one should be able to entertain the idea that the claim could be true before challenging it. Despite the sceptic's appeal to rationality, frequently their initial aversion to a claim is emotional. Rationality is then employed only after their minds have already been made up to try to affirm these suspicions.

The studies of the famous neuroscientist, Antonio Damasio, have shown that people who have a type of brain damage that leaves them unable to process emotions, are also left unable to form any quick decisions at all! Such people can only rationalise. Ask such a subject if they would like milk in their coffee, and they are left for a long time trying to determine the pros and cons of either option. If we only had rationality with which to make decisions, then almost nothing would get done.

It is unlikely that most animals rationalise to the extent of a human being. Yet animals can achieve the most amazing feats of problem solving and achievement. Consider, for instance, the complexity of a beaver dam, or a termite mound, or the intelligence of crows.[1] There is an amazing amount of problem solving in these animal feats.

One of the strangest displays of problem solving in non-humans is the Japanese experiments by Atsushi Tero from Hokkaido University, on the maze-solving capabilities of slime moulds (Tero et al., 2010). Slime moulds are, at least in appearance, a living goop, seemingly without mind or organs.

Place a slime mould in the centre of a maze, and place a small amount of oats at the exit, and after a while you will find that it has solved the maze! The slime mould achieves this by sending extensions out in every direction and, upon finding the food, the connecting tendril is strengthened and the others die off, leaving the perfect solution to the maze.

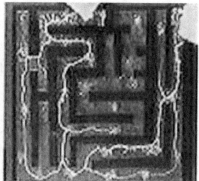

Slime mould in a maze.

The experiment was further extended by creating a map of Tokyo with subway stations represented by oats, and having the slime mould decide on the connections. The result was that the slime mould created a subway plan that efficiently navigated around obstacles. Its efforts compared favourably to what is possible by human engineers. I take from this, that rationality is merely one of our many possible modes of problem solving. Other lifeforms and organising structures are constantly

---

[1] recommend a documentary called *A Murder of Crows* (Fleming, Su10).

solving problems all around us, and many of them do it without brains. Rationality is great for humans explaining things to other humans, but even among humans it is only something we engage in with effort.

When a sceptic engages with magic, they should not initially expect to find rational explanations. A magician might not be concerned with being rational at all, as long as they can achieve what they desire. Instead, the first thing a sceptic should look for is the effect of the magic. If this effect is repeatable, as good magic ought to be, then a rational explanation can be sought after the fact. A magician who produces repeatable results will often be able to do so without being able to truly explain how the magic works themselves. Too often, sceptics dismiss interesting results simply because a magician can't rationalise their methods.

I'd like to suggest that if the goal is really to determine what is real and what isn't, then there are a number of crucial steps to being a good sceptic:

Seek to understand what is being claimed

It's very important to establish how people use their words, and to conduct any experiment based on what they mean, not on what you think they mean.

People who have seen a ghost, for instance, don't necessarily mean anything more than that they have had an extremely strong experience of a presence, perhaps one that they have seen. They don't necessarily mean that a ghost is real in the same way a particular person is real. If you are expecting to find a ghost in the way that you might locate somebody in the flesh, then your search is quite likely to come up empty. If such a person claims that the ghost is real, then often what they mean by "real" is that they have had a strongly convincing subjective experience. If many people have seen a ghost, then one ought not to dismiss the experience just because nobody was able to shake the ghost's hand.

If you interpret the individual's claim to mean that they had the experience of a ghost, then you can look for other ghost experiences. It's almost certain that you will find something to work with. Ghost experiences can be studied even if ghosts can't.

Different people have very different ideas about what is real. To a born-again Christian, a vision of Jesus is one of the most real things in their life. They might well measure reality based on their strong emotional experience, and an overwhelming sense of meaning. Such people may be ready to concede that seeing Jesus was not the same kind of real as leaning on a table, or shaking hands with somebody. Likewise, to some hardliners such as the famous cognitive scientist, Daniel Dennett (2008), their own consciousness is not real. Dennett has claimed that both consciousness and free will are illusions caused by underlying deterministic brain function. At which point one wonders if Daniel Dennett hasn't "poofed" all his agency out of existence. If everything he believes and says is the result of a deterministic automation, then why should we listen to him?

Seek to learn what the claimant is experiencing

Once you have a fair idea about what they mean, then it seems to me that the bravest and most honest thing you can do in determining the truth of a claim is to attempt to have the experience yourself. This is something I suspect many self- identifying sceptics will hate.

Can you try to copy the stimulus that caused the ghost experience? Can you spend a night in the same haunted building? To do this authentically might require letting go temporarily of preconceptions, prejudices, and maybe even strongly held beliefs.

If one was to be sceptical about the religious practice of speaking in tongues, it might mean spending a week at an evangelical church attempting to speak in tongues, before one has an authentic Holy Spirit experience on a par with those particular Christians. The effort one puts in counts. The sceptical testing of the experience can only happen once one knows what the experience is. Often the best way to start is to try to have the experience yourself.

In order not to completely flip over to cloud cuckoo land, I recommend setting a time period beforehand. If necessary, set on a calendar how long you will spend trying to gain the authentic experience. How long you will wear the believer's hat? When the due date arrives, if you have gained an insight into the claimant's inner experience, only then should you try to take it apart.

Apply regular sceptic techniques of analysis to what you have learned

Only now that you understand what it is you are testing for, can you expect to be able to test it without misunderstanding the claimant.

In debates there is often talk of logical fallacies. These are indeed a very good thing to study if one wishes to navigate truth claims. But if one wishes to really get to the bottom of something, then there's no point in looking for logical fallacies until one has applied what is often referred to as the "principle of charity".

The principle of charity explains that if one is serious about a debate that leads towards a constructive resolution, then one should first help the claimant articulate their argument. You should work together to understand exactly what it is they are trying to explain. A good technique is to repeat back to them what you think it is they mean, and then have them correct you until you both agree. Bret Weinstein, a prominent evolutionary biologist and internet commentator, has come up with his own popular term for this: steel-manning. That is, the opposite of the strawman fallacy. The "strawman" is where one redefines an opponent's argument and then attacks that new definition, rather than their actual claim. Straw-manning can be a good technique for propaganda, but not for establishing the truth.

Play with the experience

Let's say you have now had your own genuine ghost experience that is comparable to that of the claimant. If possible, discuss it with them to make sure you both agree that the experience counts. Then, and only then, should you try to find limits to the experiment.

Can you have the same experience summoning Elvis or Santa Claus?

Can you induce the same religious emotions that a Christian has during speaking in tongues, towards Mickey Mouse rather than Jesus?

Clearly, these experiments should be conducted away from judgement, lest one be crucified for blasphemy or otherwise cause upset. This step is, however, very important for understanding what is actually going on, so bravery is required here. At this step it is reasonable to be irreverent in one's approach. Only through manipulating the experiment in various ways can we expect to learn which parts produce the experience and which don't. Some, after all, claim to be moved by the spirit of Elvis in the same way that Christians can be moved by the spirit of Jesus.

At what point does the experience become something else?

I have tried these steps myself when challenged by a magician friend, Ciaran MacCoinneach, to try some hands-on magic. Ciaran is an

Some of the Major Arcana from the Rider-Waite tarot deck.

experienced fortune teller, specialising in palm reading, tarot and I Ching. For a long time, Ciaran and I would drive out to bars and he would read palms or give tarot readings to strangers we would meet, while I would observe. Sometimes, ten people in an evening would have their fortune read by Ciaran. I measured his success by establishing if the person had had a genuine uncanny experience and if he knew more about them than should be possible.

I have had many readings from Ciaran myself, where I tried to induce different outcomes, by asking different sorts of questions and by being forthcoming or withholding information from him. He was one of the first magicians I met who delivered interesting results.

Finally, he suggested that if I was to learn anything more I should learn fortune-telling myself. I took this challenge by learning tarot divination with the popular Rider-Waite-Smith deck. I used his explanations, as well as tarot literature and internet resources to write myself a tarot-reading manual. We then discussed the manual and improved it over time until we were both happy with it.

I started reading for friends, acquaintances, and strangers at parties. Something which I still enjoy doing. After practice with Ciaran's guidance, I have always seemed to deliver results even when the querent is a devoted sceptic.

I have since exchanged readings with many other fortune-tellers, some of whom have been excellent and some of whom, as one might expect, have been less than successful.

Upon reaching the level where I started to induce the same uncanny experience in the querent as Ciaran does, I then started to play with the limits of the tarot.

In this I discovered some interesting things about my tarot readings:

- The tarot can function very well as a counselling technique. The querent usually goes away with a strong feeling of having been taken seriously and listened to, as well as feeling like they have more clarification and often even a new approach to a life problem they were previously confused about.
- The tarot can provide a very plausible, useful narrative for what is going on emotionally in someone's life, especially if it's something they have previously had difficulty in articulating.
- The readings work well regardless of whether the querent is giving feedback during the reading or not.
- The tarot, disappointingly, does not reliably predict sports results, or winning lottery numbers.
- The tarot, with effort, can predict the interactions between characters in a movie or TV show that I am watching for the first time. It helps one to be aware of major plot points and character motivations, and very often before they are fully revealed in the show.

One time at a party I had been doing some readings, when a friend of a friend who I didn't know very well asked: "Can I do a bullshit reading with the cards just for fun?" He was the jokester type, and I later found out, a comedian, but I enjoyed his challenge and decided to raise the stakes.

"Sure you can, but wouldn't it be more interesting if you used the manual I made here and tried your best to do a good reading?"

He took me up on the challenge and did a reading for his friend. Neither he nor his friend had any previous experience with the tarot, and he himself expected it to be bunkum, so they were both very surprised and enthusiastic when the reading worked very well. Something about the rules of tarot as a game can work, even when the participants don't believe in it. To me, magic that doesn't rely on belief is the most interesting kind.

Another time at a different party, I did a reading for a self-proclaimed "rationalist materialist". Again, he went in with all bullshit detectors firing, eager to trip me up. By the end he was literally pacing back and forth muttering, "This shouldn't be happening," unable to decide if he was spooked or exhilarated.

My current theory on how the tarot works is that it is a narrative game. The Rider-Waite cards are specific enough to build solid and singular storylines, yet they are just general enough that they can be applied to any situation, as long as the reader is creative enough. This is why, once he was given the explanations of the individual cards, the quick-witted comedian was able to give a good reading. Tarot doesn't very often give black and white or yes or no answers. This is why something as specific as a sports result or lotto numbers won't work.

Despite my efforts to rationalise it, there is also a genuine feeling of "tuning in" that one experiences as a fortune-teller. This feeling helps one tap into emotional and intuitive types of decision making. As a fairly rational type thinker, my fortune-telling experiments have given me a glimpse of the inner world of the intuitive type of person. If I had remained critical of this intuitive feeling throughout the experimentation, then I wouldn't have gained a personal understanding of it. I think being open to this feeling is part of what makes the tarot reading work, even if there were nothing "psychic" about it. It could be as little as tapping into the right state of imagination to bring the story out of the cards. A type of flow-state. There's something similar going on when I improvise music. Very quick decisions must be made. It's less important that one decision be more "correct" than another, and more important that the decisions are made quickly enough not to interrupt the flow of the musical performance, or in the case of the tarot, the narrative performance.

Because intuitive decision making is hard to pin down, there really is an uncanny feeling that goes along with fortune-telling. I sometimes get an inspiration that feels like it's come out of the ether. I'm certain this is the same type of experience that people who engage with "psychic phe-nomena" are describing. For now, I'm quite happy to put this into the "I don't know" basket, though I hope to have an explanation one day.

If we were to combine all that I have so far discussed in previous chapters into a practice, I would call this practice "pragmatic magical thinking".

In further chapters, I will explain this approach in higher detail, and explore some of the reasons why magic frequently works, and the different kinds of magic available to us.

CHAPTER 6

Memory, narrative, and identity

You are a story you tell yourself about yourself.

—Unknown

In this chapter, I will discuss how the neurological structure of human memory causes us to create narratives. These narratives produce our past, our roles, and, by extension, our identities. Pragmatic magical thinking is a useful toolkit for becoming aware of these narratives, and playing with them in order to produce real world effects. Previously I have explained how our attention radically affects our opportunities and ability to avoid pitfalls. In this chapter, I will discuss how our mental framing also affects the way the world presents itself to us, and therefore affects what we can and can't get away with.

How memory works

In the modern world, it's common to compare our brains to hard drives that store memories. It is as if one day we might be able to reach inside a brain and be able to download everything that makes up that person. This tantalising, yet scary idea has been explored in science fiction, such as the TV show *Red Dwarf*, or the classic anime *Ghost in the Machine*.

Despite first appearances, a closer look into the science of memory shows that things aren't that simple, and such fantasies are a long way off. Memory storage in the human brain is not as similar to computer data as some might hope.

Human brains store memories in an incomplete fashion. Current neuroscience suggests that if one was capable of reading the information that is stored in the brain, one wouldn't find anything like a model of the person's experiences. Instead, we store only the amount necessary in order to reconstruct a memory when triggered by an outside stimulus or state of mind.

What's more, memories are not "things". They are processes. A group of neurons can contain multiple memories.

When one has an experience, a group of neurons will fire in a particular pattern. When one remembers the experience, the neurons will fire in a strikingly similar pattern, and the moment can be re-experienced. We are constantly walking around experiencing and re-experiencing things. If magic is the manipulation of perception in accordance with the will, as I have described earlier, then our memory creates a fertile ground for magic.

Many memories only come back to us when they receive the appropriate stimulus. Otherwise these types of memories can remain "locked" away as if we have lost the keys to the filing cabinet. In psychology, memories that require this extra stimulus are called context-dependent memories and state-dependent memories. In these cases, the conditions of the environment, or the state of mind that were present during the learning process also need to be present in order for us to retrieve the memory.

A common example of a context-dependent memory is when we leave a room to get something done, and immediately forget what it is that we wanted to do. Only returning to the room seems to restore the forgotten memory. It's as if the thought was left behind in that space. The only way to retrieve it seems to be to go back to the room where the memory "is" and collect it again. It is my strong suspicion that what is really happening is that there is some external trigger in the room that caused us to have the thought in the first place. The trigger will usually be something we sensed in the environment. However, we only experience the thought the trigger produces, and don't always notice the trigger itself. Magicians have exploited this phenomenon using "memory theatres" (aka "method of loci"). These are imagined environments that are created to hold the keys to unlock many memories. This type of technique can push the normally forgetful human mind beyond its normal limitations and enable practitioners to retain and recall huge lists of terms. This is quite an ancient method that dates back at least as far as Cicero's *De Oratore*, an ancient Roman dialogue from 55 BCE.

This very phenomenon of context-dependent memory can be used by stage mentalists, such as the famed Derren Brown (2007), to manipulate a volunteer from the audience to uttering a preselected phrase, or drawing a predetermined picture, preordained by the magician. The victim of the trick believes that they are coming up with a random phrase or picture, but they have been psychologically conditioned, by unconscious memory triggers, to recall an exact idea that was chosen by the mentalist.

This is not an easy task to pull off, and requires a scripted set-up, as well as visual and verbal cues that play on the senses. It works so well, because most of us believe that the ideas that we have always come from our own minds. Frequently, however, they don't. We are just unconscious of the external source, influence, or trigger. Carl Jung, the pioneering psychoanalyst and magician, said *"You don't have ideas, ideas have you."*

This is the same underlying principle behind subliminal advertising. A sign might be recognised unconsciously. As a result, by psychological conditioning, the target will remember the experience of, say, drinking a Coke, and desire one. They will remember the sensation, but not always recall seeing the sign that triggered it. Afterwards, they will tell themselves that they made a decision to purchase a Coke of their own free will. For our purposes, I consider this effect real magic.

> Studies suggest that characteristics of the environment are encoded as part of the memory trace, and can be used to enhance retrieval of the other information in the trace. (Mastin, 2010)

The most famous study of context-dependent memory is the "scuba diver experiment" (Godden & Badderley, 1975). Divers were asked to remember a list of terms both above water and underwater. When asked to remember the information, the divers remembered best when they were asked in the same environment that they memorised the list in. Again, it's as if the memories were left in the location.

This can be problematic for those who need to practise for a performance or an exam, as there is no way to practise in the exam room itself. One way around this is to try to practise in more than one location, so that the memory becomes "detached" from the scenery and is more easily retrieved under pressure.

As a professional musician and guitar teacher, I have noticed that I often have to pick up a guitar in order to remember a song. My students have often mentioned this as well. It can feel as if the memory is "in the guitar", because the interaction with the guitar offers the stimulus to bring forth the memory.

For non-musician music lovers, a similar phenomenon can be experienced by trying to remember the lyrics of a favourite song. Often the entire song must be sung through in order to retrieve the lyrics that are, for example, in the third verse. I remember as a child trying to sort items in alphabetical order, and having to sing the alphabet song from the beginning every time, in order to remember where a particular letter was placed. At the time, I felt perplexed by the inefficiency of my own memory.

You can work this type of magic yourself. Try choosing a place that you frequent, such as a landmark somewhere along your daily travels. Purposefully assign a memory to that particular landmark. For instance, a favourite tree might be assigned to a positive childhood memory. You can use this mind-hack to "landmark" important reminders in places where they will be relevant. Maybe a pot plant just outside your house will store a trigger to check your pockets for your phone, so that you don't leave it behind. Start playfully. Try it on a willing friend or family member.

Similarly to context-dependent memory, state-dependent memories happen when a state of mind, such as a mood, is encoded with a memory, and that state is required for recall. Being angry makes it more likely that you will remember other times you were angry. Being sad makes it more likely that you will remember other times you were sad. This can have an impact on whether these states of mind lead to habits. It also might be why emotional states of mind can create a kind of momentum that can be hard to shift. Once angry, it takes some effort to come back down to calmness, perhaps in part because of the flood of angry memories. If you often feel the world is plotting against you, then you might have formed such a state-dependent "thought habit". Being aware of this phenomenon might be the first point of leverage to shift the unwelcome habit.

A person in a gloomy mood is more likely to recall gloomy information, a person in a happy mood is more likely to remember cheerful information. Patients with clinical depression have been found to recall more negatively focused information than non-depressed controls. (Goddard, 2012)

Studies have also been done with stress hormones such as epinephrine, showing that particular memories can also be attached to the hormonal state:

> Extensive evidence suggests that stress hormones such as epinephrine play a critical role in consolidating new memories and this is why stressful memories are recalled vividly. Studies by Gold and van Buskirk provided initial evidence for this relationship when they showed that injections of epinephrine into subjects following a training period resulted in greater long-term retention of task related memories. This study also provided evidence that the level of epinephrine injected was related to the level of retention suggesting that the level of stress or emotionality of the memory plays a role on the level of retention. (McGaugh & Roozendaal, 2012)

While changing one's emotional habits is certainly no walk in the park, understanding how state-dependent memory can create a kind of emotional momentum gives us an angle of control we might not have had before. If it's something you want to try, I recommend starting in a frivolous fashion rather than on something too serious. Perhaps a morning coffee, and the associated caffeine rush can be wilfully attached to a reminder to let go of yesterday's stress and focus on starting a new day with a clean slate.

For these reasons and more, I don't believe it is exactly accurate to say that memory is entirely in the brain. I think it is clear that memory is an interaction with the environment. This environment includes the human body, the places the body inhabits, as well as communication and social interaction with other people.

When we write a shopping list, we are externalising our memory into the environment. The books, movies, songs, and other media that we interact with are also our memory triggers, and are as necessary for what is expected of us in the world as that which is contained within our skulls.

Just as bees function as a hive as well as individually, our externalised memory functions like an extension of our individual brains.

Our memory has evolved to work with these external stores and reminders. If one was to take a human away from all these triggers, it would result in a lessening of their self. One not-so-pleasant way to look into this is with research accounts of prisoners held in solitary confinement: dark lonely rooms that cause sensory deprivation. Not only does the mental health of these subjects deteriorate rapidly, but their brain starts to invent triggers to compensate, which can result in the hallucinations sometimes referred to as "prisoner's cinema". This is usually described as a series of dancing lights, or "phosphenes", that appear in front of the eyes out of the darkness, generated by the observer's own visual cortex, but it can also progress into full hallucinations.

A safer and more enjoyable way to try this is with a sensory deprivation tank. Friends who have tried this have reported to me very odd, and sometimes psychedelic, experiences.

The power of narrative

In Merlin McDonald's fantastic book *A Mind So Rare* (2002), he explains that our memories of experiences are laid out in small chunks, each of which never exceeds about fifteen seconds of actual time. Ponder that! All of your memory of past events is like many momentary stepping stones. We join these remembered moments together like a join-the-dots puzzle to create narratives which we think of as our past. This process requires creativity, and the way we frame and connect these moments is alterable after the fact.

This momentary "stepping-stone" memory also explains why memories can change over time. Often future experiences can radically reconfigure a past memory. Therefore, our remembered past is not as fully "fixed" as we might expect. For example, one might have a childhood memory in which Santa Claus visited the family home one Christmas. Later, the memory might be reconfigured when one realises that a particular uncle was missing from the room, only to reappear later, after Santa had left. The narrative can change the context of the memory. New stories can rewrite the past!

The narratives we create to join these gaps inform our identity. The ego plays a part. We often reconfigure the past in order to point out what a fine fellow we are, or to support our cognitive biases.

History, on a much grander scale, is also a great joining of the dots. Usually, the historian looks at available evidence in order to line up events in accordance with their pet narrative. An entertaining and exaggerated example of this can be seen with conspiracy theories, such as moon landing hoaxers, or "chemtrail" enthusiasts. The joining of the dots can be stretched and shaped to absurd levels. All history suffers to some degree from this uncertainty, and conspiracy theories are only an extreme example, not the exception.

The power of roles

A collection of personal narratives, supported by an individual's past, and their projected future, can be generalised into a role. A role is a subpersonality within an individual with its own drives, values, and even its own beliefs (which we will explore in the next chapter). Roles are acted out in the world and interact with other roles. These roles allow us to frame the interactions we have with other people, so that we can more easily understand each other's behaviour, what is expected of us, and make better predictions as to how a person will behave. Without these roles, we wouldn't be able to track such relationships as friend or foe, buyer and seller, or parent and child. Each of us has multiple roles, and these various roles inform what we can get done in the world.

For example, a particular woman might spend some of her time in the role of a mother, and another part in the role of a saleswoman. As a mother, the nurturing protection of her children might seem quite contradictory to the salesperson's view of people as opportunities to earn commission. In the mother role, the children ought to be encouraged into their independent selfhood. In the sales role, other people must often be reduced to an opportunity to score sales.

It is normal for human beings to have different roles that have contradictory values. The term "cognitive dissonance" has been used to describe two or more sets of values that are at odds with each other, causing stress in the individual. I would like to propose that most of the time we live in "cognitive harmony". That is, we are able to compartmentalise our values in such a way that they don't conflict, even if they contradict. A nurse may behave as a nurse whenever they wear their uniform and, in that role, they must care for their patients. Their uniform will necessitate a certain code of conduct, and others will have certain expectations of anybody wearing that uniform. Later, the nurse might come home, change into black clothes, go to a band practice, and become a death metal singer who sings enthusiastically about violence. The ritual of shedding one costume for another keeps one role from interfering with the other.

If you have cognitive dissonance between the values expressed by one role and another, try forming a ritual to compartmentalise each role. Perhaps you can treat the front door of your house as a magical portal which sheds you of your job stress as soon as you walk through it. Maybe have a container next to your front door in which to place your work phone, so that you can leave the work role behind and embrace the home keeper's role. My friend, Alice Flett, once told me a story about a time when she was working with a difficult boss. Rather than letting her worries pollute her free time, she would meditate on the image of putting her boss in an imaginary chest and then throwing away the key!

Rituals such as graduation ceremonies, christenings, initiations, the wearing of badges or name tags, or the carrying of a clipboard, can have a big effect not only on a person's own mindset, but also in the way they are treated by other people. Sometimes, such as is the case with a police officer's uniform, these rituals can be legalised. That is, a uniformed cop has certain legal responsibilities to uphold that may be shed when the uniform is taken off. In other cases, the rules are unwritten but the effects are just as real. In future chapters, I will explore the magical implications of this line of thinking in much more depth.

Archetypes, the mythological role

Many roles have cross-cultural universality. The psychoanalyst and magician Carl Gustav Jung and his followers termed these roles "archetypes". A good introduction to these archetypes can be found in Joseph Campbell's TV series, *The Power of Myth* and book of the same title (Campbell & Moyers, 1988), or in his famous book, *The Hero with 1000 Faces* (1949).

Archetypes, such as the wise man, the hero, the villain, the trickster, the maiden, the mother, or the warrior, pop up again and again in our stories. They are patterns of meaning that have specific tasks or values. Yet they are still general enough that we can find them in universal examples throughout media, from journalism to fiction and to our own behavioural patterns. This is similar to the "Red Toyota Corolla" syndrome I have described earlier. As ethologists point out, even animals can express archetypes.

Archetypes can be symbolic, biological, and social. They underlie the things people find important. So any story, including a news report, is necessarily going to draw from archetypes. They can be thought of as an ordering structure for roles.

Depending on one's chosen framework, archetypes can range from a few to numerous.

As with most creative thinking, it's not so important whose structure we adopt, as what we do with that structure and the results it produces.

Archetypes can be considered instinctual behaviours that we act out. Typical human experiences that may shape our lives consciously or unconsciously. Feeling like you are on a crusade is identification with the hero archetype. Feeling ostracised is identification with the outsider archetype. We can read about these types of characters and then use them to frame our own behaviour. Such is the many layered nature of the human condition.

For the sake of a very brief introduction, here are a few of the more central archetypes that Carl Jung discussed:

- **The Self:** The central archetype which structures our identity. We project the self onto people and the characters we want to be like through identification, empathy, and solidarity. The self is the inner part of you that observes your interactions.
- **The Shadow:** Anything as yet unrealised by consciousness, as well as all the parts of ourselves we don't like to look at. The shadow often reveals itself through the imagined intentions we project onto others. Carl Jung maintained that discovering our shadow and consolidating it into the self is necessary for healing and progressing towards our full potential.
- **The Persona:** Our social mask. It can be explored by asking ourselves what we feel is expected of us, and how that governs our behaviour. The persona is also governed partly by our desire to court those who hold power. Carl Jung proposed that problems happen when we over-identify with one persona, rather than many. An overly rigid persona can cause a disconnection with our inner self. He considered the persona and the shadow to be opposites in that the persona is what we look at, and the shadow is what we avoid looking at.

- **Anima/Animus:** The anima is the feminine aspect in men, and the animus is the masculine aspect in women. The gender discussed here is traditional, and it might be easier to understand in a modern context to say that the anima is the reactive nature of an individual (like how an audience reacts to a performer), and the animus is the proactive nature of an individual. Carl Jung proposed that both the anima and the animus have a big effect on our close relationships, especially those that involve one individual dominating another. This domination need not necessarily be negative, such as a mother protecting a child. The recognition of this kind of interaction can be the beginning of addressing any interpersonal issues. He believed that owning one's anima/animus can help stabilise the individual emotionally.

My views about the "archaic remnants", which I call "archetypes" or "primordial images," have been constantly criticized by people who lack sufficient knowledge of the psychology of dreams and of mythology. The term "archetype" is often misunderstood as meaning certain definite mythological images or motifs, but these are nothing more than conscious representations. Such variable representations cannot be inherited. The archetype is a tendency to form such representations of a motif—representations that can vary a great deal in detail without losing their basic pattern. (Carl Jung, 1964)

The power of reframing

One way that narrative can be harnessed purposefully to help us is through the psychological concept of "reframing". Narrative therapist Stephen Madigan (2009) says "we speak ourselves into meaning".

Narrative therapy works from the standpoint that our inner narratives can be negotiated and changed in order to improve mental health. Narratives that are low in meaning, or full of negative emotion, can harm an individual, and should be exchanged, if possible, for narratives that are high in positive meaning. I believe that this effect is part of what is going on in many forms of divination, such as the tarot that I discussed in the previous chapter, especially if the goal is to counsel the querent.

In narrative therapy, one seeks to separate a problem from one's identity. Instead of telling yourself "I am a worrier," you would externalise the problem as a separate will: "The worry voice is trying to sabotage the situation."

Most counselling approaches utilise narrative in one way or another. A friend of mine, James Driver, who is a practising psychotherapist, has outlined some examples in our conversations:

> For example, if we get anxious in social situations we might—consciously or unconsciously—have a narrative that this anxiety is protecting us from rejection.
>
> The anxiety makes us nervous, which causes us to hold back from expressing ourselves. As a result we prevent anyone from judging or criticising us. However if we look at this narrative more closely, we see something different. Holding back results in feeling rejected, alone, feeling not good enough, feeling disliked. The anxiety might appear to be protecting us, but instead creates this negative outcome. In a sense, it claims credit for something it is not actually doing. If we can reframe this narrative, by recognising that the anxiety is not helping us, then we have more freedom to act. Rather than seeing the anxiety as a warning of potential rejection, we can instead see it positively as the possibility of being accepted.
>
> This reframing of narratives can occur in a range of ways. One example would be a reframing of causality, telling a different story about why something happened. For example, perhaps we made a mistake at work and our boss yelled at us about it. We could easily fall into a narrative like: "My boss yelled at me because I'm no good at my job, I always screw up, I'm hopeless."
>
> This is a story where a problem happened because of who we are. If we can view this from a different perspective, we can create a more realistic and healthier narrative such as: "My boss yelled at me because she was frustrated about that particular mistake, but in general I do my job well and I have had good feedback at other times."
>
> This is creating a different story for the cause—in this case, this happened because of what I did, but not who I am.
>
> Another way would be to say: "This happened because my boss was having a bad day, perhaps the mistake was actually inconsequential." This example excludes both our identity and our actions.
>
> We might believe that the purpose of our anxiety is to warn us of risk of rejection—but on closer examination, we might discover

that the purpose in reality is to ensure that we keep feeling the way we always felt—perhaps when we were belittled or dismissed as a child. It serves to maintain that which feels familiar and "normal" to us.[2]

As we can see, narrative and roles are core to human memory and identity, and, as such, techniques such as reframing can have an enormous power to redirect us. A pragmatic magician should look to narrative as one of the primary tools underpinning magic. Narrative has the power to radically alter the past and future, to widen our ability to see opportunities to fulfil our will and to protect ourselves from obstacles, dangers, and setbacks. The stories we tell ourselves help determine the way we are treated by other people, the way we feel about ourselves, and therefore the ways we can act in the world.

---

[2] (Driver, James. Registered Psychotherapist. Interviewed by Ari Freeman, 12 December, 2019).

CHAPTER 7

Believing different things
on different days

Everything that gets into your brain affects your reality tunnel, your worldview or your belief system, which I abbreviate B.S. The two major things I've been trying to teach in all of my books is: Never believe fully in anybody else's B.S ... I don't care who it is, don't swallow all their belief system totally.

The second rule is like unto the first: Don't believe totally in your own B.S ... Which means that any belief system or reality tunnel you've got right now is gonna have to be revised and updated as you continue to apprehend new events later in time.

—Robert Anton Wilson (1993)

In this chapter I will look at the idea of "cognitive harmony" from a different angle. In music, harmony is the ordering of stacked notes into complementary patterns. Likewise, cognitive harmony is my term for the ability to function well with multiple belief systems, in the same individual.

Cognitive dissonance, defined here as the stress caused by conflicting beliefs in an individual, cannot be fully relieved by reducing one's life to one simple set of rules. Nor can it be resolved by ignoring everything that doesn't fit in with one's personal narrative. No matter how inconvenient it is, reality always has a way of crashing the party. In psychology, this behaviour of shutting out contradictory information is referred to as the "distortion defence mechanism", a gross reshaping of external reality to meet internal needs.

As previously discussed, the world is filled with more information than is able to be processed by a single individual. Similarly, as a society we have not succeeded in generating a unified theory with which to explain everything. Therefore, given the many tasks and roles we must undertake, the only path left to us is to switch between belief systems. I propose that having multiple belief systems is actually the normal state of a healthy functional human being, and that trying to operate with only one belief system is, in large part, what causes cognitive dissonance.

Before I go any further, I must explain what I mean by "belief". The type of beliefs I am interested in are those that one acts out in the world as if they were true. I am less interested in what people say they think is true, especially if they act differently. Very often, we aren't fully aware of our own beliefs. For instance, someone might say that money is the root of all evil, but still spend a lot of their time trying to acquire as much of it as they can. Their behaviour betrays their narrative. To use money is to believe in it.

Cognitive dissonance can also occur if an individual's beliefs differ from the ideology of a group to which they belong. For instance, they might be asked to behave in a certain way at work, which conflicts with their personal principles.

We can see this frequently in our modern society when issues such as environmentalism clash with capitalism. For example, a fast food company might decide to switch from plastic to wooden cutlery in order to appear more sustainable to its environmentally concerned customer base. Even though everybody in the company might believe that this is a good move, it is possible that a shareholders contract might prevent it. Often companies are legally bound (via "lawyer spells") to try their best to produce a profit for their shareholders, and can be sued if they fail to do so. Cases like this are not only breeding grounds for cognitive dissonance among employees, but also show that a company's apparent belief system can be quite separate from the belief system of the people who run the company.

Likewise, many people attend church on Sunday and then behave in an "unchristian" manner the rest of the week. Consider the Italian mafioso, often highly Catholic in personal belief, yet at the same time a member of an organised crime group that breaks multiple Christian commandments and principles.

I come from New Zealand, a country with a statistically high degree of atheism and agnosticism. Many New Zealanders report a distrust of religion, and our country has a low church attendance in comparison with its traditionally Christian past. As a teenager in the late 1990s, I spent a year in Germany as an exchange student. Church attendance was still common for German families. Even though I was agnostic, I attended a Catholic church with my host family, and I considered it part of the cultural experience.

As part of my curiosity to understand the culture, I would ask people if they went to a church or mosque, and what sort of religion they followed. The answers from the Germans were almost universally, "Yes, I go to a Catholic church," "Yes, I go to a Lutheran Protestant church," or "Yes, I attend a mosque."

Something seemed off, though. If I probed further, the same individuals would often reveal that they were agnostic about the existence of God, or some other aspect of their religion such as the infallibility of the Pope.

I started adding the question, "But do you believe in God?" To my surprise, the answer was usually, "Oh, I'm not sure if there is a God or not."

Unlike the New Zealanders of the late 1990s, the Germans attended church as a matter of tradition, regardless of their individual personal beliefs.

The German churches flourished undeterred by the widespread agnosticism. Despite what many non-religious people think, religions usually accept a certain amount of agnosticism among their participants. Attendance and participation are what count if you are trying to keep a church going.

There are people who claim to live under one set of rules all the time. Considering the complexity of the world, I think these people are either not telling us the truth, not telling themselves the truth, or are otherwise in a near-constant state of stress at trying to squeeze a complex world into a belief-shaped hole.

More nefarious still are the cults that prey upon this type of stress. Some set an impossibly high spiritual goal, then use the guilt of not living up to that standard as leverage to control their members.

On the flip side, if used in a positive way, the pursuit of an unobtainable perfection can be used to provide an endless source of inspiration, like a guiding star. As long as one knows that while one can perpetually improve, one can never actually achieve an ideal state. Allowing oneself to slip up, then learn from the experience and move on, is healthy. Forever judging oneself or someone else for not reaching a bar set too high is destructive.

Another way to explain believing different things on different days is through the concept of collective beliefs. This has been written about by social scientists Margaret Gilbert and André Orléan. They seek to explain, much like my earlier fast food company example, that a group may hold a belief which causes its members to behave in a certain way, even if none of those members hold that belief individually:

> Foreign exchange brokers, like everybody else, may know perfectly well that the currency is undervalued and yet continue to sell it. What counts for them when they operate on the market is not their opinion of the true value of the currency, insofar as they can esti- mate it, but how they believe the market is going to behave. Brokers make profits on a market by correctly predicting the evolutions of group opinion. This is the rule of the game.
>
> As a broker, however much I believe in a rise in the euro, I'm powerless when I see all around me that the other operators on the exchange market are selling euros. For the same reason, even if I judge that the euro deserves to be worth more against the dollar, I still hesitate about buying the European currency. If I'm the only buyer up against fifty brokers that are selling, I'm sure to get my fingers burnt … I don't necessarily follow my own personal convictions … (Orléan, 2004)

As one can infer, it is quite possible that the majority of the fifty bro- kers mentioned in the quote might believe the euro is undervalued and yet still behave as if they believe the dollar to be stronger. They not only have their own personal beliefs, but also their belief about the group-belief of the market.

This is a common situation that can arise in any group. All that is required to relieve one of the cognitive dissonances caused by the group's belief being different to one's own is a rationalisation. As the broker explains, he would lose money if he were to act on his own values, and therefore his hands are tied.

Another example might be seen in a member of a political party who is trying to get a particular bill to pass. They might strike a quid pro quo deal with the rest of their party to vote yes on a different bill in return for support on the one they care most about. From the point of view of the vote count, only the party belief can be observed, not the individual's. No wonder these groups seem to behave like they have their own will, separate from individual values, or sometimes from common sense. The group behaves as if it is an entity in its own right, and sometimes that is the best way to think of it. We will explore this idea further later on in the book.

Perhaps when an individual is at odds with the beliefs of a group entity, rather than fighting as one against the group, it can be more effective to create a new group entity, in order that the battle might be fought at the same level of abstraction. Fun examples of this can be found in New Zealand's history, with satirical political movements such as the Wizard of New Zealand's own Imperial British Conservative Party[3] or the McGillicuddy Serious Party.[4] Both of them humorous political parties that ran for Parliament, partly in jest and partly in protest.

Belief as a tool

> *Alice laughed: "There's no use trying," she said; "one can't believe impossible things."*
>
> *"I daresay you haven't had much practice," said the Queen. "When I was younger, I always did it for half an hour a day. Why, sometimes I've believed as many as six impossible things before breakfast."*
>
> —*Alice in Wonderland* (Carroll, 1898)

Once a magician has accepted that it is quite ordinary for a single individual to hold multiple, conflicting beliefs, they can then turn this to their own advantage. One of the underlying principles behind magic as laid out by the writer and chaos magician Peter J. Carroll (1987) is the idea that belief can be used as a tool. If you don't like what you are getting from your life, consider changing your belief system.

---

[3] (ArhWizard of New Zealand, 1997).
[4] (htps://en.wikipedia.org/wiki/McGillicuddy_Serious_Party).

My term for the ability of an individual to juggle different belief systems in order to fulfil different roles is "spiritual code-switching". Code-switching is a concept I have borrowed from linguistics. It refers to the ability of a person to switch between thinking and communicating in one language and another instantly, often within the confines of

The Wizard of New Zealand (right) and myself (left) in 2018.

a single conversation. Likewise, spiritual code-switching is the ability to change spiritual frameworks like tools, as if one were exchanging a spanner for a screwdriver.

Just as one reality tunnel can highlight aspects of one's environment while rendering others invisible, one belief system can open up opportunities for certain behaviours and actions while rendering others impossible.

The master role is the magician. He knows he is acting, but there is still no greater role.[5]—The Wizard of New Zealand (as he stated when he was appointed the official Wizard of the University of New South Wales in 1969).

> Once you have a belief system, everything that comes in either gets ignored if it doesn't fit the belief system, or gets distorted enough so that it can fit into the belief system. You gotta be continually revising your map of the world. (Robert Anton Wilson, 1993)

There is another matter that must be confronted by both the psychologist and the magician before belief can successfully be harnessed for change.

In Western culture, it is usually taken for granted that thought precedes action. Many self-help and therapy modalities seek to first control thought, in order that they may positively affect behaviour and habits. However, this is often not quite right. We often find out how we think and what we believe by our habits and actions. These can be unconscious. For instance, how do you know you are angry? Do you have an angry thought and then turn red? I think it's often the case that we have a bodily response first. We often find out we are angry because of increased heart rate, flow of blood to the head, or tensing of the muscles. In psychology, this concept is called "embodied cognition". One of the first explanations of this effect was laid out by William James, in his essay "What is an Emotion?" (1884). This is the same William James who laid the foundation for the philosophy of pragmatism which is core to this book:

---

[5] The Wizard of New Zealand quoted this to me himself while we were sitting at his dining table in 2019).

Common sense says: We lose our fortune, are sorry and weep; we meet a bear, are frightened and run; we are insulted by a rival, are angry and strike. The hypothesis here to be defended says that this order of sequence is incorrect, that the one mental state is not immediately induced by the other, that the bodily manifestations must first be interposed between, and that the more rational statement is that we feel sorry because we cry, angry because we strike, afraid because we tremble, and not that we cry, strike, or tremble, because we are sorry, angry, or fearful, as the case may be. Without the bodily states following on the perception, the latter would be purely cognitive in form, Pale, colourless, destitute of emotional warmth. We might then see the bear, and judge it best to run; receive the insult and deem it right to strike, but we could not actually feel afraid or angry. (James, 1884)

Embodied cognition is still a relevant theory in psychology today. Often, we get the thought and the feeling around the wrong way, thinking that we act on thoughts rather than, is often the case: our thoughts explain our actions to us.

Gazzaniga (2000) has suggested that people explain their behaviours by fabricating stories. In his research, brain-damaged patients who could not explain their behaviours accurately were nevertheless quick to provide plausible, though obviously false, explanations for their actions. More recent research has demonstrated a similar phenomenon in normally functioning adults (Johansson et al., 2005). This work employed sleight of hand to dupe participants into explaining decisions they did not make. Most participants failed to notice that these were not their decisions. Furthermore, they had no problem providing quick and elaborate explanations for why they made them, even though the explanations could not have possibly been true.The general pattern thus seems to be that people are unaware of their own behaviours. If the conscious self cannot recognise its own actions, it is unlikely that it controls them. (Morsella & Poehlman, 2014)

Because of this, not only can one effect change in oneself or a willing subject by thought control, but also, often more effectively, by behaving differently. Acting as if you believe something to be true can be a quicker way to change one's inner beliefs than trying to think differently.

This is one of the primary factors that underlies ritual as a magical concept. For instance, psychological tests show that people usually value a group more if they have undergone a difficult initiation rite before they are allowed to join. No wonder initiation is core to so many magical traditions from shamanism to the Golden Dawn.

> Elliot Aronson and Judson Mills (1959) studied whether the cognitive dissonance created by an initiation process could explain how much commitment students felt to a group they were part of. In their experiment, female college students volunteered to join a group that would be meeting regularly to discuss various aspects of the psychology of sex. According to random assignment, some of the women were told that they would be required to perform an embarrassing procedure before they could join the group (they were asked to read some obscene words and some sexually oriented passages from a novel in public), whereas other women did not have to go through this initiation. Then all the women got a chance to listen to the group's conversation, which turned out to be very boring.
>
> Aronson and Mills found that the women who had gone through the embarrassing experience subsequently reported more liking for the group than those who had not, and Gerard and Matthewson (1966) found that having to take some electrical shocks as part of an initiation process had the same effect. Aronson and Mills argued that the more effort an individual expends to become a member of the group (e.g., a severe initiation), the more he or she will become committed to the group in order to justify the effort put in during the initiation. The idea is that the effort creates dissonant cognitions (e.g., "I did all this work to join the group"), which are then justified by creating more consonant ones (e.g., "Okay, this group is really pretty fun"). The women who spent little effort to get into the group were able to see the group as the dull and boring conversation that it was. The women who went through the more severe initiation, however, succeeded in convincing themselves that the same discussion was a worthwhile experience. When we put in effort for something—an initiation, a big purchase price, or even some of our precious time—we will likely end up liking the activity

more than we would have if the effort had been less. Even the effort of having to fill out a purchase agreement for a product, rather than having the salesperson do it for you, creates commitment to the purchase and a greater likelihood of staying in the deal (Cialdini, 2001). (Stangor, 2011)

Perhaps this offers a partial explanation as to why ritual is such a common part of traditional magic—from a witch doctor's blessing, to singing hymns in a church, to an orientation party for freshmen at a university.

A magician can experiment with this phenomenon. Things to try:

- When struggling with destructive belief, try behaving as if the opposite is true, and then seeing if a new, more healthy belief follows.

  For instance, when confronting impostor syndrome, the fear that you might not compare well to others of a similar skill level, a "fake it till you make it" approach might allow one to overcome personal doubts.
- Ritualise beliefs through costumes. Wear a business suit and carry a clipboard, a janitor's coveralls, bucket and mop, or a hi-vis vest and hard hat, and see if that grants you access to places you don't normally have access to. What you wear and how you behave determines how people treat you, and whether they pay attention to you at all.
- Adopt the attitude that "everyone has something to teach you" for a week. See if by the end of the week you have learned some new things. The following week, adopt the attitude that everyone else is a fool. See if by the end of the week you have discovered the loose ends and logical fallacies in most people's pet ideas. Consider the opportunities and obstacles each belief has created and consider each attitude a tool that can be switched out at will in order to get different things done.

CHAPTER 8

Outside voices vs. inner voices

Where do your ideas come from? Do they originate from your own mind? Or do they originate from outside your mind, either in the environment around you, or in your cultural sphere?

The concept of inspiration, which draws from the same linguistic root as the word "spirit", underwent a radical shift in the post-Enlightenment era. In the past, as evidenced in literature, folk stories, and myth, people mostly described inspiration as if it came from outside sources. God's Holy Ghost would reach down to spark an idea in an individual's mind, or the Muses would whisper inspirations to poets, artists, and musicians.

Many of us hear a voice in our head when we think something through, or when we read a book. It's considered normal to interpret this voice, or inner monologue, as being part of our self. In some contexts or states of consciousness, this very same voice might be interpreted instead as an outside entity. In rarer moments, these disembodied voices can be indistinguishable from talking to a real person.

In the past, hearing "outside" voices was a commonly accepted part of life. In many traditional societies, nary an important decision could be made without the guidance of gods or spirits, through prayer, oracles, or divination. These outside voices were often given more authority than a human being. No decree could be spoken without invoking gods or spirits at least in lip service. Many today, for instance, still believe that the Bible was dictated to humans by God's Holy Spirit.

The psychologist Julian Jaynes (1976) put forth the idea that the development of writing might have played a role in devaluing the role of spirits:

> These limitations of gods were both relieved and greatly exacer-bated in the second millennium B.C. by the success of writing. On the one hand, writing could allow a civil structure ... to remain stable. But, on the other, it was gradually eroding the auditory authority of the bicameral mind ... Once the word of god was silent, written on dumb clay tablets or incised into speechless stone, the god's commands or the king's directives could be turned to or avoided by one's own efforts in a way that auditory hallucinations never could be. The word of a god had a controllable location rather than an ubiquitous power with immediate obedience.

Before writing, people regarded the phenomena that many now attempt to explain through psychology, as spirits, symbolism, animism, cosmol-ogy, and myth. It is widely accepted that most pre-agricultural cultures were animistic. That is to say, each and every important aspect of one's environment and culture had a spirit with which one could negotiate.

Even today, there are examples of animistic cultures which regard animals and aspects of nature as people. In the culture of the Kluane, who reside primarily in Yukon, Canada, animals have been said to talk to shamans and others on occasion. The rituals behind hunting and the associated taboos and allowances are said to be negotiated with the ani-mals themselves, both as spirits, and through physical interaction:

> Although Kluane people do recognise a metaphorical relationship between hunting and reciprocity among humans, this does not mean that they see animals as being "like people." For them, ani-mals **are** people.
>
> In stories, animals regularly speak to northern hunters in human languages and in so doing convey important information (such as how they wish to be treated). Because many contemporary hunting practices are rooted in these stories (Tanner, 1979, p. 137), they take

for granted that animals really are as they appear in them, and this includes an ability to understand human language, whether spoken or thought. Similarly, animals encountered in dreams (as well as in occasional waking experiences) are reported to sometimes speak in human languages. Indeed, I was told explicitly more than once that although animals in Kluane country probably cannot speak English, they most definitely can "speak Indian." (Nadasdy, 2007)

In cultures that moved into cities, polytheism began to replace animism as a belief system. Polytheistic cultures often look to oracles for guidance in important decisions. One of the most historically important examples is the ancient Greek Oracle at Delphi, which was a major cultural hub from around 800–400 BCE. For nine holy days a year, as many as 35,000 people might visit and partake in the rituals at the temple of Apollo. There, the Pythia, an oracle and high priestess, would become possessed by Apollo to inform the most important political, strategic, and cultural decisions.

At the most famous oracle, that of Apollo at Delphi, there was a queer cone-like stone structure called the omphalos or navel. It stood at the reputed center of the earth. Here presided on certain days, or in some centuries every day throughout the year, a supreme priestess, or sometimes two or three in rotation, selected so far as we know on no particular basis (in Plutarch's day, in the first century B.C., she was the daughter of a poor farmer).

She first bathed and drank from a sacred brook, and then established contact with the god through his sacred tree, the laurel, much as conscious Assyrian kings are depicted being smeared by tree-cones in the hands of genii. She did this either by holding a laurel branch, or by inhaling and fumigating herself with burnt laurel leaves (as Plutarch said), or perhaps by chewing the leaves (as Lucian insisted).

The replies to questions were given at once, without any reflection, and uninterruptedly. The exact manner of her announcements is still debated, whether she was seated on a tripod, regarded as Apollo's ritual seat, or simply stood at an entrance to a cave. But the archaic references to her, from the fifth century on, all agree with the statement of Heraclitus that she spoke "from her frenzied mouth and with various contortions of her body." She was entheos, plena deo.

Speaking through his priestess, but always in the first person, answering king or freeman, "Apollo" commanded sites for new colonies (as he did for present day Istanbul), decreed which nations were friends, which rulers best, which laws to enact, the causes of plagues or famines, the best trade routes, which of the proliferation of new cults, or music, or art should be recognised as agreeable to Apollo—all decided by these girls with their frenzied mouths. (Julian Jaynes, 1976)

Compare this with the modern landscape where "hearing voices" is code for insanity. Only within certain groups, such as evangelical churches, is hearing voices, such as that of God or Jesus, encouraged, and even then one can be in hot water if one hears the "wrong" voices. Neuroscientist Oliver Sacks (2012) offers:

Up until about 1800, anyone was allowed to have visions, or hear voices. They were assumed to have some spiritual origin; gods, demons, the muses, ancestors, the dead; and around two centuries ago [this] business became medicalised and hallucinations were seen as a disorder of the brain. Probably associated with madness.

In my attempts to understand both religion and magical thinking, things started to click when I came to a decision to treat "inside voices" and "outside voices" as the same mental phenomena described in different ways.

Due to the privacy of our thoughts, our moments of inspiration can never be completely shared with others. As such, it is difficult to study these accounts other than through anecdotal evidence. The only recourse for an enquiring magician is to try to have the experience yourself.

Regardless of a voice's origin inside or outside the mind, it either results in an action, or it doesn't. My hypothesis is that the propensity to hear inside voices vs. outside voices is mostly a product of one's cultural framing, and/or disposition. The practical outcome, all other things being equal, is the same.

In psychology, the term for hearing voices is "auditory-verbal hallucinations". We will work with this for the time being, even though it negates the prospect of real outside entities, for which I will provide a pragmatic framework in the following chapter.

Dr Kristiina Kompus, an associate professor from the Department of Biological and Medical Psychology at the University of Bergen, gives an explanation for the difference between the inner voice that most of us hear and the "external" voices that some people hear:

> Every one of us has an inner speech, or in fact an inner dialogue, or this imagined conversation happening in our head, and the big difference is most of us do not hear this out loud. We can clearly distinguish the thoughts, and in this case the verbalisations we make up inside our own head, but in this case [with] the hallucinations, the hallmark is that they are just as clear and just as loud as an actual sound coming from the outside.
>
> So there is basically one major model of hallucinations ... This one model suggests [that] we all have inner speech, and the auditory-verbal hallucinations are generated by the same process that makes inner speech in all of us, but due to some problem, the brain treats the inner speech as if it would be real external speech ... The suggestion has been, inner speech is, essentially, almost like a motor act. So you have to prepare a kind of motor sequence ... to speak it out, and the hypothesis is that absolutely all plans of motor actions are accompanied by a sort of warning signal to the sensory cortex, to just ignore that movement you are about to make. So in that signal, the sensations are self generated, and [the warning signal] dampens the response to these. This would be the same reason as to why we can't tickle ourselves. It's because the plan has been sent to the sensory cortex and it's dampened. And what it is that you see in experiments is that the auditory cortex response to speech that you generate, is actually suppressed compared with ... external stimulation. So then the hypothesis behind inner speech theory is that the internal voice is accompanied by preparing the auditory system to ignore it, but in hallucination patients, this preparation doesn't work. So the inner speech is perceived as if it would be a real external stimulus, attributed to an external agency ...
>
> But the thing is, people who hallucinate, they are also capable of having inner speech. This theory doesn't completely explain why people with schizophrenia don't hear all of their thoughts out loud all the time ... In people who hallucinate there seems to be a pretty clear delineation between the voice and [their] own thoughts. (Kompus, 2017)

As a side note: I have a small disagreement with the beginning of this quote. "Every one of us has an inner speech." While perhaps most people can relate to this, there are some people who claim to have very little or no inner speech. This is sometimes an aspect of a condition like autism, but there are also some "neurotypical" people who say they do not do much of their thinking in language at all.

Despite the fact that we all have thoughts, the question of what we, as individuals, experience when we have thoughts is, strangely, not often asked. Normally, I experience a narrator in my mind, though I can also switch to thinking in image, text, sound, or music. In situations where I need to comprehend a problem from different angles, I split my inner voice into a kind of committee that takes on different viewpoints. It's as if I'm having a group discussion. At no point do these voices feel like they are anything other than parts of myself. They just take on different roles in a conversation like lawyers in a courtroom, or Greek philosophers at a symposium.

After they have done the task of discussing the problem, they meld back into my singular voice. It's not a great stretch to imagine these "split selves" taking on a more permanent separation in some people. In certain individuals they can, either wilfully or unwillingly, become sub-personalities in their own right.

Can voice hearing be a skill that an ordinary person can learn? Could a magician learn to "code-switch" between an inner monologue and perceiving an external entity? I decided, in experiment, to allow myself to experience outside voices. If one is to communicate clearly and openly with a variety of different subcultures, for instance evangelical Christians or witches on one side, and materialists on the other, then it's important to experience both points of view. For both the scientist and the pragmatic magician, it's the outcome that should matter most, not the mode of thinking.

My most interesting interaction with spirits came with the help of two tabs of LSD and a long walk through the "red zone" in Christchurch, my home city in New Zealand. The red zone is a land reserve created after hundreds of houses were demolished. This was due to a series of earthquakes that severely damaged our city starting on September 4, 2010, and reaching a peak on February 22, 2011.

Some might dismiss the use of psychedelic drugs as opening oneself up to "delusion", but I make no truth claims from the experiment other than the fact that it's possible for an individual to willingly experience talking to spirits, whether they are "real" or not. Furthermore, it's possible for this to happen without becoming insane. My encounter gave me first-hand experience that allows me to relate to others who claim to talk to spirits, and that was more than enough to make it interesting for me. Psychedelic drugs work by making the user highly suggestible. For this reason it's important not to take any idea you have on them as gospel. Just acknowledge the experience for what it is. Psychedelic drugs can, if treated properly, be a useful tool for exploring the limits of one's mind, and for breaking out of bad thought habits.

The red zone consists of a large number of formerly residential streets, with the houses removed. It now functions as a kind of park. Despite the houses being gone, much of people's former gardens remain. This has formed a new ecosystem of both introduced and native species of plants and animals. Parts of the red zone are easily walked through, while other parts are quite overgrown and swampy. Birds gather at sunken bits of land that become ponds after it rains. The ghostly remnants of pavements, driveways, signposts, and street names impart an eerie quality, and one can't help but feel that the whole place is currently being reclaimed by natural forces.

Carving of Tāne-nui-a-Rangi at the entrance of Auckland
Zoo by Lyonel Grant, Ngāti Te Arawa.

My main interaction during the experience was with two spirits who claimed to be the Māori god, Tāne Mahuta, and a young feminine nature spirit which I called Hine, who, in this case, described herself as Tāne's lover. Tāne is the male nature spirit of trees, birds, male beauty, and the masculine, "active" aspect of fertility. Hine came forth as the receptive feminine drive towards procreation. She stood for the trees and plants that were repopulating the red zone, changing its landscape from the suburban to the wild.

Hine talked about being happy with "the sacrifice" the city of Christchurch had given her; some land to use as she pleased, with minimal human interference. Since the red zone was set aside, a diversity of plants has been restored, and bird and animal life is increasing. Tāne discussed being disappointed that so many people in our modern culture live in a disheartened and depressive state. He wished that men would "pick up their 'Taiahas'" (a traditional Māori weapon, which he used as a metaphor for our tools and strength) and create "wonderful things and be proud."

These two gods that I interacted with might be my own invented constructs, real outside entities, or a mixture of cultural characters and my imagination. Talking to spirits is a subjective experience that we can't test scientifically. To try to draw certain conclusions, either spiritually or sceptically, is futile. Others might try the same approach as I did and have their own experience, and those stories can be collected and studied, reported as phenomena. That's the most we can do. There is much evidence for spirit contact, but it might always be impossible to draw conclusions on their reality.

I believe the worth of the idea is more important than the way it was experienced. As in the example of the artist that can see fairies (see Chapter 2), it is not so important whether that person created the fairies in their mind or was actually visited by spirits. Pragmatically speaking, all we can be concerned with is whether a spirit experience produces an outcome. The red zone experience gave me a new interest in the ways that plants and animals regenerate when left to their own devices. Once experiencing plant life as having a will and intention, I began to pay much more attention to it. After watching several scientific videos about plants, my entheogen-induced experiences were validated. Plants are territorial, they have numerous senses, they are aware of the presence of other life forms in their vicinity, they learn from their experiences, and they have purposeful ways to convince animals to pollinate them or disperse their seeds. Some of this may seem like a given to plant fans, but I had never particularly paid attention to plant behaviour before these experiences.

Since giving myself permission to spiritually "code-switch" in this manner, I have found myself now able to relate in common experience with all sorts of spiritual people from pagans, psychics, Christians, Jews, and Muslims, and indigenous people such our New Zealand Māori. All of this despite having started from a materialist rationalist worldview.

Hearing voices as mental illness

Now I hear some of you protest: "Ari, have you gone off the deep end? Hearing voices is delusion, plain and simple!"

This concern would be a genuine one if it wasn't for some sort of grounding point. That grounding point is pragmatism. If a line of thinking is not producing beneficial change for the individual, those around them, or the world at large, then it must be dropped. The deluded person is the one who keeps expecting particular results, even when they fail over and over. The wise thing would be to change one's method or one's expectations.

Schizophrenia can be a very real and serious affliction. Many people diagnosed with schizophrenia hear voices that instruct them to commit acts that are out of character. These thoughts can be paranoid or even violent in their expression. Public concern over schizophrenia, along with the unfortunate Hollywood trope of the murderous madman, such as the character Norman Bates in Alfred Hitchcock's classic film *Psycho*, have created stigma for voice hearers. Less discussed are those people who hear voices, yet remain functional and stable. Some studies suggest a certain proportion of the population has at least one or more voice-hearing experiences in their lifetime.

> In a longitudinal New Zealand study, 803 adults of European descent were assessed at age 26 using a standard psychiatric interview (Caspi et al., 2005). Thirteen percent reported at least one hallucinatory experience (voices, strange smells or tastes, unusual bodily feelings and/or visions when completely awake), and 3.4% reported hearing things or voices that other people cannot hear. (Beavan et al., 2011)

It's important to note that most of these people who hear voices do not require any medical intervention. In most cases these people are not mentally ill by any useful definition. Certain life events can influence voice hearing. During grief, many people have experiences involving talking to recently passed loved ones.

> There are, for example, bereavement hallucinations. These especially occur if people have been happily married for half a century or whatever, and if the husband or wife dies, there's a 50% chance that the remaining spouse will see them or hear them, and this sort of hallucination is not frightening; it's often very comforting, seem[ing] to be part of the mourning process ... a sudden hole is left in one's life and this helps it to heal over. So there I would say the hallucination is highly adaptive and not dysfunctional. (Sacks, 2012)

The Hearing Voices Movement[6] proposes an alternative treatment for voice hearers who are suffering from a psychotic breakdown. Instead of expelling the voices, as is the usual goal of psychiatric treatment, they are instead taught to manage and have stable relationships with their voices. These voices become regarded as sub-personalities, or aspects of self, that need to be taken into account, but not necessarily obeyed. The movement also proposes that many people who have episodes in which they hear voices do not always require psychiatric assistance.

While this is controversial as an approach, there are people who claim to have stabilised their schizophrenia, and have gone on to lead functional and successful lives.

Eleanor Longden is one such person who has become a public advocate for the destigmatisation of those who "hear voices". Here is an excerpt from a talk she gave at TED in 2013:

> And the voice persisted, days and then weeks of it, on and on, narrating everything I did in the third person; "She is going to the library," "She is going to a lecture." It was neutral, impassive and even, after a while, strangely companious [sic] and reassuring. Though I did notice that its calm exterior sometimes slipped and occasionally mirrored my unexpressed emotion. So, for example,

---

[6] http://wwaring-voices.org/.

if I was angry and had to hide it, which I often did, being very adept at concealing how I really felt, then the voice would sound frustrated.

Otherwise it was neither sinister nor disturbing. Although, even at that point, it was clear that it had something to indicate to me about my emotions. Particularly, emotions that were remote and inexpressible.

Now, it was then that I made a fatal mistake. In that I told a friend about the voice and she was horrified. A subtle conditioning process had begun. The implication that "normal" people don't hear voices, and the fact that I did meant that something was very seriously wrong ...

Suddenly, the voice didn't seem quite so benign anymore, and when she insisted that I seek medical attention, I duly complied, which proved to be mistake number two. I spent some time telling the college GP about what I perceived to be the real problem. Anxiety, low self-worth, worries about the future, which was met with bored indifference ... A hospital visit followed, the first of many. A diagnosis of schizophrenia came next, and then, worst of all, a toxic tormenting sense of hopelessness, humiliation, and despair about myself and my prospects.

But, having been encouraged to see the voice, not as an experience, but as a symptom, my fear and resistance towards it intensified. Now, essentially, this represented taking an aggressive stance towards my own mind. A kind of "psychic civil war", and in turn this caused the number of voices to increase, and grow increasingly hostile and menacing ... Culminating in commands to harm myself in a particularly dramatic instruction. "You see that tutor over there, you see that glass of water. You have to go over there and pour it over him in front of the other students"...

After a difficult time in the mental health system, including some mistreatment and abuse, she gradually found people who encouraged her to recover.

Together they forged a blend of courage, creativity, integrity, and an unshakable belief that my shattered self could become healed and whole ... They empowered me to save myself. And crucially, they helped me to understand something which I always suspected: that my voices were a meaningful response to traumatic life events. Particularly, childhood events, and as such, were not my enemies, but a source of insight into solvable emotional problems.

When the voices warned me not to leave the house, then I would thank them for drawing my attention to how unsafe I felt, because if I was aware of it, I could do something positive about it. But go on to reassure both them and myself that we were safe.

She is now a member of the organisation *Intervoice*, part of the Hearing Voices Movement.[7]

The cultural and social framing of hearing voices seems to have a big effect on the outcome for the voice hearer. Some voice hearers who have had trouble in societies that don't accept outside voices have found successful treatment by training with shamans. Shamans have the role of being mediums for spirits in their communities, and are regarded as medicine-people and seers.

The following excerpt from an article published in *Nautilus*, discusses a young American man who sought treatment from a shaman, after psychiatric treatments had failed:

> When Malidoma (a shaman) first met Frank (a schizophrenic) one evening over dinner in Jamaica, he recognised the man's likeness to himself instantly. "The connection we had was immediately clear," he says. As soon as [the] schizophrenic met [the] shaman, the latter shook his head and clasped Frank's hands as if they'd known each other for years. He told Dick that Frank was "like a colleague!" Malidoma believes that Frank is a U.S. version of a titiyulo; in fact, there is a version of a titiyulo in pretty much every culture, he says. He also believes that one cannot choose to become a titiyulo: It happens to you.
>
> "Every shaman started with a crisis similar to those here who are called schizophrenic, psychotic. Shamanism, or titiyulo journeys, begin with a breakdown of the psyche," he says. "One day they're fine, normal, like everyone else. The next day they're acting really weird and [acting] dangerously toward themselves and the village—seeing and hearing things that aren't there, acting paranoid, shouting" ...

---

[7] https://wwtervoiceonline.org.

Had Frank been born into the Dagara tribe, and experienced the same breakdown at age seventeen that led him to run from his friend's apartment, Malidoma tells me that the community would have immediately rallied around him, performing the same rituals that his sister experienced. Following this intervention, his tribe members would begin the work of healing Frank and re-integrating him back into the community; once he was ready, he'd receive a prominent position. "He'd be known as a man of spirit, who'd be able to provide insight into the deep problems of the people around them," he says.

Today, Frank Russell is finding his symptoms easier to manage. He also has a deeper relationship with his father, who says their journey into shamanism has changed the way he thinks about health and illness. (Neilson, 2016)

As we can see, the culture of the voice hearer has a huge effect on the way they frame their illness, which in turn affects their capacity to cope with the voices, and their prospects for healing.

Inner monologue

Now that we have addressed the pathology that can accompany voice hearing, let's compare that with the typical "inner monologue" that most of us experience.

Charles Fernyhough is a leading psychologist in this area of study. Here is an excerpt from one of his interviews (2016) where he discusses the concept of "inner monologue":

If you ask someone to reflect on their inner experience, you find that it's full of words. People often say they have a voice going on in their heads the whole time. And the key thing here is not to assume that inner speech is like external speech. So we shouldn't assume that when we talk to ourselves in our heads, it's going to sound exactly like it sounds when you talk to another person, or even ourselves out loud. To give an example, imagine you're sitting quietly in your living room late at night, and you hear a loud clattering noise outside the window. You are probably not going to say to yourself, "The cat has just knocked the dustbin lid off." You are probably going to say to yourself quietly in your head, "The cat." Or you might say, "The dustbin lid."

Inner speech, I think, often has this condensed note-form quality. It's almost like external speech is the full text, and inner speech is the notes you make for yourself on that text …

We are coming to a view of hearing voices as something that is much more than just an auditory experience. It's something that is accompanied by all sorts of other sensations. For example, a common thing that is described by polar explorers, is the sense of a presence being with you, a sort of a benevolent entity following you, and saving you from peril. And some voice hearers that I've spoken to have said, "It's not like having a voice inside me, it's like having a person living within me. It's like being inhabited by another person." And as we start to understand hearing voices, as a communicative process, as something that results from a particular kind of communication, just like inner speech does, we get a much better sense of how it is that our inner speech can represent all of these social agents, but also how these social agents can pop up in hearing voices, and talk back to us.

The Russian developmental psychologist Lev Vygotsky, in his book *Thinking and Speech* (1934), put forward the idea that inner speech develops from social speech. Infants start talking to parents and other family members. This progresses to them talking to themselves out loud. Over time, this self conversation becomes the inner monologue that most of us are familiar with. Current child development studies have confirmed this idea, which is now the dominant theory of language development in children. The theory suggests there is a close relationship between inner thinking and actual conversation with another person. Perhaps this is why voice hearing comes across for many of us as a kind of "blurring" between self and non-self?

Talking to God

Psychological anthropologist Tanya Luhrmann (2017) has presented a study of Christians who routinely experience conversations with God at the Vineyard Protestant Church in Chicago. Her aim was to take part in their experience in order to get as close as possible to understanding them. I think that her approach, as well as her findings, are useful to help us understand the nature of how even mentally well people can hear voices:

My question is, how does someone learn how to do this? How do you come in from the outside, as somebody new to faith, and you end up in a church like this, and God becomes an invisible person amongst people, who just "hangs out" at your side ...

Knowing God in this church wasn't so much about acquiring the ability to utter a proposition; to say "I believe in God." I thought I saw that knowing God was a skill. It was something that you learned, and that the vehicle for the learning was prayer ... People learned to think about their mind differently. They acquired what I call a "new theory about their mind". I thought I saw that they had a kind of comfort with imaginative play. Let me be clear. It's not a world that thinks of God as imaginary, but they became comfortable with using their imagination to experience God more vividly ... You'll be praying for someone else, and sometimes the ideas that come to you, they aren't yours, they are God's ... Members of the church describe this as "discernment". They say you have to discern whether you are talking to God or not ... The pastor said to me, "You know, if you think God is asking you to jump off a bridge, that's not God."

She goes on to describe the ritual of the prayer circle which she took part in and studied:

Two things are going on. The person who is being prayed for is typically crying. They are demonstrating that this is rare, it's hard, it's weird; it's hard to understand how much they are "loved". And the people in the prayer circle are acting out the part of God. They are saying things to the person that they think that a loving God would say. So [that is]:

"Lord, we know that Mary is getting on a flight tomorrow. Lord we know that you know that she is scared of flying. Lord we pray that she will feel enveloped with the warm arms of your embrace and she will feel your love when she is in the plane." ... They talk of God coming "alive".

This type of prayer is a form of evocation. An act of magic, usually acted out through a ritual, that draws a spirit into the presence of a magician or group of magicians.

Luhrmann discusses how social the prayer experience is. There are prayer training sessions, with experts and students. They comprehend God as a person-like presence. Similar to the presence one might feel of a loved one who has recently passed away. Not everybody, she observed, was able to learn how to feel God's presence. The members of the prayer circle would explain that prayer was hard to do and that some people were better at prayer than others and how people would experience a personal change when they learned how to pray "correctly".

> One of them says: "Recently when I was praying for someone, I heard a voice that was outside of myself say 'Put your hand on their head and pray.'"
>
> Someone else: "The Lord spoke to me clearly in April, like May or April, the start of school," and so I say: "You hear this audibly?" "Yeah."
>
> "Were you alone?"
>
> "Yeah, I was just praying, I wasn't praying for anything really, I was just thinking about God and I heard, 'Start school.' I immediately got up and I said, 'Okay Lord, where?'"

Dr Luhrmann differentiates strongly between those who heard God in prayer, and those with forms of psychosis.

> Back in the day ... I spent a lot of time in uptown [Chicago]. And uptown used to be the area in Chicago that had the highest density, per capita, concentration of people with psychosis in the entire state of Illinois apart from Cook County Jail. And so I know a lot about people who experience psychosis and what I wanted to say is that the experiences that people were reporting to me did not sound like psychosis. They sounded like something different.

The audible experiences were brief, and were not distressing, unlike most of the experiences reported by schizophrenics undergoing treatment, which are often invasive. Perhaps the ability to compartmentalise the experience mostly within the confines of prayer prevented the voices from invading the rest of their reality? The social framework, as well as personal boundaries around the phenomenon of hearing voices, seem to make all the difference. Most ritual magic to invoke spirits has very clear procedures to begin and end the evocation session, and these serve to compartmentalise the experience as something special and separate from mundane activities. It is likely that this helps prevent the kind of distress felt by schizophrenics when they are are unable to control their interaction with "outside" voices.

At the Vineyard Church, which Luhrmann attended, they valued prayer practice and the gaining of inner experience as a more important aspect of their ritual than belief. Experience is paramount to these kinds of people. This is in stark contrast to the suspicions of many sceptics who assume that belief comes first, and that people talk themselves into voice-hearing experiences. Luhrmann's study instead shows that even a sceptic such as herself can have the experience regardless of their faith in the reality of God or other spirits.

Imagination seems to play a big role in these prayer circles. The members of the prayer circle use imagination as a tool to help frame the God experience. They do not feel that this use of imagination negates the reality of God, but rather consider it a way to train the mind to become receptive. C. S. Lewis describes the act of pretending as a useful skill to contemplate God in his famous book, *Mere Christianity* (1952).

> Very often the only way to get a quality in reality is to start behaving as if you had it already. That is why children's games are so important. They are always pretending to be grown-ups—playing soldiers, playing shop. But all the time, they are hardening their muscles and sharpening their wits, so that the pretence of being grown-up helps them to grow up in earnest. Now, the moment you realise "Here I am, dressing up as Christ," it is extremely likely that you will see at once some way in which, at that very moment, the pretence could be made less of a pretence and more of a reality. You will find several things going on in your mind which would not be going on there if you were really the Son of God. Well, stop them. Or you may realise that, instead of saying your prayers, you ought to be downstairs writing a letter, or helping your wife to wash-up. Well, go and do it. You see what is happening. The Christ Himself, the Son of God, who is man (just like you) and God (just like His Father) is actually at your side and is already at that moment beginning to turn your pretence into a reality. This is not merely a fancy way of saying that your conscience is telling you what to do. If you simply ask your conscience, you get one result. If you remember that you are dressing up as Christ, you get a different one.

The type of prayer described by Luhrmann and Lewis is a kind of intuitive divination that appears very similar to the Delphic oracles of ancient Greece which I discussed earlier.

Entheogens

As briefly mentioned previously, psychedelic drugs can offer an opportunity for spiritual experiences, which sometimes include auditory hallucinations and voices. It's no wonder that almost every culture has used entheogens at some point in their history. That is, the use of mind altering substances in order to contact spirits. Many religious movements exist even today around ritual drug use. The operative word here is "ritual". As psychoactive substances work in part by making the user highly suggestible, the context by which one takes the drug can be as least as important, sometimes more important than the chemical effects. This is why people usually report very different experiences between recreational drug use, say at a party or a music festival, and drug use undertaken for spiritual or magical purposes.

The aforementioned neurobiologist, Oliver Sacks, has discussed his use of LSD and amphetamines, and how it helped him to understand his patients who experience hallucinations as a result of brain damage, dementia, and psychiatric disorders such as schizophrenia. Here is an account from his book *Hallucinations*:

> On the West Coast in the early 1960's, LSD and morning glory seeds were readily available, so I sampled those, too. "But if you want a really far-out experience," my friends on Muscle Beach told me, "try Artane." I found this surprising, for I knew that Artane, a synthetic drug allied to belladonna, was used in modest doses (two or three tablets a day) for the treatment of Parkinson's disease, and that such drugs, in large quantities, could cause a delirium (such deliria have long been observed with accidental ingestion of plants like deadly nightshade, thorn apple, and black henbane). But would a delirium be fun? Or informative? Would one be in a position to observe the aberrant functioning of one's brain—to appreciate its wonder? "Go on," urged my friends. "Just take twenty of them—you'll still be in partial control."
>
> So one Sunday morning, I counted out twenty pills, washed them down with a mouthful of water, and sat down to await the effect.

Would the world be transformed, newborn, as Huxley had described it in *The Doors of Perception*, and as I myself had experienced with mescaline and LSD? Would there be waves of delicious, voluptuous feeling? Would there be anxiety, disorganization, paranoia? I was prepared for all of these, but none of them occurred. I had a dry mouth, large pupils, and found it difficult to read, but that was all. There were no psychic effects whatsoever—most disappointing. I did not know exactly what I had expected, but I had expected something.

I was in the kitchen, putting on a kettle for tea, when I heard a knocking at my front door. It was my friends Jim and Kathy; they would often drop round on a Sunday morning. "Come in, door's open," I called out, and as they settled themselves in the living room, I asked, "How do you like your eggs?" Jim liked them sunny side up, he said. Kathy preferred them over easy. We chatted away while I sizzled their ham and eggs—there were low swinging doors between the kitchen and the living room, so we could hear each other easily. Then, five minutes later, I shouted, "Everything's ready," put their ham and eggs on a tray, walked into the living room—and found it completely empty. No Jim, no Kathy, no sign that they had ever been there. I was so staggered I almost dropped the tray. (Sacks, 2012)

While psychedelic drugs, particularly LSD and, in some cases, psilocybin mushrooms, can produce auditory "hallucinations", they tend to be background sounds: mumbling crowds of voices and atmospheric noises. Experiences of spiritual contact on psychedelic drugs is more likely with psychological priming, as discussed previously with ritual evangelical Christian prayer. Shamanic rituals often combine elaborate and dramatic processes with the use of "plant medicines" such as peyote, tobacco, ayahuasca, and psilocybin mushrooms.

What can be gleaned from studying accounts of both shamanic practice and recreational use of psychedelics, is that the drugs are not usually enough in and of themselves to have a clear or controllable experience. Without exception, all magical traditions, as well as recent studies on the use of psychedelic drugs in the treatment of depression, post-traumatic stress disorder, and anxiety show that the ritual and the environment in which the ritual is situated are vital.

One such drug used in traditional spirit magic throughout the Americas is tobacco. To those most familiar with tobacco in theform of cigarettes, it might seem surprising that tobacco can be a powerful hallucinogen. The reason that regular cigarettes aren't hallucinogenic is two-fold.

First, native North and South American shamans use a particular species of tobacco, not normally found in cigarettes called nicotiana rustica.

This strain of tobacco contains nine per cent nicotine or more, compared with the one to three per cent in the commercial tobacco species, nicotiana tabacum.

Second, regular smokers are imbibing relatively small doses of nicotine regularly, which means that they build up a tolerance. The shamans, known in South America as tabaqueros, by comparison imbibe extreme doses less often and usually after a week or more of fasting and abstaining from sex. These large doses can be smoked, chewed, drunk as a tea, consumed as a ground-up paste, or occasionally applied in the form of an enema. Furthermore, the additional chemicals added to commercial cigarettes are not present, so some of the carcinogenic content is reduced. At these nicotine doses, the tobacco becomes an entheogen: a substance that induces spirit experiences.

In his book, *The Cosmic Serpent—DNA and the Origins of Knowledge* (1999), the anthropologist Jeremy Narby discusses ritual tobacco and ayahuasca use by the Ashaninca, an indigenous people living in the rain forests of Peru. In particular he relates his conversations with Carlos Perez, a forty-five-year-old Ashaninca shaman, who used tobacco and ayahuasca to talk to spirits:

> My uncle was a tabaquero. I watched him take lots of tobacco, dry it a bit in the sun and cook it. I wondered what it could be. "That's tobacco," my uncle told me. And once the mixture was good and black, he started tasting it with a little stick. I thought it was sweet, like concentrated cane juice. When he ate his tobacco, he could give people good advice. He could tell them, "This is good," or "This is not good." I don't know what the intellectuals say now, but in those days, all the Adventist missionaries said, "He is listening to his bats, to his Satan." He had no book to help him see but what he said was true: "Everybody has turned away from these things, now they all go to the missionary. I do not know how to read but I know how to do these things. I know how to take tobacco, and I know all these things." So when he talked, I listened. He told me:

"Listen nephew, when you are a grown man ... you must not only learn how to write, you must also learn these things."

Listening to Carlos's stories, I gradually became familiar with some of the characters of Ashaninca mythology. For instance, he often talked of Avfreri: "According to our ancient belief, he is the one of the forest, he is our god. He was the one who had the idea of making people appear." Carlos also referred to invisible beings, called maninkari, who are found in animals, plants, mountains, streams, lakes, and certain crystals, and who are sources of knowledge:

"The maninkari taught us how to spin and weave cotton, and how to make clothes. Before, our ancestors lived naked in the forest. Who else could have taught us to weave? That is how our intelligence was born, and that is how we natives of the forest know how to weave."

Hypnagogia and hypnopompia

Hypnagogia and hypnopompia are the liminal states between wakefulness and sleep. The former refers to the state during onset of sleep, and the latter to the state that precedes waking. It is during these sleep phases that phenomena such as lucid dreaming, sleep paralysis, and hallucinations can happen. These hallucinations can feel much more vivid and real than regular dreams, and can be terrifying or transcendent.

These phenomena are most prevalent when the person is particularly close to their waking state, due to factors such as an ongoing background noise in their environment. Dreams and hypnagogic/hypnopompic hallucinations can be much more vivid when normal REM sleep has been suppressed due to sleep deprivation, drugs, or drug withdrawal.

I became especially interested in lucid dreaming and these hypnagogic/hypnopompic "threshold states" when I was a teenager. Other youths around me were experimenting with drugs, and reporting their experiences, but I wanted to know how far my mind could go without the interference of drugs. I purposefully abstained from all recreational drugs, apart from very moderate alcohol consumption, until my first experiences with magic mushrooms and LSD at the age of thirty-six. I thought that if I could explore some of these borders of the consciousness and imagination then I might have a better understanding, and therefore an easier experience if I ever did choose to take drugs or engage in magical ritual later on.

These threshold states of sleep can be either voluntary or involuntary. Normally, when an individual is asleep, their brain induces a paralysis of the body in order to prevent them from acting out their dreams. This is because when one is dreaming of moving, the motor cortex is still active, running the same "circuits" as if one was actually moving. Without this paralysis, the sleeper, who may be dreaming of running, will actually act out the running. This phenomenon has been studied with cats. In 1959, the French neuroscientist Michel Jouvet experimented with cutting specific parts of cats' brains which are responsible for paralysis during sleep. These cats have been shown to chase imaginary prey and run and leap even though they are asleep! In situations where the paralysis is not properly activated, the sleeper will act out their dreams. Sleepwalking is a common example of this. The opposite of sleepwalking is sleep paralysis: an involuntary state during hypnagogia or hypnopompia where the paralysis of the body is not properly "switched off". During sleep paralysis, the sleeper is aware of what is going on around them, almost as if they were awake, but they feel as if their body is frozen, a state that many people report as terrifying. To complicate matters, they also hallucinate, commonly experiencing entities entering their space and holding them down, sitting on their chest, or otherwise restraining them. Anyone who has experienced this can tell you that these hallucinations do not feel at all like dreams, and are very difficult to distinguish from reality.

Throughout history, writers and artists have tried to depict or describe sleep paralysis, and it has given rise to many legends such as the fabled "night hag", a demon who holds the sleeper down. Other examples of sleep paralysis entities include succubi and incubi, demons who try to have sex with the sleeper in order to interfere with their chastity.

As a teenager and young adult, I enjoyed trying to reach the state of hypnopompia voluntarily. Usually I would attempt this while travelling on trains, as the constant gentle noise would provide an "anchor" on which to remain partly conscious, as well as providing a mesmerising sensation. The results were very strange and thrilling. Dream-people would turn up, sit opposite me and engage in fascinating conversation, only to suddenly and shockingly disappear as soon as I awoke. These entities would feel like real people right until the moment that they disappeared. In one such attempt, this same experience happened over and over about fifteen times! Each time, a new person would turn up, an old wise man, an attractive woman, a young man, etc. Every time I would have forgotten about the previous hallucination, and every time I awoke, they would disappear and I would feel the same shock, suddenly realising "It's happened again!" Each conversation felt fascinating, deep, and emotionally engaging, but to my frustration, as I suddenly awoke, all specifics about what was said would disappear along with the apparition.

John Henry Fuseli—The Nightmare 1781.

I have been able to repeat this experience many times, such as while travelling on a ferry. Something about an unfamiliar environment and a constant gentle noise seems to help. Unfamiliar sleeping environments make these experiences more common. Apparently, we tend sleep less deeply when we aren't at home, perhaps an evolutionary trait that kept our hunter gather ancestors safe from attacks by predatory animals and rival hominids.

These threshold states offer an opportunity for the magician to engage with voice hearing and "spirits" without needing to fear going mad. As with my other recommended experiments, an open-minded approach is advocated. These experiences can feel very real and intense, but cannot actually harm you.

Likewise, learning to control these states can be a therapeutic way to learn to overcome the fear that can come with involuntary sleep paralysis, voice hearing, and nightmares.

Tulpa and servitors

Now that I have outlined some varieties of voice hearing as a result of sleep states, drugs, prayer, grief, and schizophrenia, let's compare these with a couple of examples of spirits purposefully summoned by magic.

Tulpa is a term from Tibetan Buddhist traditions for spirits that are created through imaginative meditation practice. These thought-forms are considered by some to be adult imaginary friends, and by others to be real spiritual entities, that are brought into existence by magic.

The term tulpa is an adaptation of the Tibetan term *Tülkus* and it began circulating in the West following the 1929 publication of *Magic and Mystery in Tibet*, by the Belgian-French explorer and theosophist, Alexandra David-Neél. She was, in turn, heavily influenced by her fellow theosophists Annie Besant and Charles Webster Leadbeater, especially from their book *Thoughtforms* (1901), in which they discuss various ways to manifest thought through magic and meditation.

More recently, since the 2010s, tulpa magic has found popularity on some internet forums, with "how to" guides and tulpa communities appearing on social media and YouTube.

The practitioners report their experiences with tulpas as sub-personalities that share their body, or as accompanying spirits that follow them around.

In traditional Tibetan Buddhist magic, these types of incarnations were often used to help expel negative parts of one's psyche, or unwelcome thoughts. The magician might create a tulpa that represented an internal fear, or an addictive tendency. They would then have an "entity", which they could compartmentalise, negotiate with, or banish. The hope was that the original negative aspect or behaviour would disappear once the thought-form was done away with. This is similar to the concept of exorcising demons, except that in this case the spirits are deliberately created as personifications of energies, intrusive thoughts, or bad habits in order to separate these unwanted quantities from one's self. Demons, in contrast, are usually considered to be pre-existing entities, and are therefore less deliberate.

The more recent "Western" tulpas seem to be more often used to provide companionship. They appear to have initially arisen from fanbase communities for anime and specifically the mostly male fanbase of the *My Little Pony: Friendship Is Magic* cartoons, who refer to themselves as "Bronies". As amusing as that may sound, genuine magical experimentation can be found in even the most unlikely of interest groups!

Tulpas in these communities are said to arrive out of daily meditations and it can take more than a year of practice until they gain their own "agency". They are often explained as the practitioner's mental processes being "divided", so that they become two personalities sharing one body. The resulting tulpa personality does not normally fully possess one's body but instead hangs around as a presence. In situations where the experiment becomes negative or unwanted, it is said to be possible to dissolve the tulpa with further meditation.

The following is an excerpt from an academic study (2015) of tulpa phenomenon by Dr Samuel Veissiere, assistant professor of psychiatry at McGill University in Montreal, Canada:

> Of 73 tulpamancers tested on this question, 37% reported that their tulpas felt "as real as a physical person," while 50.6% described their mental companions as "somewhat real—distinct from physical persons, but distinct from [their] own thoughts" and 4.6% claimed "extremely real" phenomena, where tulpas were "indistinguishable from any other agent or person." Only those 4.6% claimed to hear and see their tulpas "outside" their heads. The median length of tulpamancy experience for these respondents was one year. Tulpamancers with more than two years' experience reported higher degrees of somatic experience.

Related to the tulpa is the concept of a servitor. Servitors are a concept used in chaos magic that are similar to tulpas, except they are created to fulfil certain tasks, and then usually destroyed by the magician once the task is complete:

... At least in the type of magick developed by Spare, Carroll, and
Phil Hine, a servitor is a part of the magician's psyche, or a part of
the Deep Mind that the magician evokes to perform a task. Do these
entities have an existence prior to their evocation? Perhaps. Magick
is trans-temporal, trans-spatial. (Marik, 2000)

I think that the use of servitors is more widespread than most people
might think, and goes beyond the sphere of those who consider themselves magicians. People personalise their cars with nicknames, and
imagine them to have personalities. They have imaginary friends as
children, or develop complex emotional relationships with their toys.
They personify "lucky" objects, or can find their personal obsessions,
or addictive habits morphing into "demonic" sub-personalities with
which they have arguments. All of these can be considered projections
of "spirit". Servitors and tulpas are just very deliberate examples of the
types of spirit we might create.

As we can see, the subject of hearing voices is complex and diverse
and offers many opportunities for a curious magician. For many cultures and subcultures, hearing voices is a part of regular experience,
rather than merely a symptom of psychosis. As such, regardless of our
starting point, we ought to accept that hearing voices is probably something that most of us are capable of given the right context, and something that we can learn to control.

Would you take the effort to induce your own spirit-hearing experience? As strange and scary as it may sound, if you are interested in
magic, I recommend it.

Next, we will make an exploration into what spirits really are, and
how they relate closely to some everyday concepts that we interact with
all the time.

CHAPTER 9

Spirits

Our laws are based upon values which, without their divine pendency, would be empty and unenforceable. Our national mottos and hymns of state are usually divine invocations. Our kings, presidents, judges, and officers begin their tenures with oaths to the now silent deities taken upon the writings of those who have last heard them.

—Julian Jaynes (1976)

Non-physical entities

In times past, nearly all human cultures considered the world to be imbued with spirits. In the modern era, many feel that these beliefs have fallen away and that spirits are mere superstitions from primitive people. Contrary to this common modern viewpoint, I will explain how we all still engage with spirits, using other terms.

Many everyday concepts can be framed pragmatically in terms of spirits, without recourse to superstition. While superstitions or false beliefs that harm the believer can be a genuine concern, many traditional spirit beliefs can be shown to serve a practical purpose. Misunderstandings have left us in a confused state, which not only has resulted in the frequent dismissal of traditions from other cultures, but has often left us unable to discuss aspects of our *own* culture. We do indeed live in a spirit- filled world, even if not explicitly in the "paranormal" sense.

Many of us take for granted that psychology was the first "real" field of inquiry to engage in the study of the mind. Stated so simply, it is easy to see how this couldn't be further from the truth. People have surely tried to comprehend the human mind for as long as there have been people with minds. If we have lost touch with older understandings, it is only because it takes effort to understand the worldview of other cultures, including the cultures of our own ancestors. Because of the ethereal nature of mind and thought, and our limited understanding of the brain, previous systems of explanation looked very different to that of modern science. Often they used stories, analogies, and symbolism to describe thoughts, thought-forms, and the entities that exist in thought-space.

In many older traditions, the mind was explained using dense terminology that looks as impenetrable to the modern psychologist as psychology today can look to the layperson. This serves as a roadblock to our understanding. Systems such as Kabbalah, Buddhist or Vedic cosmology, the Egyptian *Book of the Dead,* as well as all the countless mythological systems from around the globe, have made maps to explore the human psyche. These spiritual cosmologies include many different ways to discuss the same concepts explained by psychology today, and we will look at two of these: the sephiroth from Kabbalah, and the chakra system from yoga and tantra in the later chapter, Ladder Cosmologies (Chapter 19).

First, I offer you a small challenge. Go and read a passage from a spiritual book; perhaps in the Bible, or another religious text, and replace the words "soul" and "spirit" with the word "mind" and see if you can still make sense of it. I usually find that the terms are, with a few exceptions, interchangeable. I also find, as a person living in the early twenty-first century, that the text often becomes much more relatable when I exchange these terms. Perhaps this will allow one an initial understanding of spiritual texts that was prevented before, and the missing nuance can be filled out later. When you learn a foreign language, you must first speak it badly before you can speak it well.

Rather than regarding the spirit world as a secondary plane of existence that only rarely engages with our tangible experience, let's instead think of it, for the sake of thought experiment, as the category of concepts that contains thought, intention, influence, and form. Because we humans are creatures who alter our environment to suit us, ideas influence almost everything that we do. As such, is there really any quantifiable difference between a spirit, as understood as a bodiless entity with its own willpower, and a powerful idea that leaps from mind to mind, influencing people's behaviour as if it had intentions of its own? At first it might seem easy to find differences, but I have found the more one learns about spirit traditions, the more these differences disappear.

One thought experiment I sometimes put to people in order to understand this mental roadblock between the modern Western conception of reality and the spirit world, is to have them imagine what it would be like to try to explain the internet to a medieval person. I imagine it going like this:

21st Century Man:	"In the twenty-first century we use something called the internet to send each other messages instantly."
Medieval Man:	"Instantly? How so?"
21st Century Man:	"We send the information, like you would write in a letter, through wires and radio waves."
Medieval Man:	"What are these wires?"
21st Century Man:	"A bit like strings that energy runs through."
Medieval Man:	"What does that look like?"
21st Century Man:	"We can't see the information as it's travelling directly, it's invisible until it arrives on a screen."
Medieval Man:	"What is a screen?"
21st Century Man:	"It's a glass window of sorts through which we see writing and pictures."
Medieval Man:	"Oh, right. I've heard of that, it's similar to what we call 'scrying', and it's done through a looking glass by wizards and witches."
21st Century Man:	"I guess that's one way to look at it."
Medieval Man:	"What are radio waves though?"
21st Century Man:	"Well, instead of the information passing through wires, this time there are no wires."
Medieval Man:	"How does the information travel then?"
21st Century Man:	"Through energy waves, a bit like light, only again, we can't see them."
Medieval Man:	"How confusing, it sounds like spells. And you use this to send letters?"

21st Century Man: "Well, not just letters, but pictures, moving pic-
                     tures, sounds and music too."
Medieval Man: "Oh, so you send the information through
                     sound?"
21st Century Man: "No, we can't hear it until it arrives, and also we
                     can send the information over immense distances
                     anywhere in the world, much further than sound
                     will travel … Hmm … I'm starting to realise how
                     hard this might be for you to understand."
Medieval Man: "Actually, I think I understand now. We have
                     witches and soothsayers who claim to send com-
                     munications over great distances instantly. They
                     do it by communicating with spirits, or projecting
                     their own spirit beyond the reaches of their bodies.
                     Clearly your internet is on the spiritual plane. Are
                     you all magicians in the twenty-first century?"

Idea constructs

Does an idea get trapped in a person, or does a person get trapped in
an idea?

Are ideas, laws, memes, identity, fads, cultural characters, and other
similar concepts spiritual? In my personal experience, magicians from
numerous backgrounds readily accept this idea.

How many parts of what we consider our "self" are non-physical?
Your persona? Your charm? Your reputation? Your influence? Your
legacy?

I would argue that most of what you think of as "you" is non-physical,
and these parts of yourself live as an exchange of ideas, impressions,
influence, and stories. One might argue that all these forms of information are transferred by physical means, but often these means can prove
impossible to pin down.

When I was a child, I kept a diary for a short time. Quickly growing
bored of the standard daily entries, I realised that I could skip pages
and leave messages from my past self for my older self to read. Weeks
later, upon reading the entries, I wondered: who was the Ari that was
communicating from the diary? He no longer had a body. My body is
only ever controlled by the present version of myself. Yet, there on the
page, that spectre from the past existed as an intangible aspect of my
selfhood. This is, in part, what your spirit is. The past *you* that lingers

when you are no longer physically present, and the aspects of you that continue to affect people when your body is elsewhere.

So, now that I have set the stage. Let's conjure up some spirits. We need a definition. One that is wide enough to compare many things, but not so vague that it isn't practical.

Depending on who I am talking to and their set of beliefs I tend to juggle between two definitions:

- For hardened sceptics, I discuss spirits as: ideological constructs that operate in the world as if they have will.
- For spiritualists, I discuss them as: non-physical beings, with which we can interact.

I feel any difference between these two definitions is unprovable, as we have no way to run a test. What is the practical difference between something that appears in every possible way to exist and one that actually exists? There is, until further evidence is discovered, no pragmatic difference.

We live in an age of media that claims to have given up on old gods, yet is saturated with TV shows and movies about superheroes, who are, in many cases, themselves based on old gods. For a bit of fun, I will use Batman as an example.

Most people would not describe Batman as being a spirit. Yet, many people have told stories about Batman, dressed as Batman, and have otherwise engaged with the concept of Batman. New stories about Batman are probably being written as we speak.

Despite not being an entity confined to a single human body, Batman has definable characteristics that allow us to recognise him. In his stories, Batman has particular character traits: a personal history, relationships, intentions, strengths and weaknesses that are relatable to our human experience.

There are ways to tell stories about Batman that are acceptable to an audience. There are also ways to get Batman wrong.

Although he is arguably more vague in concept than a particular human being, Batman's fans still easily recognise him when he appears in print, image, and film.

Batman and his nemeses serve as metaphors for aspects of the human morality struggle, but his stories also generate wealth and jobs for an entire media infrastructure through comic books, games, toys, clothes, and films. Some people are also influenced by Batman, for better or for worse, exactly as they could be influenced by a real person they have met. Although not "real" in the sense that your physical body is real, Batman has a very similar, or perhaps the same kind of reality as a mythological god, or indeed as your own past self.

Swearing at your car, and other spirit interactions

Sometimes people swear at their cars when they won't start. It's as if, in the moment, they believe the car is alive and they wish to punish it for not behaving. Under times of stress and pressure, even people who might consider themselves rationalists will often revert to magical thinking, such as swearing at the imagined personality of an object. There are scientific studies that show that swearing can literally decrease our perception of pain, so it appears that there can be small practical payoffs to these actions (Stephens et al., 2009); some catharsis or stress relief at the very least. In order to swear at an object and get the emotional and analgesic payoff, you have to first imbue the object with an imagined spirit.

These small spirit interactions reveal that even "modern" humans are still wired for animism. Animistic cultures are those that believe that everything has a spirit that can be communicated to or negotiated with. The beliefs of the Lakota people from the North American prairies in the United States give us an example:

> Depending on the context, animals, spirits, ghosts, rocks, trees, meteorological phenomena, medicine bundles, regalia, weapons, and other objects were seen as persons or subjectivities, selves with souls, capable of agency and interpersonal relationship, and loci of causality. Personhood was extended to most things in one's environment with which one communicated and interacted, and the potential for personhood was ever present. This animist worldview effectively dissolved the boundary between what Westerners call nature and culture. As Oglala author Luther Standing Bear writes. (Posthumus, 2017)

Memes and mind viruses

The following is a quote from the famous antitheist and geneticist, Richard Dawkins (1976). Here, while introducing his concept of "memes", he comes peculiarly close to describing the existence of spirits:

Examples of memes are tunes, ideas, catch-phrases, clothes fash-
ions, ways of making pots or of building arches. Just as genes propagate themselves in the gene pool by leaping from body to body via
sperms or eggs, so memes propagate themselves in the meme pool
by leaping from brain to brain via a process which, in the broad
sense, can be called imitation. If a scientist hears, or reads about, a
good idea, he passes it on to his colleagues and students. He men-
tions it in his articles and his lectures. If the idea catches on, it can
be said to propagate itself, spreading from brain to brain. As my
colleague N. K. Humphrey neatly summed up an earlier draft of
this chapter: "... memes should be regarded as living structures,
not just metaphorically but technically. When you plant a fertile
meme in my mind you literally parasitize my brain, turning it into a
vehicle for the meme's propagation in just the way that a virus may
parasitize the genetic mechanism of a host cell."

Despite being a polemicist against religion and often magic too, here
Dawkins is himself using pragmatic magical thinking. The only difference between his "meme" and a spirit is the attribute of will. Spirits
have wants. They are trying to get certain things done. Dawkins says
memes are replicating structures, similar to living organisms, as if they
have a will to live and manifest. Spirits in some sense are like personified memes, who likewise wish to manifest and to replicate and
develop.

Just like the other memes, they need our involvement (or that of
other living things) if they are to manifest in the physical. Similar to
a computer virus, which uses the computer's processing power, or a
biological virus, which hijacks the replicating "machinery" of the cell,
the meme/spirit puts our minds to work in order to engage with the
human world.

Later in the chapter, Dawkins even describes how memes can grant
us a kind of afterlife:

We were built as gene machines, created to pass on our genes. But
that aspect of us will be forgotten in three generations. Your child,
even your grandchild, may bear a resemblance to you, perhaps in
facial features, in a talent for music, in the colour of her hair. But as
each generation passes, the contribution of your genes is halved.
It does not take long to reach negligible proportions. Our genes
may be immortal but the collection of genes that is any one of us

is bound to crumble away. Elizabeth II is a direct descendant of William the Conqueror. Yet it is quite probable that she bears not a single one of the old king's genes. We should not seek immortality in reproduction.

But if you contribute to the world's culture, if you have a good idea, compose a tune, invent a sparking plug, write a poem, it may live on, intact, long after your genes have dissolved in the common pool. Socrates may or may not have a gene or two alive in the world today, as G. C. Williams has remarked, but who cares? The *meme complexes* of Socrates, Leonardo, Copernicus and Marconi are still going strong.

Not only can a person continue to influence us after they die, but their ideas can still carry aspects of their will. Companies that last generations will usually continue some of the original ambitions of their founder. Part of their willpower can become detached from their individuality to continue their mission.

One of the strangest ways I have come across in which this has happened is with L. Ron Hubbard, the founder of Scientology. Scientology is a mixture of a religion, a self-improvement racket, and a space cult. There were many moments in Hubbard's life where he behaved in a paranoid fashion. During his lifetime he was accused by his wife Sara of being a paranoid schizophrenic. She said that he himself had come close to being institutionalised during their marriage. There are other reports from throughout his life that reveal that Hubbard had moments of severe mental illness, and it was likely that he sometimes suffered from paranoid schizophrenia (Miller, 1987).

Hubbard targeted any person who spoke out against Scientology, calling these people "suppressive persons". Sometimes these were detractors from the general public, and other times they were ex-Scientologist apostates. These people were to be shunned by Scientologists, even if they were family members, and were considered dangerous influences who might poison the minds of the initiated.

To deal with any polemicists who spoke out against Scientology, Hubbard wrote a set of guidelines he called "Fair Game". This encouraged Scientologists to stalk, film, photograph, and attempt to ruin the reputation of these people (Anon, 1979; Hubbard, 1967).

Because the very rules of Scientology were informed by Hubbard's personality, including his apparent mental illness, Scientologists today are still, in some cases, acting out under these orders of Hubbard's paranoia.

Although Hubbard died in 1986, his paranoia still lives on in the institution he founded.

This could easily be thought of as a "spirit" that started in Hubbard, and now exists in the rules of Scientology, jumping from body to body in order to enact its will.

Demons and invasive thoughts

Demons are spirits, or idea constructs, who take more than they give, or otherwise disrupt an individual's well-being. They often try to blur themselves into the person so that the person can't tell which is their own personality and which is the unwanted invader.

Here, we will look at two belief systems, one from Christianity and one from Islam, which have long equated demons with invasive thoughts. These invasive thoughts can be considered as parasites hijacking our mental processes. Much like the computer virus comparison mentioned earlier with memes, invasive thoughts, obsessions, and cyclic thinking can cause an individual to behave in ways that trigger the same unwanted mental phenomena in other people. They can be contagious, just like viral memes, jumping from head to head.

It's now common to explain invasive thoughts and cyclic thinking as internal psychological phenomena, even if the sufferer themselves feels as if they are interacting with an outside entity. Although the term "demons" can be vague, it is clear that, especially in Christian orthodoxy, including the writings of the Desert Fathers (the first monks in the third to fifth centuries CE) that the particular demons in question are the same phenomena that psychologists now refer to as "invasive thoughts".

> Since obsessional thoughts are inconsistent with one's sense of self and threaten one's self-image, they possess a quality that psychiatrists refer to as "ego-dystonic" or "ego-alien", as if coming from outside the person's normal sense of self. Obsessions are typically experienced as "an uninvited guest popping into my head". Or as psychiatrist Jeffrey Schwartz puts it, obsessions "seem to arise from a part of the mind that is not you, as if a hijacker were taking over your brain's controls, or an impostor filling the rooms of your mind.

The sufferer feels like a marionette at the end of a string, manipulated and jerked around by a cruel puppeteer ..."

... as Gregory the Great wrote in the sixth century, the demons constantly "besiege [*obsidentes*] the minds of men with bad thoughts ... If you have blasphemous thoughts, do not think that you are to blame. God knows what is in our hearts and he knows that ideas of this kind come not from us but from our enemies [the demons]." (Graiver, 2016)

Orthodox nun, PhD, and author, Mother Melania of the Holy Assumption Orthodox Monastery, describes the relationship between spirits and invasive thoughts in this interview excerpt from the documentary *Battling Darkness* (2013):

The [Desert] Fathers say it is worse to be possessed by your passions, than it is by a demon, and the reason is the possession by passions is in fact, a worse form of possession by demons. I might want to stop here and define passions, because in the context of our culture we tend to use that in a positive sense, but the word passion, it comes from "to suffer" ... and therefore it's a passive type of a thing, it's something that's happening to me. So when the fathers talk about the passions ... when they are using it in the negative sense they are talking about those bents inside us that are leading us away from God. There are demons associated with them. There are demons of gluttony, there are demons of pride, there are demons of lust. If I am putting my effort of mind and will towards thinking about, you know, that really good-looking guy, or you know, "I can't believe Sister so-and-so did that" ... these dumb things that we get into, we're making ourselves homes of demons.

It was understood that there was mental illness at least 300 years before Christ, and the fathers of the church, they don't have a problem with that [concept].

To those sceptical of demons, the idea of external entities sending thoughts into human minds can seem superstitious. The alternative is that we generate our own invasive thoughts and therefore, when we have them, it's a kind of malfunction of our thought process. A "broken self". I would argue that in some cases, thinking of invasive thoughts as demons can be pragmatic. It allows the sufferer to more easily compartmentalise which thoughts they want to keep and which thoughts they want to "exorcise". We have discussed this in the previous chapter when talking about tulpa. There exist ritual practices to split off the unwanted habits into a sub-personality and then exorcise them. With this clearer distinction between self and non-self, does one stand a better chance of regaining control over one's thoughts? It could be worth a try for those who have had little success with the idea that their invasive thoughts happen because they have a broken mind.

In Islam, there is similar concept: whispering demons that are called Waswâs. These are also often equated with the type of cyclic thinking and invasive thoughts that affect sufferers of mental disorders such as obsessive-compulsive disorder, anxiety, and post-traumatic stress disorder. Spirit believers can attribute these distractive and negative thoughts to outside entities who interfere with human concerns in the same way as we discussed with the Christian examples.

> Waswâs al-Qahri is a manifestation of some kind of "obsessive-compulsive disorder" commonly expressed in Muslim populations. Muslims who suffer from Waswâs al-Qahri showed, beyond acceptable behaviours, extreme acts and behaviours in acts of worship and their daily activities. For example, Muslims with Waswâs al-Qahri have anxieties or fear that their acts in the process of ablution or the prayer itself are somehow inadequate and that the acts must be repeated until reaching a self-defined perfection. The strength of these Waswâs may vary, so much so that they appear, to non-specialists, to be very strong and it seems that the sick person is doing that willingly. From an Islamic perspective, these unwanted thoughts are whispered into the minds and hearts of people by Jinn. There are different types of Waswâs al-Qahri including: Waswâs al-Qahri Fee Aqeedah, obsession related with belief; Waswâs al-Qahri Fee Taharah, obsession related to purification; and Waswâs al-Qahri Fee Kwaf Min Fuqdan al Saytara [fear of losing control], obsession related to cognitive and affective experiences of losing control of one's life. (Rassool, 2020)

The following is a transcription from a YouTube video of Muslim imam Muhammed Tim delivering a sermon about Waswâs at his mosque in 2008.

... And then there are those people who get Waswâs, whisperings
of the shaitan [devils or evil spirits] in matters of belief, for example about Allah, about whether Islam is true ... And then there are
those people who get Waswâs of the shaitan in issues relating to
al ibadat—relating to acts of worship. Like people who get confused in their purification. Or people who get confused in their
salah—prayer ... And likewise those people who get Waswâs of the
shaitan, as it relates to their muamalat—their dealings with people.
For example, decision making ... and people who get Waswâs in
relation to their relationships and their friendships, and they start
thinking that someone meant something that they didn't mean, or
they start having problems in their marriage because they are getting this whispering that their husband is not being true to them or
honest with them or the wife is not being faithful to them and so
on and so forth.

While many Muslims believe in the existence of shaitan (devils), we
can see that the concept also functions to explain intrusive thoughts,
just like traditional Christian beliefs in the besieging of the mind by
demons. It would be oversimplifying to say that beliefs in demons are
only a way to frame mental illness symptoms, but it is clear that there
is a lot of crossover. This is one angle that can help believers and non-
believers relate. After all, the goal to try to remove unwanted phenomena from the mind is the same.

Roman genius and other tutelary deities

In connection with the idea that one's influence can be regarded in
terms of spirit, let's take a look at the guardian spirits, referred to as
tutelary deities. One of the most common conceptions of a tutelary
deity is that of the guardian angel: a spirit assigned to a person, place,
nation, or institution which guides and protects. Despite the fact that
many Christians believe in personal guardian angels, this concept is
surprisingly absent from the Bible. While guardian angel type spirits
can be found in many traditions, I will focus on a particular concept
from the ancient Roman religion, the "genius", which has had a great
influence on Western society.

The word "genius" is now usually used to describe either a very
intelligent person, or more specifically, and to me more importantly,
a person whose work transforms the way their society understands

the world. The word genius, however, originally had spiritual connotations, which only serve to make the modern interpretation more intriguing.

In ancient Rome, a genius was a spiritual aspect of a person, place, institution, or thing. Each family had a genius; a guiding male spirit attached to the paternal family line and an accompanying female "juno" spirit attached to the maternal line. These dual spirits came together in union to guide the father and mother of the household respectively. They were especially invoked to ensure the fertility and good fortune of a clan or family line. Sacrifices and prayers would be offered by members of the household to their genius and juno, especially during ceremonies such as anniversaries and rites of passage.

Roman family genius sculpture from the first century.

Another related guardian spirit was the "genius loci", a spirit of a place, that could be similarly invoked in order to protect that place. These can be seen depicted in artwork and sculpture at temples, and other landmarks, both in Roman ruins as well as on modern buildings and landmarks. The term "genius loci" has since been co-opted by architects and town planners to describe the emotional effects of a place on its inhabitants, and how these effects can be modified by designers; another form of magic.

As Roman culture progressed, genii were increasingly invoked by governors and generals to influence their subjects. Libations had traditionally been offered from an individual to their own genius at ceremonies, especially when celebrating achievements that brought honour to a household.

A breakthrough was made when Roman Emperor Octavius, who later became Augustus, transformed his own genius into something for his whole nation to invoke and worship. In 30 BCE, libation offerings to the genius of Augustus were made mandatory at public and private ceremonies. Augustus and his predecessor Julius Caesar, like the Egyptian pharaohs before them, set up the concept of the imperial cult, or nation under a god-emperor.

This was a very powerful, yet risky, act of magic. By transferring the focus of power from a human to a spirit, that power of authority can reach much further in its influence. However, the will and intent of that spirit is now partly shaped by its worshipers and can take on a "life" of its own, like a tulpa, separating from the will and control of its originator. By detaching the will of the individual from the person in this way, the spirit and its influence, like a meme, can also stay around much longer than a single human lifetime. Certain genius spirits, such as Jesus Christ, grow huge and seemingly immortal, and so detached from their source that we can't always know much about the person who began the process.

It is important to note that the genius of a person was not the same as that person. In a similar way, the influence or legend of a person can be considered a separate aspect from a person contained in a body. When we discuss the genius of Einstein, we are usually more interested in the ideas and influence that Einstein set in motion, his genius, than we are in Einstein the corporeal human being.

In the case of a royal family, or similar dynasty, the genius, through heirdom (the Crown), can be passed from individual to individual.

With powerful genii, it's not often very clear whether the genius is serving the person, or the person is serving the genius. This type of genius represents all the rules and expectations of the people it governs. It contains a symbolic container for a common identity, and can be the focal point for ideology.

We can see an example of this today on the images on our coins and banknotes. Most often they depict people who now act as genii to uphold the currency's value. Sometimes these genii are historical figures, but they can also be cultural characters, such as Marianne, the personification of the French Republic, who was depicted on the franc as well as on postage stamps. Or the Statue of Liberty, which depicts Libertas, a politicised Roman goddess, who has been depicted on ancient Roman coins, as well as on the US dollar. The Roman concept of genius was later compared by theologians such as Augustine with the idea of a Christian soul. The influence and what we remember of a person, their genius, survives death, and offers us a conception of the afterlife, albeit one without the ego.

In the British Commonwealth, Queen Elizabeth II could be considered to have been a living vessel for the genius, which is the Crown. In most of her public appearances, she was like a priestess who adds spiritual authority to a ceremony. Jesus Christ is the genius of the Christian religion, and in Catholicism, the Christ genius is communicated with via the genius loci of the Vatican, which is served by the pope, another human priest who serves as a focal point for the genius of the guiding "spiritual father".

As we can see, these genius spirits are to be found throughout all cultures, and can be useful for understanding the symbolism by which we structure society.

Legal personhood

Corporate personhood is the legal concept under which a corporation can have some of the same legal rights and responsibilities that a person holds. Although it might initially seem strange to those who have never considered it, legal personhood serves the practical purpose of allowing corporations to enter into contracts with other parties. So, for instance, an individual can sue a corporation instead of an individual within that corporation. It also allows corporations to sue individuals and other corporations, especially when it comes to debts, payments, and ownership. This concept has actually been around for a long time, with some historical precedents in ancient India, ancient Rome, and in the Catholic Church.

Lawyers and written law are a phenomenon of cultures that use writing and written records. These are spells that manipulate the perception and behaviour of human beings. Before they were written, laws were created through public counsels and spoken ceremony. This might involve gift exchanges, monuments, and importantly to us, the invocation of spirits.

Under modern conventions, a punishment for breaking a law might result in a fine or imprisonment enforced by police, judges, bailiffs, and prison guards. Many cultures, however, have used more spiritual forms of magic, enforced by magicians and chiefs. The punishment will often be a curse. A curse can function using the spirits and invasive thoughts which I have already discussed. A magician uses the target's own mind against them, causing cyclic thinking, anxiety, stress, or other mental or psychosomatic ailments, until the person's ability to function is severely affected. A powerful magician will know ways to achieve this trickery even if the target regards themselves as a non-believer in magic. Such is the powerful nature of suggestion. We will explore this further later on in Chapter 21.

Added to this, if the other villagers are horrified by the broken taboo, then the perpetrator can be shunned. They may be expelled, attacked, given the cold shoulder, or treated like a ghost. In living situations where members of the group are co-dependent on each other, this can result in the perpetrator being cut off from food or other resources necessary for survival.

Recently here in New Zealand, there has been a fascinating case of national law combining with Māori spiritual beliefs, in order to protect their homelands. The Ngāi Tūhoe Iwi (tribe) has had a long historical battle to protect their North Island homeland of Te Urewera since colonisation by the British, and later the Government of New Zealand. Invoking their traditional spirituality, which describes the land as a living entity and ancestor, and modern state law, Ngāi Tūhoe successfully won a court case in 2014 to have their homeland Te Urewera recognised as a legal person under national law.

> Te Urewera is a legal entity, and has all the rights, powers, duties, and liabilities of a legal person. (Te Urewera Act, 2014)[8]

---

[8] https://wwgislation.govt.nz/act/public/2014/0051/latest/DLM6183601.html

Te Urewera was previously considered by New Zealand law a national park protected by the Crown. Below is a direct quote from a Tūhoe writer, Linda Waimarie Nikora describing her beliefs regarding her homeland:

> Te Urewera is very much part of Tūhoe. If Tūhoe talks to Tūhoe, then you are talking to Te Urewera as well. You cannot separate the two. We are all around and within it.
>
> We have relations here, there and there. And we are all intertwined. Tūhoe and Te Urewera are one. It is incomprehensible to see them as separate. I cannot for the love of me make them separate. (Te Awekotuku & Waimarie Nikora, 2003)

These rulings show that the invocation of spirits to protect places and resources is still powerful and can be combined with the law-spells of national legal systems to cross cultural boundaries and align guardianship values between indigenous cultures and nations. "Legal persons" must be cared for as if they were a spirit. The acknowledgement of the Māori spiritual beliefs and the granting of custodianship is an acknowledgement of the spirit of Te Urewera.

Furthermore, the legal success of the Tūhoe has set a legal precedent. In 2017, legal personhood was granted to the Whanganui River, settling a 140 year old land rights dispute between the New Zealand Government and Māori. After this, also in 2017, legal personhood was granted to the Ganges and Yamuna rivers in India, both sacred to Hindus.

As we have seen, spirits do not denote a simple singular concept. Experiences of non-physical entities are common, and probably an unavoidable intrinsic part of the human experience. Many of the ideas that we consider modern and rational have more in common with spirit belief than may be initially acknowledged. It is no triviality that cultures have always personified institutions, places, objects, and people's influence, and it makes little sense to dismiss these without first considering their practical purpose.

CHAPTER 10

Why you aren't just your brain

Reductionism is the belief that observing the smallest parts that make up matter will allow us to explain everything else. This ideology is an inversion of an earlier one in which all things emanate from a single all-connected source called the monad. Using the monad, the most abstract conception of God, religions and mystical traditions have sought to explain all existence from the top down. Until recently, scientists and engineers have explained things from the bottom up. As science has progressed it has been discovered that the smallest things, particles, can not be so easily reduced. Electrons and photons do not always behave separately, displaying mind-boggling entanglements with each other that belie our understanding of them as separate objects.

Though it had a precursor in ancient Greek atomism, reductionism became all the rage with the marvel of clockwork. Life started to be compared with machines. Animals began to be explained as if they were robotic automatons. Nowadays, this metaphor has developed for the computer age, and we are often compared to computers, with robot bodies. Our brains are described as mere processors, and the entirety of our personalities, thoughts, feelings, and memories merely a result of an operating system running in our skull.

Many people ponder if a personality could be downloaded as data to a computer, or if a computer could, given the right sequence of ones and zeros, gain conscious self-awareness, or even a soul. The more fervent of the transhumanists can hardly wait for a new bodiless age, where personalities live in a digital cloud and can be downloaded into a variety of human or robot bodies. The implications of this are highly dualistic, like a kind of sci-fi Gnosticism. The body is thought to be something that restricts. An imperfection that prevents us from reaching the potential of pure mind or spirit. If we were pure spirit, or pure information, then we could be boundless and free. Wouldn't that be nice? No?

These science fiction fantasies send us down the wrong track. When we restrict our studies of consciousness and perception to the brain, we end up asking the wrong questions and that has painted the scientific study of consciousness into a corner, now popularly termed the "hard problem". I propose that the pragmatic magic approach we have been exploring in this book can help us to see these issues, and I will attempt to reframe the question of consciousness and the mind here, in the hope that it will allow us a better understanding of the problem—in order that we may ask better questions, and hopefully perform better magic.

Hives

The science of behavioural biology, in particular, has already let go of reductionism.

Consider the bee. If one is to understand what a bee is, the temptation for the reductionist would be to take a bee, and put it in a laboratory environment. The bee would be prodded, pulled, given a bunch of tests, and eventually dissected in order to find out what the bee can and can't do, how it came to be, and what it is made of. The problem with this is that the bee didn't evolve in a clean spartan laboratory. That's just the place that is most ideal for scientists to do their testing. The bee, as an individual being, isn't really where "beeness" ends. Though a single bee seems at first like a simple thing, incapable of living for very long on its own, the hive of bees is something much more complex and capable.

The hive lives on a higher level of abstraction, unbound from a single body, allowing it to interact with its environment and solve problems to a much higher degree of complexity. The hive as a nest is necessary for the bees' long-term survival and should therefore be considered as an extension of their organism.

Note that while human beings and many other creatures reproduce in pairs of individuals, bees reproduce as a hive, normally having only one queen. Therefore, each bee is something more akin to an organ serving the nature and will of the hive rather than a truly separate individual entity.

Like other creatures, bees are in a constant feedback loop with their environment, which is rife with other organisms, all so interconnected in their interactions that it is very hard to fully understand all the ways in which one is affecting the other. This is particularly noteworthy in bees' symbiosis with flowers. Studies show that bees operate frequently on this group level, and are capable of perceiving the world symbolically. We can tell this by scientific studies of bee dances. The cutely named "waggle dance" of a bee can communicate the location of a nectar source by representing the distance and the direction, via the direction of the sun in relation to the hive. Not only are the sun and flowers' locations represented symbolically by the angle of the bee's dance, but it has also been found that individual bees get better at interpreting the dances the more they observe them. The bees teach each other as if by a form of language. This shows us that the hive is not merely an emergent quality of a complex of robotic bee bodies, but a feedback loop between multiple elements from the physical to the social. Waggle dances appear to be a form of protolanguage, and show that bees are capable of at least a basic level of abstract thinking.

Abstract thinking has previously been mistaken as a type of perception that only humans or a few "higher" mammals and birds are capable of. If bees are capable of it, then perhaps all creatures are able to do it to some degree. If we were to compare this hive/body dichotomy to humans, one will see that we have different levels of existence at different layers of organisation. From here I will start with parts of the body and colony of life forms that live in us and work "upwards" to the mind.

The body is a colony

While it is often useful to think of your body as a single "you", it is also a colony of independent life forms. Many of these parts of the greater "you" are also capable of independent action and treat your body as their environment. We depend on a complex colony of bacteria, which reside primarily in our guts, to digest our food. Modern medical science now shows that these bacteria have a strong effect on our over-all behaviour and mood, and therefore influence our conceptual, social, and emotional world. Gut bacteria are responsible for the production of serotonin, a vital chemical for brain function and mental health.

On a nervous system level, our brain, brainstem, spinal cord, and the nerves that branch out along our body all behave as an interconnected system. Some of our reflexes, such as the age-old hammer-to-the-knee test that doctors sometimes perform, don't require the brain at all, but are triggered from the spinal cord. Does this mean that the spinal cord must be considered part of the brain?

To complicate matters further, humans have a second, less under-stood neural centre in our gastrointestinal tract. Called the enteric nervous system, and sometimes referred to as the "second brain", this nerve cluster has roughly 500 million neurons; more powerful than the spinal cord, which has about 100 million neurons, but less powerful than the cranial brain which has about 86 billion neurons. We are not fully aware of the function of the enteric nervous system. However, we know it is capable of functioning independently from the main brain and brainstem. The enteric nervous system is deeply wired into the larger brain via the vagus nerve and prevertebral ganglia. It seems that this "gut-brain" might be necessary for some automatic and subconscious processes.

As we make new discoveries, the idea that we have only one brain, and that it alone is responsible for our consciousness, becomes more dis-tant. It has recently been discovered that the heart also contains neurons and does some of its own neural processing. Perhaps these discoveries will continue until we are forced to treat most of the body as a think-ing extension of the brain? At the very least, the idea that our person-hood is contained entirely within the cranium must now be put to rest. The transhumanist's dream of becoming bodiless and immortal by having their minds uploaded to computers may be dashed by the necessity of also modelling the human body in order to function, and perhaps many of the restrictions that a body brings with it.

Embodied cognition and enactivism

One of the problems in the contemporary neuroscientific study of consciousness, I think, is really sort of a basic fundamental one, which is that we've been looking for consciousness in the wrong place, we've been looking for it inside of us. For me that's a profound mistake. That's a bit like trying to find the dancing in the musculature of the dancer. Or trying to find the value of money in the chemical composition of the dollar bill. It's the wrong kind of place to look. The idea that I've had in my work is that instead of thinking of consciousness as something that happens within us, in our brains or anywhere else, why don't we try and think of consciousness as something that we do, or enact, or perform in our dynamic involvement with the world around us. (Noë, 2012)

Here, I will summarise two related philosophical theories that look beyond the brain to explain cognition:

- Embodied cognition: A theory which purports that any full understanding of the human brain should also take into account its relationship with the rest of the body.
- Enactivism: The idea that much of our cognition arises from interaction with our environment, rather than entirely in the brain.

Whatever assists you in solving a problem can be thought of as part of the cognitive process. Because we have been told so often that our brains are "us", and that all cognition happens within our brains, at first it seems hard to swallow that part of our cognition could take place outside the body.

Perhaps the first hurdle for many is the common metaphor of an environment as a backdrop, like a stage set in a theatre, which is somehow separate from the actors. Instead our environment is constantly negotiating itself with us, containing its own actors and actions. Our behaviour in the world affirms our existence. If we push, the world pushes back.

It is not usually necessary for the brain to contain a complete model of anything that we interact with. This includes our own bodies. The brain is already a very energy-thirsty organ, consuming around twenty percent of the energy required to fuel our entire bodies. When there is a way to conserve body energy, it can result in an evolutionary advantage.

For this reason, we only need to store the amount of information in our brains required to interact with our environment. We do not need to model the parts of our environment that take care of themselves, which is to say, most of it. Much of our memory and perception consists of workarounds, shortcuts, heuristics, and hacks, rather than the maps, lists, or files one would expect to find in a computer. Solving problems in the environment often takes less cognition than trying to solve them entirely in your head. Consider working out a complex maths problem on paper compared to trying to keep track of all the terms in your memory. This "offloading" of cognition into the environment allows us to perform tasks that are too much for our brains alone.

In 1986, an Australian roboticist, Rodney Brooks, conducted experiments to see if robots consisting of multiple modules could perform tasks without the use of representations, models, maps, or any unified operation. One of his robots in particular, named Herbert, proved this was possible.

Herbert was designed to move around the lab, collecting Coke cans. It did this despite not being able to maintain any internal processing for longer than three seconds. Furthermore there was no communication between any of Herbert's separate modules. Each behaved like a separate robot. One set of sensors allowed it to avoid obstacles such as walls. Another allowed a mechanical arm to position itself in relation to a can. A mechanical hand made a grasping motion when it was in a particular position in relation to the arm, and so forth.

By a clever chaining of completely separate functions, Herbert was able to collect the Coke cans despite having no unified program to do so (Symons & Calvo, 2009).

Brooks's idea, named "subsumption architecture", became influential in robotics, theories of intelligence, and embodied cognition. If a robot can complete complex tasks that arise out of separate chained functions, perhaps life forms, including human beings, sometimes exploit this approach also.

Kirsh (1995) provides a classification of ways in which humans arrange objects and features of their environment in ways that help them compensate for the limitations of their relatively limited cognitive resources. In Kirsh's scheme, we use the spatial arrangements of objects in order to regulate certain task choices, to simplify perception, and to simplify internal computation. By initially gathering all the ingredients one wants to put in a salad near the sink, one thereby simplifies subsequent task choices. This provides a visual cue concerning what items are to be used and what is to be done with them. Moving the washed items over to the knife and cutting board indicates what is to be done next. In stacking spare pieces of wood appropriately, a carpenter can facilitate the later choice of pieces for use in protecting the work piece when clamping and hammering. In working around a sink with a garbage disposal unit, it is often convenient to block the drain opening to prevent something from falling into the unit. This spares the user having to choose a safe place to put an object that might fall into the unit. These are cases in which the use of space facilitates certain task choices. (Symons & Calvo, 2009)

If we are a mind-body system, it is incorrect to frame the environment as something completely separate from us. Much of what we like to think of as our mind is an interaction with our environment. This is one of the reasons it is so hard for many people to understand how minds relate to brains. Our cognition contains so many shortcuts that we are forever cut off from any pure reality, including much of our own nature and the workings of our own bodies. We simply never evolved with the end goal of understanding ourselves.

A person needs only to store instructions with which to skilfully manipulate a tool, rather than storing a model of the tool. The tool does what it does. We do not need to understand every aspect of its make-up in order to use it. We need only to respond to feedback, such as the sensation of operating a hammer, and react accordingly. Writing things down helps us think, as does talking a concept through. Many of us have realised that when we try to teach something to another person, we end up learning it better ourselves. The interaction with the person helps us order our thoughts.

Enactivist theory holds that this external interaction with the environment should be considered as part of your cognition. External tools like shopping lists, notes, computers, and calculators free up short-term memory. Given that we have very limited short-term memory, the cognitive boost acquired by memory-aids, such as writing, is *enormous*.

Furthermore, the world of ideas is as much a part of our environment as the physical world. For instance, a human being who lacks language is going to be severely restricted in how they can operate in the world where language is pervasive. It is here especially that the extended mind and enactivist ideas start to converge with magic and magical thinking. Magical rituals will frequently alter the environment on purpose, to alter perception towards particular outcomes. We can see this going on with theatre, musical performances, and religious rituals such as the Catholic Mass.

Put simply, an individual, their mind, their environment, and their social sphere are so interconnected that it's not fully possible to say where one ends and the other starts!

Social and cultural realms

Just as the bee has evolved to be part of a hive, so the human being has evolved to be part of a social sphere: small group relationships with other human beings or animals, such as livestock and pets. This social sphere interaction is almost always necessary for finding a mate, and must therefore be treated, in evolutionary terms, as real. Awkward or crass people often find their social opportunities diminished. Charming people often find them increased. Already we have a sphere of reality where interactions, such as charm and persuasion, have a profound effect. Charm and persuasion are, of course, a huge part of magic.

At a body level, humans reproduce through sex. But at a social level, as we have discussed with Dawkins's meme theory, we also reproduce through ideas. Above the social level is the vast network of social groups that we call culture. Here, we find categories of action and identity such art, music, tradition, and social hierarchy. All of these have a profound influence on the individual and their opportunities to act.

These non-physical influences are so fundamental to being a human being that it might not make sense to speak of a "self" without other people, let alone a physical environment.

So let us lay out clearly what this tells us:

- Your consciousness is not a "thing", nor is it "in your head". It is a process constantly reaching out into the environment and affirming itself. Human consciousness requires a brain, and an environment to interact with. Part of that environment is a network of other brains doing the same thing.
- You are in constant process with your environment, and it's that process that creates the feeling of "you". Your selfhood is developed among other people. You are a collection of roles, and these roles are regularly in negotiation with others.
- Your memories (as we discussed in an earlier chapter) are not stored in a complete fashion. You only retain enough information so that

they can be recomposed when you get stimulus from outside. Your self-awareness requires these constant triggers. Without them, we lose the "keys" to access many memories. Because of this, it is not a given that a brain raised in a vat without feedback from the senses, or a body, would be conscious at all.

- The "environment" is not merely a bunch of objects. The environment, considered properly, happens at every level you can perceive patterns at. At the tangible level, the material level, the individual level, the social level, the societal level, the moral level, the cultural level, the idea level, and at the spiritual level. Learning new fields of study opens up new conceptual environments. All human environments involve symbolism, and our relationship to symbols can be manipulated through magic.

- We are constantly negotiating what we can and can't do with the environment. What we can do, in large part, determines who we are. Changing the environment changes us. Because we don't ever take in the world all at once, even shifting our perception of our environment can radically affect our opportunities to act. If magic is the ability to manipulate the perception in accordance with the will, then acts of magic can also radically affect who we are.

Ideas can change the way we perceive and interact with objects. The abstract is in a constant interaction with the concrete, and therefore magic and magical thinking are not only unavoidable, but present us with powerful tools to alter reality as we understand it. Ideas form the self as much as bodies do. Environments are as necessary as brains, and social environments are just as formative to us as physical environments.

For all these reasons, it does not make sense to restrict all that you consider to be you to the functions of your brain. For the same reasons, hard-line materialism is not a tenable position for an effective magician.

In the next chapter, I will take a break from neuroscience and discuss some common ways that magic affects us day to day.

CHAPTER 11

Magic is around us every day

C ontrary to those who would suggest that magic belongs to the past, I would argue that the technology and ideology of the contemporary world has thrust us into the most magical age we have yet seen. We live in a world full of charms. Our attention is constantly funnelled and manipulated by the magicians that call themselves advertisers, artists, musicians, political campaign managers, PR people, and publicists. To name but a few.

If magic is the ability to shift perception in accordance with the will, then aren't the advertisers who are trying to peddle you things that you don't need, magicians? Aren't advertising logos just spells in the form of symbols that engage our attention and manipulate our desire? I used to think I was too smart for that. I had my impulses under control. My will was my own ... Here's how I discovered I was wrong.

The charm magic of advertising

One day I was driving down a road in the city where I live, Christchurch, New Zealand. I wasn't paying much attention to anything other than the road, and for once my mind was fairly quiet. Suddenly a strange thought came into my head: "You want a can of Coca-Cola."

Possibly, we have all felt that impulse. Only, the thing was, that I don't drink Coke. I hadn't bought a Coke in over a decade. What was going on? This impulse felt like a deep familiar habit, but I had never been in the habit of craving Coca-Cola. How had this foreign desire infiltrated into my mind under the guise of one of my own thoughts?

The cognitive dissonance caused by this desire came to a sudden reprieve when I passed a Coca-Cola sign on a dairy (convenience store). I knew the road well enough to realise that I had passed at least two or three other dairies in the last two or three minutes. Because I was off-guard, the magical Coca-Cola sign had infiltrated its way into my subconscious and re-manifested itself as pure desire. I was stunned at this realisation. I had heard about subliminal advertising, but this was the first time I had knowingly felt its effect.

Another time around 2009, I was at home and had begun to watch the Tim Burton remake of the film *Charlie and the Chocolate Factory* on TV. Television advertisements in NZ at the time were placed so that you were able to watch only about twenty minutes of the movie undisturbed. After that, the ad-breaks would increase in frequency as you became more invested in the film. By the last quarter, there was almost as much ad-time as film run-time.

I got to roughly halfway through the movie and a very similar, strange, detached desire came to me: "It's the ads now. If you hopped into the car you could probably make it to the dairy and buy a chocolate bar (again something I almost never did) and make it back in time."

Before I knew it, I was back in my chair holding a Pinky bar. Not my favourite type of chocolate bar by a long shot.

"How the fuck did that happen?" I thought.

Pretty soon it was ad time again and an advert for Pinky bars came on. During a movie themed around chocolate. I had been charmed! I swore off TV after that. I had always been annoyed by ads, but now I also started to fear them. I had come to the realisation that they are a type of magic spell.

After I stopped watching TV, I began to feel better. More in control. Less pressured. My willpower felt stronger. I was out of the range of TV advertisers.

Having read about witchcraft, charms, and curses from a young age, I started to see many aspects of our culture as having something in common with magic. As previously discussed, one of the primary ways a curse works is by using someone's mind against them. The worst ads do this too. They play on our subconscious fears or desires. Later on, I took a sales-service role at a bank. I was told to use a particular curse to sell insurance to bank customers. Something called "creating doubt". If the customer said they were not interested in having insurance, we were told to say things like: "But what if your house burned down, would you have enough to get started again?" or "If you were to have an accident and lose your job, would your family have enough to get by?"

I was being asked to make the customer afraid, in order to part them from their money for the benefit of the bank. I am not adverse to insurance, but I found the proposal of using fear as a lever of manipulation very distasteful. I didn't stay at that job for much longer.

Logos as sigils

In occult magic, a sigil is a symbol created by a magician as a charm in order to manifest their desire, or control the behaviour of other people. Sigils abound in most magical systems. Here are three examples:

- **Galdrastafir.** A variety of Icelandic magical staves, which were used as charms in Icelandic witchcraft from the seventeenth century onwards.
- **Vévé.** Sigils used to invoke the Lwa (or Loa), the primary spirits of the Voudou religion, which is found in various forms in Latin America, the Caribbean, and the Southern States of the US, and has its roots in the religion of the Yoruba and Fon peoples from West Africa. During ceremonies, the elaborate Vévé are

Ægishjálmur "Helm of terror". Used to create fear in enemies, protect the warrior, and promote success in battle.

drawn, usually on the ground. They are specific to each of the spirits.
- **Sigils.** Austin Osman Spare, the English occultist (1886–1956) created a method for creating sigils to manifest wants by manipulating the subconscious of the magician. Later the method was popularised

The *Vevé for Papa Legba,*
Guardian of the spirit world.

by the Chaos Magic movement which started in England in the 1970s, and is still popular today. The magician creates a sigil by writing out a desire. Then removing the vowels and repeating letters. Finally, the remaining characters are rearranged to create a design. This is then used to prime the magician's subconscious in order to manifest a desire.

I will see a red toyota corolla
w l s   r d t y   c

Sigils don't only appear in the realms of the occult. Advertising logos are also sigils. The McDonald's "Golden Arches" and the aforementioned wavy Coca-Cola logo have become so recognisable that they now act as lures, pulling in customers. They don't just present themselves as to say, "food and drink available here". They also operate through conditioning to generate the very hunger and thirst that would cause you to buy them in the first place. They can appeal directly to our animal drives, sometimes bypassing the rational mind completely. This would sound like superstitious nonsense if it wasn't backed up by market research:

> Using the techniques of so-called motivational research, advertising
> firms first identify our often hidden needs (for security, conformity,
> oral stimulation) and our desires (for power, sexual dominance and
> dalliance, adventure) and then they design ads which respond to

these needs and desires. By associating a product, for which we may have little or no direct need or desire, with symbols reflecting the fulfillment of these other, often subterranean interests, the advertisement can quickly generate large numbers of consumers eager to purchase the product advertised. (Arrington, 1982)

The even more direct link between production and wants is provided by the institutions of modern advertising and salesmanship.

These cannot be reconciled with the notion of independently determined desires, for their central function is to create desires—to bring into being wants that previously did not exist. (Galbraith, 1958)

Like Pavlov's famous experiment in which ringing a bell would cause a dog to salivate in anticipation of being fed, the sight of the Golden Arches signals "snack time". People will often submit to this desire even when they were not initially very hungry.

Once when I was fourteen, around 1995, I was on an evening school trip. My mother had given me ten dollars for dinner, and we were let off the bus in Timaru, a town in New Zealand not particularly known for its sophisticated dining options. In an attempt to see how much food I could get for my money, I took advantage of a McDonald's special for 95c hamburgers. I bought ten hamburgers for dinner, expecting to have to give some of them away to friends. I found myself, to my shock, to still be hungry after eating all ten. What kind of culinary witchcraft was this? High calorie food that doesn't fill you up?

From then on I became suspicious of McDonald's. I stopped considering it a meal and instead treated it like a type of confectionary. I found myself craving it often, even though every time I bought it, I found the flavour to be very disappointing. It took quite an act of will to see the Golden Arches and not suddenly forget that I didn't actually like McDonald's. By the age of seventeen, I had given up on McDonald's for life. I must, however, give them credit for my first awakening on the charm magic of manufactured desire.

Music as charm magic

On a more positive note, charm can also be used for good. When I first started studying magic, I began looking for a way to engage with it that utilised my talents. In my late teens, I encountered the graphic novels of the writer/magician Alan Moore.

> There is some confusion as to what magic actually is. I think this
> can be cleared up if you just look at the very earliest descriptions
> of magic. Magic in its earliest form is often referred to as "the art".
> I believe this is completely literal. I believe that magic is art and
> that art, whether it be writing, music, sculpture, or any other form
> is literally magic. (Moore & Vylenz, 2003)

This wide definition of magic got me started on the journey that has
produced this book. Alan Moore chose writing as his primary approach
to magic. My primary approach has been through music. I took Alan
Moore's take on magic as a challenge and decided to treat my musical performances as magical spells to charm people into having a good
time. I learned to keep a careful eye on the audience while I performed.
My performances normally involve a large amount of improvisation,
centred upon a blues or funk groove. I also frequently perform as a one-
man-band, which gives me full scope to transform the music as I play
without the restriction of requiring bandmates to follow my lead.

Alan Moore.[9]

Pretty soon, the audience reactions radically improved. I was taking
more risks and getting bigger payoffs. Removing songs and approaches
that didn't work as well, and developing those that did. If people are

---

[9] By Fimb—Alan Moore, CC BY 2.0, https://commons.wikimedia.org/w/index.php?curid=4686143.

dancing, I will play more dance songs to keep them there. If the dance floor is dwindling, I will play something lower key to give them a break, and then time the energy to come back up when their energy is restored, something I learned from watching good DJs.

I've often heard other musicians blame the audience for a performance that has not met their expectations. This can be a self-defeating trap. I believe that the performer must hold themselves responsible for the performance. They need to be able to adapt to each context, and to give the audience what they need in order to have a good time.

Prior to my magical awakening, perhaps half of my performances would meet my expectations, while the other half would not work out as well as I hoped. After reframing my music as a set of charm spells, almost every gig has been successful, with great audience feedback.

The author in action.

Now, you might dismiss this as merely a state of mind, and I would agree, except that there is nothing "mere" about it. States of mind, as discussed earlier, radically affect what you can and can't get done in the world. The ability to positively influence people's state of mind is a huge power, and it is fundamental to how and why we use music. I was no longer a hobbyist. I had become a professional musician.

Art is, like magic, the science of manipulating symbols, words or images, to achieve changes in consciousness. The very language of

magic seems to be talking about writing or art as much as it is talking about supernatural events.

A grimoire for example, the book of spells, is simply a fancy way
of saying "grammar". Indeed to cast a spell, is simply to "spell" to
manipulate words, to change people's consciousness, and I believe
this is why an artist or a writer is the closest thing in the contemporary world, that you are likely to see, to a shaman.

At the moment, the people who are using shamanism and magic
to shape our culture are advertisers. Rather than trying to rile people up, their shamanism is used as an opiate to tranquilise people.
To make people more manipulable, their magic box of television
and by their magic words, their jingles, can cause everybody in the
country to be thinking the same words and have the same banal
thoughts, all at exactly the same moment. (Moore & Vylenz, 2003)

Acting as invocation

For another wonderful description of how performance can function as
magic, I would recommend Keith Johnstone's book *Improvisation and
the Theatre* (1979). Especially his chapter on "Masks and Trance". It discusses the nature of invocation, and possession which is a large factor
in all successful acting.

> We had a Mask that had a thick droopy nose and angry eyebrows.
> It was a deep, congested red in colour, and it liked to pick up sticks
> and hit people. It was quite safe so long as the teacher knew this and
> said "Take the Mask off!" sharply at the critical moment. Someone
> borrowed it once—Pauline Melville, who had taken over my classes
> at Morley College. Next day she returned the Masks and said that
> someone had been hit on the arm. I had to explain that it was my fault
> for not warning her. (And I pointed to the Mask that hit people.) I once
> saw three similar droopy-nosed Masks—they were Kabuki Masks,
> and they were on the hanamichi (the platform that runs through the
> audience) and yes, they had sticks and were threatening people.
> Another Mask was called Mr Parks. This one used to laugh,
> and stare into the air, and sit on the extreme edge of chairs and fall
> off sideways. Shay Gorman created the character. I took the Mask
> along to a course I gave in Hampshire. The students were entering
> from behind a screen and suddenly I heard Mr Parks's laughter.
> It entered with the same posture Shay Gorman had adopted, and

looked up as if something was very amusing about the ceiling, and then it kept sitting on the extreme edge of a chair as if it wanted to fall off. Fortunately it didn't, because the wearer wasn't very athletic. It really makes no sense that a Mask should be able to transmit that sort of information to its wearer.

Once students begin to observe for themselves the way that Masks compel certain sorts of behaviour, then they really begin to feel the presence of "spirits". I remember a Mask I'd just made. A student tried it out and turned into a hunched, twisted, gurgling creature. Then a latecomer arrived, picked up the same Mask, and the identical creature appeared.

Another example of the way that acting intersects with magic can be found in this 2012 interview with Nicolas Cage, a Hollywood actor, famous for his outrageous in-character freakouts. Here, he discusses his magical acting method, which he amusingly calls "nouveau shamanic":

Interviewer: You've developed an acting discipline that you've referred to as Nouveau-Shamanic, is that correct?

Nicolas Cage: Yeah.

Interviewer: What are the core principles?

Nicolas Cage: I've been told that all actors really hail from the early medicine men, and the shamans in the villages pre-Christianity, where they would put on masks and act out, and really they were probably pretty crazy, but they would go in and find answers to questions. Today you are called psychotic if you do that, but it's all semantics. So what I would do is I would put on Afro-Caribbean paint [gesturing to his face]. Like a white and black paint and black out my eyes so I look like this sort of Afro-Caribbean Voudou icon, and then I would sew in bits of Egyptian artifacts that were thousands of years old into my costume, and gather some onyx or tourmaline or something that was meant to have "vibrations", and who knows if it works or doesn't, but for me it was an idea of trying to stimulate my mind, or trick my mind into believing I was this character from another dimension, and I would walk on the set and then wouldn't speak to anybody. Wouldn't say a word, so I projected this aura of horror which created fear in my fellow actors, which then inspired me to believe I really was this character.

I would argue that both the Johnstone's masks and Nicolas Cage's self-transformation can be considered "invocation". That is, the drawing in of a different personality, or spirit, into oneself. As we have previously discussed with spirits back in Chapter 9, it may be the case that outside entities are entering the body of the actor and enacting their will, or it could be that the actor is temporarily constructing a second identity, which can appear to have its own will for the duration of the scene.

Either way, the outcome appears outwardly to be exactly the same, and it can not only be difficult for an observer to tell the difference, but also difficult for the actor. Some method actors find that the best performance results come not only from seeking to live out the experience of the character, but also bending their own identity towards believing they *are* the character.

For a pragmatic magician, these examples hint at the kinds of everyday magic that one should look out for. Understanding the ways in which we can be manipulated, for better or for worse, is the first step towards being truly free to choose the way one reacts. Taking the art of performing seriously as a game of influence upon one's audience can radically focus a performer, in ways that can be beneficial to both them and their audience.

For those pragmatic magicians who are just getting started, I would suggest beginning by working with whatever it is that you are already good at. Once one's confidence is rewarded by real world results, one can then move on to try more difficult types of magic.

Nicolas Cage, from *Vampire's Kiss* (Bierman, 1989).

CHAPTER 12

The origins of modern science

In the next six chapters I will correct some frequent misunderstandings of history involving science, magic, and religion. Beware. What is to follow might upset some who prefer to not have their worldview upended. Any piece of history is always somebody's narrative. My own one here sets out to disprove several incorrect common narratives that I feel have gone unquestioned for too long, causing a deep distortion in our worldview. These need to be corrected if we are to really understand magic. I have the type of personality that prefers complex truths to false certainties. It's often within these complex and uncertain areas that we can find the best leverage points to create magic.

Among the common beliefs about magic, religion, and science in the contemporary world that don't live up to historical scrutiny are:

- The idea that science has been practised throughout history in a way that we would recognise today
- The idea that science and religion are natural enemies that have been in conflict for most of history
- The idea that science and magic are of different origin and necessarily at odds with each other.

Secular science is recent

The word "scientist" was coined by William Whewell, a science historian, theologian, natural philosopher, and Anglican priest. The term was first published in 1833, in his review of Mary Somerville's "On the Connexion of the Physical Sciences", in the *Quarterly Review*, a literary and political periodical published in London.

Previously, those who we now call "scientists" were referred to as "natural philosophers".

As an interesting side-note, William Whewell also coined the terms "physicist", "linguistics", "astigmatism", "electrode", "cathode", "anode", "dielectric", and a several other important scientific terms. In the eighteenth and nineteenth centuries, it was common for Christian clergy to be interested in natural philosophy. They often held to a doctrine referred to as "the Book of Nature", where it was thought that good Christians ought to study and understand two "books" with equal zeal: "God's word", the Bible, and "God's creation", nature.

Portrait of William Whewell, 1794–1866.

Until the late sixteenth century, natural philosophy was one of many branches within the core subject philosophy. After that, it gradually become a specialised field, eventually evolving into science as we understand it today.

Modern science is rooted in empiricism, where evidence is acquired by observation and experimentation, and then the collected data is analysed. Empiricism has only become the dominant approach to studying nature since the Enlightenment, which historians usually place as beginning around 1715, the year that Louis XIV, King of France died. This event sparked an anti-monarchy movement that led to the French Revolution. Before that, and contrary to popular belief, natural philosophy had always had a strong tie with both religion and magic. During the Renaissance in particular, natural philosophy was deeply intertwined with Christian humanism, old Jewish lore, Kabbalah, and magic; especially divination, astrology, invocation of spirits, and scrying (communicating with spirits visually through objects such as a crystal ball).

Many science historians treat Renaissance alchemy as a type of protoscience. A careful look however, will reveal that alchemy is not merely a primitive version of modern chemistry. It is also a moral system of self-improvement, a highly mystical framework for understanding "God's creation", and a collection of systems for magical communication with spirits.

If an alchemist had trouble with a chemical experiment, it was not unusual for him to summon an angel or spirit through automatic writing or scrying in order to help "inspire" him towards a solution. This is well documented in the Enochian magic of John Dee and Edward Kelley, or in Paracelsus's invocations of the Elementals: Gnomes, Sylphs, Salamanders and Undines, which were used to express the classical elements earth, air, fire, and water. Removing the moral, mystical, or magical components of alchemy would have seemed to be defeating the point to an alchemist.

One of the best sources I have found for explaining alchemy and its nuances is the modern alchemist and educator, Dennis William Hauck (2019):

> Alchemy dates back to a time when our two cultures of science and religion were part of one true philosophy, a collection of ideas that has been called the perennial philosophy because it keeps popping up in many different guises no matter how hard people try to suppress it. Basically the philosophy of alchemy consists of three general principles. The first is that the universe is striving towards perfection. The whole universe is becoming aware. The levels of awareness comprise a gradient of reality from lower frequency to

higher, from lead to gold, from utter darkness to whitest light, from dead matter to pure mind …

The second principle is that consciousness is a force in nature … and if you can fortify or concentrate your own consciousness, you can project that power into the world around you, just as the "one mind" fashioned the cosmos from the chaos of the "one thing" … Furthermore, when mind acts on matter it imposes its essence or truest nature on it, and thus everything, everywhere carries the archetypal signature of its creator.

The third principle of alchemy: all is one. The levels of creation are determined by the interplay of the one mind and the one thing. Or the forces mind and matter, spirit and soul in the universe.

Matthieu Marrian, the alchemical tree, standing under the influences of the heavens. Seventeenth century (Emblem 5-Avri potabilis chimice preparati).

Alchemy has regained a cult following in large part through the influence of Carl Jung, who used its symbolism as a framework for explaining the psyche. Although I am a fan of Carl Jung's ideas, his "spiritual", which leaves the chemistry out, can be a roadblock to understanding how the Renaissance alchemists truly thought. To them, chemistry was a means to understand the spiritual nature of God's world, and the spiritual cosmology of alchemy was a means to understand the chemistry. Modern chemistry, where matter is treated as a mindless substance, would look very alien to them. Likewise, "spiritual alchemy" would seem to them untethered to the world, without the grounding purpose of understanding nature.

Spiritual alchemy was also incorporated into the magical practices of the Hermetic Order of the Golden Dawn, perhaps earlier than Jung. The Golden Dawn is one of the most influential societies of modern magic, being the formative training ground for famed magicians such as Aleister Crowley, Dion Fortune, and Israel Regardie, as well as the source material for movements such as Wicca, Neo-Paganism, and the psychedelic movements of the 1960s and 1970s. For those drawn to ritual occult magic, the Golden Dawn is a popular, and appropriate, place to start.

The Islamic golden age and the Western Renaissance

In the West, the Renaissance forged a movement to discover the universe's secrets, a drive that continues today with modern science. This movement was rooted in the theology and morality of Islamic and Christian humanism. Using ancient Greek knowledge preserved by the Byzantine Empire (the eastern remnant of the Roman Empire), the Islamic Empire, which was itself largely built upon the earlier Persian Empire, underwent a mathematical and alchemical golden age, which lasted roughly from 786 to 1258 CE. As well as the writings of the ancient Greeks, the Islamic Empire had access to Chinese, Indian, and Persian writings, which allowed them to form great libraries and the academies known as "madaris".

Thus began a movement to translate the wealth of ancient scholarship into Arabic, creating a culture of education that made great advances in maths, astronomy, medicine, and medieval chemistry. This golden age was underpinned by the Islamic ideals of education, government sponsorship of scholars, and the dominance of the Arabic language. All of these advancements were thoroughly intertwined with scholarship of the Quran.

Contrary to common narrative, which tends to describe Europe and the Islamic world as separate entities, the Islamic world had a steady influence on medieval Western scholars. No more so than during the Islamic occupation of Spain, a state known as Al-Andalus, from 711 to 1287 CE. Western alchemy was based on the many Islamic works which were translated into Latin, especially those of Jābir ibn Hayyān, who is better known in the West by his latinised name "Geber", and those of Abu Ali Sina, also known in Latin as "Avicenna".

Jābir ibn Hayyān, died 806–816 CE.[10] Abu Ali Sina, 980–1037 CE.[11]

In the West, the Renaissance began with Petrarch (1304–1374), who brought forth the idea that if God has granted us our great intellectual and creative capacities, then it is our duty to use these faculties to their fullest extent. Discovering and pondering His universe was considered a devotional act. Petrarch wished to combine his Catholic faith with his deep interest in classical Latin and Greek literature. He considered the study of ancient wisdom to be both a moral and a practical pursuit.

---

[10] https://commons.wikimedia.org/wiki/File:Jabir_ibn_Hayyan_Geber,_Arabian_alchemist_Wellcome_L0005558.jpg
[11] From the collections of the Bibliothèque interuniversitaire de santé.

Unlike earlier religious thinkers he regarded the acquisition of knowledge, both philosophical and empirical, as a way to understand and venerate God, for it was believed that God ordered the universe. This created the humanist ideal which powered the Renaissance, and is still a powerful belief today, albeit in secular form.

Later, during the Enlightenment, God was replaced with "nature". Gradually, the idea of a divine will began to dissolve. The acquisition of knowledge shifted gradually from a pious humanist value, to an individualistic one. Over time, religion became increasingly mistrusted, and natural philosophy gradually became detached from religion and the clergy. The term "science", a Latin word for "knowledge", and the value that knowledge ought to be pursued for its own sake, go hand in hand. With the onset of modernism in the mid nineteenth century onwards, there was a gradual value shift from venerating the great wisdom of the past, especially the classical Greek and Roman philosophers, towards a fervent faith in progress towards a bright future. New became better than old. The common beliefs of our ancestors became passé, often seen as foolish. Usefulness became a primary value, replacing salvation and duty to please God. Technology and science were expected to fix all the world's ills, and send us towards "Utopia": a concept itself, perhaps ironically, inspired by the Christian idea of God's "Kingdom on Earth" as predicted in the Book of Revelation.

One of the primary drivers for technological breakthroughs since the Renaissance has been the industrial complex, especially during wartime. The main criterion for this type of science has not been the discovery of God's universe, nor nature, but utility. Canned food, duct tape, digital photography, and the internet are all examples of inventions developed initially for needs during wartime.

The long view of science vs. the short view

Now some may protest that I have taken an overly short view, and that an all-inclusive history must trace science back even as far as the ancient Greeks; especially Aristotle, Pythagoras, and the Atomists, Leucippus and Democritus.

Although the influence of these ancient thinkers is clearly fundamental to the development of science right through until modern times, any history of science that draws such a long, unbroken line will have to contend with an issue: today we consider science to be a secular undertaking. In the past, however, there has been no easy distinction to be made between science, religion, and magic. Only since the scientific revolution, starting in the mid sixteenth century, has science slowly become secularised. Even then the influences of magic and religion still often creep in. Any long view of science reaching back into the Renaissance, or medieval, or even ancient times, will have to contend with the fact that the old "scientists" have so often been magicians, diviners, clergy, mystics, astrologers, and monks.

Add to this that the ancient and medieval seeker had no consistent scientific method. "Scientific method" evolved as a term in the mid nineteenth century just like the word "scientist". Before that, "science" was much less unified, less consistent, and less empirical. There do exist earlier approaches that propose a type of systematic method, like those put forth in Francis Bacon's *Novum Organum* (1620). Still, these approaches to testing and forming conclusions took a long time to evolve into the scientific method which we recognise today.

Heroes of science, or magicians?

Isaac Newton (1642–1727), one of the fathers of calculus, is often discussed as an early scientist by modern historians, particularly those with a limited understanding of the Renaissance worldview. At a closer look, however, he was more correctly, in both attitude and method, one of the last alchemists. This becomes clear when reading his works directly, which are filled with mysticism, symbolism, numerology, and religious ideas. Newton spent a large part of his life trying to decode the biblical Book of Revelation in order to understand its esoteric wisdom. He considered himself a magician, in particular a numerologist, penetrating the mind of God in order to produce an absolute frame for the universe. His concept of gravity, for instance, was that of a mysterious unexplained force, or "spooky action at a distance" (a phrase coined by Einstein to disparage what he saw as incomplete scientific claims). His understanding of optics, which has left us with the legacy of the "seven colours of the rainbow", was informed, not by empiricism, but by his desire to align the light spectrum with the seven notes of the major scale in music, as well as the seven heavenly spheres in astrology. He was a believer in Musica Universalus, or "Music of the Spheres", a principle in which the underlying patterns of the world are to be understood within a musical cosmology. These are clearly not the attitudes of a modern scientist. Now that Newton's writings, as well as those by other alchemists, can be easily accessed first hand on the internet,[12] the idea that these thinkers fit neatly into a modern materialistic worldview must go up in an alchemical puff of smoke.

Sir Isaac Newton, 1642–1726 (portrait by Godfrey Kneller, 1689).

Likewise, many in the modern Western world who view religion and science as opposing forces, cite early science "martyrs" such as Giordano Bruno (1548–1600), and Galileo Galilee (1564–1642), as evidence for religion's spite towards scientific inquiry.

Both of these figures were persecuted by the Catholic Church for their worldviews and antics. As such, it is popular today to view the Catholic Church in particular, and Christianity in extension, as being opposed to the scientific worldview. Looking historically, this can be shown to be little better than a conspiracy theory, one which will be closely explored, and debunked, in the following chapter.

Giordano Bruno, for example, exemplified by such modern science celebrities as Neil DeGrasse Tyson (2014) for his discussion of life on

---

[12] Sir Isaac Newton Online http://sirisaacnewton.info

Giordano Bruno, 1548–1600.[13]

other worlds, was, in fact, a magician. Bruno wrote several books on magic, in particular, *De Magia*, *Theses De Magia*, *Magia Mathematica*, and *De Vinculus in Genere*. He was also a reactionary theologian, preaching Arianism; the idea that Jesus was not divine, but merely an enlightened human being.

This view directly undermined Catholic authority, and Bruno was particularly scathing in his criticism of the Catholic Church's doctrine. Aside from a hypothesis that other stars might be suns with their own planets, and perhaps their own life forms, Bruno can not be easily argued to be a scientist. For his religious and magical crimes in particular, as well as his loud opposition to the Catholic authority, he was burned at the stake as a religious heretic. Not, as is often suggested, for being a scientist.

Galileo is another historical figure considered to be a "science martyr" by many. Popularly thought to have been persecuted for his scientifically influential heliocentric model of the universe, Galileo was in fact also a polemicist railing directly against Catholic authority. After his writings on heliocentrism caused a stir, the Catholic Church commissioned a book from him in Latin, the language of scholars, to "teach the controversy". The only condition was that he dedicate it to the pope, and not be rude about it. Galileo instead wrote a platonic dialogue, in common Italian, where the Church's doctrine was personified in a caricature of the pope, whom he named "Simplicio" (Simpleton). He particularly quoted the conversations he had with the pope in private. For this insult, he was not executed as many claim, but was put under house

---

[13] (Mentzel, Johann Georg, Public domain, via Wikimedia Commons).

arrest, where he was attended to by his daughter, and was allowed visitors. This may seem harsh, but it can, in the context of the times, be regarded as a lenient punishment, considering that many of the more militant Catholics were after his blood. This, after all, was not the age of freedom of speech that we now take for granted. (Freedom of speech was first legalised by the United Nations in the Universal Declaration of Human Rights, 1948).

It should be noted that many scientists who come up with theories far outside the currently accepted model are still censored and critiqued like heretics today,

Galileo (1636 portrait by Justus Sustermans).

albeit without a literal burning at the stake. While religion has had its draconian moments, it should perhaps not be considered any differently from other forms of politics when it comes to censorship.

Religion's support of the sciences

Contrary to common anti-religious sentiment, much of proto-science, and science into the modern age, has in fact been funded by religious institutions. In particular, Catholic monks, especially the Jesuits, have had a huge impact on science, as did the Islamic madrasas (academies), which preceded Western universities.

The Catholic Church is still the largest non-governmental provider of higher education in the world, and almost all of its institutions allow non-Catholic students.

The Catholic Church has also been active in astronomy since 1580, completing the construction of the Gregorian Tower, a Vatican observatory built to collect astronomical data for the Gregorian calendar, in 1582. Since then, it has owned a number of observatories around the world, and has funded a steady number of astronomers. Their most prestigious achievement has been the Big Bang theory which was first proposed by Georges Lemaître, a Belgian Catholic priest, in 1927.

A list of Catholic clergy who contributed to science includes: Nicolaus Copernicus, Gregor Mendel, Albertus Magnus, Roger Bacon, Pierre Gassendi, Roger Joseph Boscovich, Marin Mersenne, Bernard Bolzano, Francesco Maria Grimaldi, Nicole Oresme, Jean Buridan, Robert Grosseteste, Christopher Clavius, Nicolas Steno, Athanasius Kircher, Giovanni Battista Riccioli, William of Ockham, Georges Lemaître, to name a few out of thousands.[14]

The Anglicans and other Christian denominations have also produced scientists from their clergy, especially during in the movement of the Parson-Naturalists in the nineteenth century. These were clergy who saw the study of natural philosophy as an extension of their religious work. The ordered complexity of the world was often used by them as evidence for a creator.

As we can see, it is problematic to view all of history under the lens of a modern set of values. In the next chapter, I will explore where the origins of the idea of a war between science and religion began.

---

[14] https://en.wikipedia.org/wiki/List_of_Catholic_clergy_scientists

CHAPTER 13

The fake war between science and religion

If science and Christianity have often been in harmony (not to mention Islam, Judaism, and other faiths), where does the popular idea of science and religion being in conflict throughout history come from?

A good place to start looking would be the French Revolution, which began in 1789. During massive economic downturn, including crop failure and difficulties in supplying bread, the hungry masses grew resentful of the privileges of the aristocracy and the Catholic Church. At the time, the Church and aristocracy didn't pay tax. A revolution took place based on Enlightenment ideals of individual liberty, democracy, reductionism, opposition to monarchy, and a new deep mistrust of religion. This fervour escalated until attempts were made to replace all traditional religion in France with an atheistic cult of "Reason", and a rival deistic cult of the "Supreme Being". (Deism is the belief that while God might have created the universe, He no longer participates in it.) Despite the horrendous violence of mass executions, the French Revolution was unsuccessful in most of its goals. The removal of the aristocracy eventuated in their replacement by the Emperor Napoleon and his house of Bonaparte, which became its own aristocratic dynasty. The attempt to remove religion severely depleted the property and resources of the French Catholic Church, but Napoleon eventually reinstated Catholicism as the national religion of France in 1801.

During the revolution and its aftermath, attempts were made to wipe out old traditions, including a movement to replace old measurement systems with the "more rational" metric system. Though the metric system became very influential in mathematics, it failed to take root in time measurement. Attempts to reform the calendar, such as with a ten day working week, were unsuccessful. It was unpopular compared with the seven day week partly because it offered only one day of rest on the tenth day. Decimal days were to be made up of ten decimal hours, split into 100 decimal minutes and 100 decimal seconds. Despite these failures, mass violence on a horrific scale, and a totalitarian destruction of culture and tradition, the French Revolution is still held by many people to be a "triumph" of reason over superstition.

Though there were starts and stops, the Enlightenment grew as a movement. Along with it developed the convenient but anti-historical idea that religions are an enemy of scientific progress.

The conflict thesis

Despite rarely being attested to directly, there is a highly influential source of propaganda about the history of science and religion which still holds great influence today. This is the *History of the Conflict between Religion and Science* by John William Draper, published in 1874.

In his 373 page volume, Draper proposes the "conflict thesis". This is the claim that science and Enlightenment ideals have existed since the time of the classical Greeks, and that religion and faith have always stood in the way of its progress. To Draper, only scientific knowledge holds any value. This is an ideology now known as "scientism".

Even though by now, most have forgotten his name, Draper's anti-religious outlook remains highly influential. Many have heard Draper's proposition through the popular voices of those influenced by him, especially a group of writers in the "New Atheist" movement spearheaded by Richard Dawkins with his book *The God Delusion* (2006). Despite the term "New Atheist", there is almost nothing new about the worldview of these writers. Most of their arguments can be found in writings of the nineteenth century, and Draper was a figurehead in that earlier atheist movement.

Recent atheistic polemicists who hold Draper's values include the late Christopher Hitchens, writer of *God Is Not Great: How Religion Poisons Everything,* Sam Harris, writer of *Letter to a Christian Nation,* Daniel Dennett, writer of *Breaking the Spell: Religion as a Natural Phenomenon,* as well as their successors such as astrophysicist and science educator, Neil deGrasse Tyson, and physicist Lawrence Krause.

In *History of the Conflict between Science and Religion,* Draper writes: "... Faith is in its nature unchangeable, stationary; science is in its nature progressive; and eventually a divergence between them, impossible to conceal, must take place" (1874, p. vii).

To take this statement by Draper seriously requires a radical dismissal of evidence to the contrary. Any cursory look at the history of theology or religious texts throughout time will show that religious faiths and beliefs have been in constant development as societal, political, and cultural pressures raise new questions, doubts, and challenges. It is not even right in most cases to say that a single person's beliefs will remain the same throughout their life.

Draper continues:

> As to Science, she has never sought to ally herself to civil power. She has never attempted to throw odium or inflict social ruin on any human being. She has never subjected anyone to mental torment, physical torture, least of all to death, for the purpose of upholding or promoting her ideas. She presents herself unstained by cruelties and crimes. But in the Vatican we have only to recall the Inquisition—the hands that are now raised in appeals to the Most Merciful are crimsoned. They have been steeped in blood! (1874, p. xi)

Draper died in 1882, so he never got to see the technological violence wrought by chemical warfare, fighter bombers, and machine guns in WWI, or the scientific hypotheses that underpinned the eugenics movement that started in America, and moved to Nazi Germany, culminating in the Jewish Holocaust, or the biological torture experiments in the name of scientific progress wrought by the Nazi Joseph Mengele, or Japan's hideous Unit 731, which conducted many of the worst tortures ever documented in history. Let alone the Manhattan Project, which produced the atomic bombings of Hiroshima and Nagasaki. Science, under the authority of violent ideologies, like religion at its worst moments, has had plenty of blood to its name.

Enlightenment values such as freedom of inquiry, freedom of speech, and empiricism have been crucial for scientific experimentation, but it has often been war that has driven scientific progress. Many modern technologies rely on discoveries which were made in wartime and funded by military or defence budgets. NASA's Saturn 5 rockets, which were the engine behind early American space exploration, came out of Werner von Braun's V2 rocket design through Operation Paperclip. Von Braun was one of the top German scientists of the Nazi regime before being granted employment by the US Department of Defense post-war. Georg Neumann's magnetic audio tape and microphones revolutionised audio recording and broadcasting. This gave Hitler the edge in spreading propaganda to a wide audience over his more conservative German political opponents. International travel was opened to the world via military aeroplane innovations. The silicon chip was miniaturised so that missiles could be guided without compromising payload. Even the internet, heralded as a great democratisation of information, was created by the US Defense Advanced Research Projects Agency, in the form of the ARPANET, in order to distribute military commands and other classified information transfers that would otherwise be vulnerable to a nuclear strike on a centralised headquarters.

Despite what many of us who grew up in the twentieth century were taught, technology in and of itself has no inherent morality. Its uses and aims reflect the ideology of its wielder.

As mentioned in the previous chapter, rather than being universally opposed to science, religious establishments, especially in the Islamic and Christian empires, have, in many cases, encouraged and funded science, and natural philosophy before it. To continue believing in an age-old war between science and religion requires picking and choosing from history, and ignoring all evidence to the contrary. An approach which is not at all enlightening.

In the next chapter, we will explore science's relationship with magic, the often forgotten partner to science and religion, and in the chapter after that, I will describe the similarities and differences between science, magic, and religion, so that we may better understand where it is pragmatic to use one or the other.

CHAPTER 14

Science's on and off again relationship with magic

As we have examined previously, the Renaissance combined magical practices with chemistry and religious mysticism. As alchemy gave way to the scientific age, it can be tempting to assume that all the magic disappeared, leaving only empiricism and the drive towards objectivity. Here, I will present a few examples as to how magic has influenced science into the modern period.

Pauli and Jung's unus mundus

Wolfgang Pauli (1900–1956), the famous Austrian quantum physicist who discovered spin theory and the exclusion principle (for which he was awarded a Nobel Prize in 1945), had a curiously close relationship with the famed psychoanalyst Carl Jung (1875–1961). Jung's own work delved deeply into introspective magic and the spiritual as a structure for therapies designed to help the patient towards "individuation", Jung's term for attaining one's true potential. Pauli and Jung's twenty-five year friendship lasted until Pauli's death from pancreatic cancer. They met when Pauli sought treatment for personal problems and mental illness. Jung's counselling at the time involved dream analysis, and Pauli became one of his most valued patients. Together they worked to interpret roughly 400 of Pauli's dreams, and this blossomed into a friendship and an exchange of regular letters in which metaphysics, numerology, and magic were frequently discussed. Pauli's dream therapy with Jung was documented in Jung's seminars, which have been published as *Dream Symbols of the Individuation Process: Notes of C. G. Jung's Seminars on Wolfgang Pauli's Dreams* (Jung, 1931). Pauli felt that psychology and quantum physics could be brought together and was especially taken by Jung's concept of "integration".

Carl Jung, 1875–1961.   Wolfgang Pauli, 1900–1958.

In Jungian psychoanalysis, "integration" is the reconciliation of opposing wills within an individual's mind-space, in order to cure anxiety, depression, and cognitive dissonance. In particular, one's will to survive versus one's self-destructive will, as well as the anima and animus: respectively the hidden feminine drives in the male, and the hidden masculine drives in the female. There is a symbolic symmetry involved in Jung's metaphysics, especially around the number four. For every dichotomy, such as positive and negative, or male and female, Jung said there are two more hidden quantities. Positive and negative are shadowed by "both" and "neither". Male and female are shadowed by hermaphrodite (containing male and female attributes), and androgyne (neither male nor female). This Jungian predilection for the number four inspired Pauli to look for reconciling opposites at the quantum level, something he termed "quantum symmetry", and which fuelled Pauli's work for a couple of decades.

Pauli also loved to muse about magical thinking, especially orientated around Carl Jung's idea of "synchronicities". A synchronicity is a strange type of meaningful coincidence, which seems to muddy our understanding of cause and effect. The human mind, inclined as it is to narratives, will often find coincidences to be especially meaningful. These synchronistic events can have a transformative appeal to our emotions and intuition. Jung's argument is that, while our conception of mechanics and science for the most part relies on cause and effect, the mind's world is based on meaning. Therefore, synchronicities can be especially influential or inspiring for an individual whether causation is present or not. From the "New Age" point of view, synchronicities are often considered to be messages that the universe has prepared for us in order to confirm a path we are on, or as omens to warn us of bad luck. There's another way to look at it though: the things that pop out at us as being especially meaningful give us insight into our subconscious tendencies. This information can then be used to affirm that we are paying attention to the right things in order to achieve our desires, or act as a portent that our attention is neglecting difficulties. As always, pragmatism should guide us: if the world is full of evil omens which don't eventuate, then one ought to reorientate one's attention towards opportunity. If the world keeps offering a pattern of opportunities that, when taken, put one in sticky situations, then one ought to start paying more attention to potential warning signs. In this way, synchronicities can be very useful to the pragmatic magician without the necessity of adopting a solipsistic belief system.

One particularly playful synchronicity involving Pauli was the so-called "Pauli effect": the tendency for the scientific experiments of Pauli's colleagues to be ruined by equipment failure whenever Pauli was in the vicinity. His friends joked that "a functioning device and Wolfgang Pauli may not occupy the same room". Though the Pauli effect was meant by his colleagues in jest, apparently Pauli considered the effect to be real.

Later, a physics experiment at the University of Göttingen suffered an equipment failure in Pauli's absence, and this was seen, at first, to be an end to the pattern. That is, until Pauli figured out that while on a train en route to Copenhagen, he had in fact switched trains in Göttingen at the precise time of said equipment failure. This has been documented by writer and physicist George Gamow in his book, *Thirty Years that Shook Physics* (1985), where he also joked that the more talented the theoretical physicist, the "stronger the effect"!

Eventually, Pauli's therapy sessions with Jung paid off. When he first approached Jung, he had difficulties relating to women, affected greatly by the suicide of his mother after she was abandoned by his father, and the dissolution of his own marriage where his wife left him for another man. Despite Pauli's great successes in quantum physics, his personal life had been a mess. He was prone to binge drinking sessions, getting in fights at bars, and promiscuity with women, especially in brothels. After the therapy, Pauli remarried and was able to keep a stable relationship with his second wife. His self destructive tendencies were brought under control. In the end, both Jung and Pauli considered Jung's methods a success.

As well as Pauli's therapy sessions with Jung and Jung's protégée Erna Rosenbaum (Jung felt that Pauli's problems with women might benefit from the analysis of a female therapist), Jung and Pauli exchanged many letters where they sought to find a solution to dualism, the idea that mind and matter are separate quantities. They proposed a "neutral monism", where the psyche and matter were to be seen as two different projections of the same underlying reality. Pauli felt that some of the mysterious elements of quantum physics suggested a deeper reality: "We must postulate a cosmic order of nature beyond our control to which both the outward material objects and the inward images are subject."[15]

To Pauli, Jung's archetypes were glimpses into core principles of reality that can appear either as psychological phenomena or as physical events. This key concept of Jung's was underpinned by the recent discovery of the "observer effect" in quantum physics, where, for example, the act of observing photons can cause them to collapse into a particle where they would otherwise behave as a wave, suggesting an interaction between consciousness and matter. They called their theory "unus mundus" (one world), and it has been written about as "the Pauli-Jung conjecture" (Atmanspacher, 2020).

---

[15] From a 1948 letter from Pauli to his friend Marcus Fierz.

Nikola Tesla's visions

Another scientist who engaged with magical concepts was the prolific Serbian inventor Nikola Tesla (1856–1943), who is sometimes called "the father of the twentieth century". His inventions include: the induction motor and dynamo, AC current (now powering every household), the Tesla coil, polyphase power (used by most heavy industries), wireless communication, radio and remote control, wireless lighting, neon light bulbs, to name but a few. Tesla claimed to receive many of his ideas through visions and dreams, where he would see a new machine, the outcome of an engineering feat, or an

Nikola Tesla, 1856–1943.

experiment in high detail. This type of creative experience might be common to many creative people, but nowadays it is very rare for scientists to admit to "revelation" as an informational source for their scientific inquiry. In truth, regardless of whether such inspirations are caused by spirits or the subconscious parts of the mind, it is only honest to admit that revelatory experiences happen, and have had a huge impact on many important scientific discoveries. I have previously discussed the relationship between revelation and creativity back in Chapter 8.

In his autobiography (1919), Nikola Tesla discusses the nature of the visions he had throughout his life.

> In my boyhood I suffered from a peculiar affliction due to the appearance of images, often accompanied by strong flashes of light, which marred the sight of real objects and interfered with my thought and action. They were pictures of things and scenes which I had really seen, never of those I imagined. When a word was spoken to me the image of the object it designated would present itself vividly to my vision and sometimes I was quite unable to distinguish whether what I saw was tangible or not.

For a while, these visions troubled him and he sought to rid himself of them. He found, however, that the more he tried to suppress them, the more anxious he became. He eventually submitted and began trying to work with his visions instead of fighting them.

> I soon discovered that my best comfort was attained if I simply went on in my vision farther and farther, getting new impressions all the time, and so I began to travel—of course, in my mind. Every night (and sometimes during the day), when alone, I would start on my journeys—see new places, cities and countries—live there, meet people and make friendships and acquaintances and, however unbelievable, it is a fact that they were just as dear to me as those in actual life and not a bit less intense in their manifestations.

After a while, he realised that the visions would often give him solutions to problems, and on a couple of occasions he even relates as to how they saved his life. As he began to immerse himself in the then relatively new field of electrical engineering, the visions began to intertwine with his electrical experiments.

> My method is different. I do not rush into actual work. When I get an idea I start at once building it up in my imagination. I change the construction, make improvements and operate the device in my mind. It is absolutely immaterial to me whether I run my turbine in thought or test it in my shop. I even note if it is out of balance. There is no difference whatever, the results are the same. In this way I am able to rapidly develop and perfect a conception without touching anything. When I have gone so far as to embody in the invention every possible improvement I can think of and see no fault anywhere, I put into concrete form this final product of my brain. Invariably my device works as I conceived that it should, and the experiment comes out exactly as I planned it. In twenty years there has not been a single exception.

Perhaps it is still the case that many scientists are inspired by dreams and visions, but since Nikola Tesla's time, it has become less common for them to admit it. Suffice to say, dreams and visions are never documented in scientific papers, and it is therefore very hard to quantify how often they spark the initial process of hypothesis, or the problem solving required for scientific testing.

Jack Parsons, the rocket magician

If ever there was an influential historical figure who blurred the line between magic and science, it would have to be the rocket engineer/occultist Jack Parsons. A man with a dream, Parsons was one of the first scientists to seriously propose sending man to the moon. Born Marvel Whiteside Parsons in 1914, he developed a

Jack Parsons, 1914–1952.

fascination for rocketry, inspired in large part by science fiction novels. As a young man, he founded the Jet Propulsion Lab with two of his friends associated with Caltech. They soon gained funding to develop Jet Assisted Takeoff (JATO), small jets that are attached to aeroplanes to help them take off from short runways, such as aircraft carriers. Soon after, the US joined World War II, and their organisation, now named Aerojet, became a matter of great interest to the US Air Force. As well as contributing to the design of jet engines, Parsons developed a solid rocket fuel that was later used by NASA and the US military in ballistic missiles.

Alongside his career in rocketry, Jack Parsons led a parallel life as a member of the Ordo Templi Orientis (OTO), an occult society adapted and led by the notorious magician Aleister Crowley, in order to teach Thelema, the religion that he founded. Parsons participated in and orchestrated many magical rituals, eventually becoming the leader of his branch of the OTO, the Agape Lodge, replacing its former leader Wilfred Talbot Smith at Crowley's behest. The Thelemite doctrine of "Do as thou wilt shall be the whole of the law", an order towards self-actualisation, was fuel for Parsons's unbounded ambition. Parsons structured his life, relationships, and marriages around Thelemite narratives. This included an early friendship with L. Ron Hubbard, who also joined the OTO order for a time before he founded

Scientology, a self-improvement scheme-turned-cult based on very similar self-actualisation practices. Together, they attempted a grand magical rite called "Babalon working". This was an attempt to manifest Babalon, aka the "Scarlet Woman", a goddess in Thelema who represented a liberated feminine counterpart to Crowley's alter ego, "The Great Beast". Babalon was supposed to bring about "the age of Horus", an era of spiritual awakening, centring upon the archetype of "the Child". Some propose that the hippy movement of the Sixties and the psychedelic subculture popularised in music, art, and film, was the fulfilment of this. Hubbard and Parsons's friendship ended in destruction after Hubbard scammed Parsons out of money in a yacht investment, and at the same time ran off with Parsons's lover, Sara Northrup. In retaliation, Parsons cursed Hubbard's escape, coinciding with Hubbard's shipwreck in a storm. Strange stuff indeed.

Though it is hard to quantify how much magic intersected with his science, it seems clear that Jack Parsons was a man of drive and vision; reaching one's true potential was the primary goal of the OTO. Perhaps without him, there would have been no US space programme, and perhaps without the OTO he wouldn't have set so lofty a goal as the moon, designing rockets that eventually achieved the moon landing. It's hard to remember that, at the time, an expedition to the moon seemed like a ludicrous idea, one for which Parsons received much criticism. Tragically, Jack Parsons didn't live to see the culmination of his work, as he died as a result of an explosion while trying to produce an order of explosives for a film set.

After his death, the Jet Propulsion Lab was incorporated into the newly established NASA. They were commissioned to build two of the main rocket engines for the Apollo space programme which landed men on the moon in 1969.

Science is considered a rational pursuit. But no person, not even scientists, can be rational all of the time. The validity of the scientific method lies, after all, in the testing, experimentation, replication, and the new hypotheses that form the next experiments. Great hypotheses require great creativity, and the values that drive one to see experiments through are deeply affected by the subjectivity, intuitions, and emotions of scientists as human beings. This ought to be taken into consideration when looking into the history of science, rather than being buried, or we risk the untenable fundamentalist position of "scientism": the ideology that promotes science as the only valid type of knowledge, ignoring narratives, history, values, literature, love, culture, relationships, friend-ship, faith, useful fictions, legal fictions, art, philosophy, and all other non-scientific paths to wisdom.

There will always be a tension between the scientific method, which can only work with results that can be repeated and measured, and human narrative, in which extraordinary and miraculous events are given extra attention and meaning. Almost all valued human stories involve the extraordinary, whereas repeatability is what provides the strongest scientific results. You can't test a one-off event. Yet, statisti-cally unlikely events are, perhaps ironically, commonplace.

CHAPTER 15

Science, magic,
and religion compared

Now that I have set the stage, let's compare the values of science, religion, and magic, and look at the differences in what they are trying to achieve.

Science is concerned with measuring quantities in the world in order that predictions can be made with the best possible certainty.

It is utilitarian and pragmatic. Interested in what can be achieved and repeated. In and of itself, science has no inherent morality, except for one single faith-based value: that it is always better to find more stuff out. This may seem a given to some people, but the unbridled pursuit of knowledge is not a value that is always shared by religions, where certain inquiries may be considered unhealthy or immoral. Outside this value, science may give data that informs morality, but it is itself morally neutral.

Like religion, science builds models and cosmologies. These cosmologies are built to be explanatory, and help future predictions.

Science has a few built-in limitations. It cannot form strong conclusions from one-off events. Certainty in science comes from being able to get the same results in repeated tests.

In comparison, miracles, which are extraordinarily meaningful rare events, are given a special value in religion.

Science also has trouble getting results from personal experience. Individual subjectivity does not hold much scientific value as data, for the simple reason that this type of experience is very hard to measure. Shared subjective experiences are a little better, but are still not favoured over that which is precisely measurable: objectivity. This is where science differs the most from religion and magic, which both value shared subjectivity foremost.

Science strives towards objectivity. True scientists, however, understand that objectivity is a goal, and not a destination. Scientists are merely human beings, and human perceptions and sense-making generally offer imperfect models of reality. So, science must take pains to test and measure and use logic and logical instruments, such as computers, to make sure that the data is as precise as possible.

> The term "religion", which comes from the Latin *religio*, has etymological ties to the terms "ligature" and "ligament", relating to the concept "to bind". Religion is, in a sense, "that which binds groups of people into communities through common doctrine or belief". Religions are, by this definition, group-focused. Religion discusses mankind's subjective experiences and morality, and tries to explain how these inform our place in the universe. It is chiefly concerned with meaning, and makes strong use of narrative and symbolism. Scientific testing has little use for symbolism, though it is, by necessity, used a lot in science education.

Religion tries to direct people towards what it deems moral and righteous, and away from what it deems harmful. Most often, the needs of the group are put ahead of the needs of the individual.

In contrast to science, religion values revelation. As we have discussed earlier, scientific hypotheses are sometimes informed by revelation, but even so, scientists are generally loath to formally document these experiences for fear of ridicule.

> Magic shares the experimental nature of science, and the interest in meaning and symbolism of religion. Like science, it is not a moral system in and of itself, but a utilitarian one. The goal is to be able to cause change in the world, and this is especially done by affecting

human perception. Unlike science, which seeks to remove illusion, the use of trickery is foundational to magic.

Anything goes in magic, as long as it works. Magic will keep anything that works, regardless of whether or not it can be explained. Explanations in magic are only directions for doing, not objective truths. Magic shares with religion that it works primarily on the subjective and personal level. For this reason, it also frequently deals in narratives and symbols. Unlike the group focus in religion, magic as a pursuit is directed by individuals, and very often for individuals. For this reason, though religions are usually started by magicians, magicians are often held in suspicion by religions once they are established. Nobody threatens the rules that structure a religion more than a magician. They are, after all, inclined to mess with the rules just to see what happens!

All religions contain magic. Rituals, prayers, invocations and other manipulations of conscious states all fit into the definition of magic we have been working with in this book. Many religions are suspicious of magic that is too playful, Sacrilegious, or irreverent, as it can quickly undo the faith in the rituals that religious communities rely on.

Magic, be it stage magic or the occult, is very attractive to those who want to subvert common beliefs about what can and can't be done, and, in many cases, what should and should not be done.

Science and religion can coexist, when religion sticks primarily to the subjective, moral, and symbolic, and science sticks to the utilitarian and objective. We have no working universal cosmology, no unified model that explains everything. For this reason, we are forced to operate under more than one belief system, as I have discussed in Chapter 10. Religion requires magic in order to create sacred experiences. Therefore, magic provides us an interesting vantage point by which to regard religion.

Science necessarily has to exclude faith from scientific method, whereas magic and religion are free to harness it. Scientific discoveries can cause tension with religious cosmologies when religions become too materialistic. Magic has the profound ability to fool people, which, when done overtly, such as in the case of stage magic, can be beneficial. Magic can, however, be used to scam, manipulate, and obscure. It is for these reasons that many fans of science devalue or even berate magic.

Religion and science came to challenge each other further when Christian fundamentalism began using the Bible to make "objective" claims about reality, such as calculating the age of the universe. This was in retaliation to the previously discussed antitheistic claims that science and religion have been in conflict throughout history (see Chapter 13). Both fundamentalism and antitheism are more modern ideologies than they usually claim themselves to be. Both sides use strawman arguments, and aim for certainty in places where there is little to be found. This can only be achieved by blocking out all contradictory information. As such, the conflict thesis, which proposes that religion and science have been at war throughout history is a misrepresentation of science (scientism), just as fundamentalism is a misrepresentation of traditional Christianity. I will outline the origins of fundamentalism in Chapter 16.

Magicians vs. scientists

If one is to truly attempt to obtain an objective viewpoint, then it is crucial that one also study the ways in which one can be fooled. If you don't understand the ways in which you can be deceived, then how can you be certain you aren't being deceived? In this way, magic can help scientists to form better experiments. A fun example of magicians tricking scientists can be found in "Project Alpha", a magical hoax which began in 1979, and continued for nearly three years.

Orchestrated by the stage magician and celebrity sceptic, James Randi, two trained stage magicians were planted into a scientific experiment testing psychic phenomena (Psi) at Washington University.

The two magicians, teenagers Steve Shaw (better known as Banachek) and Michael Edwards, used tricks involving spoon bending, moving objects in sealed globes, manipulating electronic clocks, and making images appear on photographic film, to fool scientists into believing they had telekinetic powers. After over a year of testing, the laboratory was ready to present its findings at a parapsychology meeting in Syracuse, in August 1981. Eventually, the two young men and Randi publicly embarrassed the lab by revealing they had been cheating using sleight of hand and other tricks.

Scientists are biased towards looking for the same results over and over, and this tendency left them wide open. Stage magicians, when talking shop, frequently mention the importance of learning how to perform a single trick in multiple ways. Various techniques will be learned to perform the same magic trick, and each of these must be made to look as similar as possible. In this way, a magician can watch to see if their mark is catching on to the trick, and if so, conceal their methods by performing the same trick in a totally different way. This will often cause the mark to let go of their initial idea about how is trick is done, even when it happens to be correct. It simply doesn't occur to most people that the magician may be switching methods. This was how Shaw and Edwards fooled the Washington University scientists. Perhaps every scientist should be taught a little stage magic theory, in order to avoid being fooled by pesky magicians? Biologists who categorise species must beware of mimics, such as stick insects, and perhaps deception ought to also be a basic assumption for other types of scientists who are trying to understand a universe which is sometimes loath to reveal its secrets?

CHAPTER 16

The origins of Christian fundamentalism

Fundamentalism is often claimed by both its believers and many of its enemies to be an ancient devout side of religion, which is absent of any flexibility of interpretation, and therefore somehow truer to the original message. It is frequently presented as the type of belief one would be certain to end up with if one was to follow the rules and beliefs of religion strictly. Here, I will frame a short history of fundamentalism that reveals it to be a very recent evolution in religious thought, younger than the aforementioned term "scientist" (1833), and younger than John William Draper's *Conflict Thesis* (1874), which is the foundation of modern antitheism, as I outlined in Chapter 13. In fact, fundamentalism can be described in part as a religious reaction against the scientism of the nineteenth century onwards.

Bible literalism

Let's start by looking at Bible literalism, which also took hold as a widespread movement in the mid nineteenth century. Literalism has its earliest roots in the Protestant movement of Martin Luther. Before the Protestant Reformation, the Church held the position of highest authority in Christianity. Scriptures were to be interpreted by clergy in accordance with official guidelines, and the Bible was not for laypeople to understand without guidance.

Starting around 1517, Luther challenged the Church's authority, leading to his excommunication by the pope in 1520. His polemics were a reaction to the corruption he saw among Catholic clergy and the Church as an institution. He proposed a new approach to Christianity, which tried to avert corruption by shifting religious authority from the clergy to the Bible alone.

Feeling that all should be their own priest, he pushed for the translation of the Bible from Latin to vernacular languages that could be printed, understood, and read directly by Christians.

The result of this was a fundamental shift towards rigidity in faith. When the clergy are the authority, they can be questioned and negotiated with, adapting their doctrine in the face of the new scientific, political, cultural, and economic challenges. This flexibility was largely lost after Protestantism. A book has no will of its own to clarify, be reasoned with, or answer questions beyond its text.

Martin Luther 1483–1546 (painting by Lucas Cranach, 1528).

Despite all of this, Luther was not himself a Bible literalist. Luther believed that scripture should be combined with reason to guide people's life. He used his doctrine of "Sola scriptura" (by scripture alone), the position that scriptures, "as comprehended by human reason", ought to be the sole infallible rule of Christian practice.

Without the translation into local languages, Bible literalism would have never taken hold, and fundamentalism would never have developed with its opposition to scientific consensus (which is not to say that quite different problems between religion and free inquiry wouldn't have arisen).

Gradually, Protestants moved away from seeing the Bible as a window into the wisdom of the past, to be understood in historical context. Instead, the Bible became a text by which to measure day to day activity, and to glean what God had in store for the individual. As an interesting magical development, it has become commonplace for Christians to use the Bible as a divinatory text, akin to tarot cards or the I Ching. Opening the Bible randomly and asking, "What does God have in store for me today?" In this way, the book can indeed answer back.

For many Christians, especially in the charismatic churches, no longer is it asked, "What did the scriptures mean in the context of their time," or "How did the worldview of the Old Testament Hebrews differ from that of today?" By assuming that the Bible speaks directly to the modern reader, fundamentalists have cut themselves adrift from traditional Christianity.

In comparison to the Catholic Trinity, Luther's Christianity replaced the Holy Spirit with the Bible itself. In the later "charismatic" movements that eventually evolved into tele- evangelism, the preacher themselves became a surrogate for the Holy Spirit.

Despite the translations of the Bible and the Sola scriptura doctrine, Christian fundamentalism did not start to take hold as a popular movement until the 1878 Niagara Bible conference. Also known as the "Believer's Meeting for Bible Study", it was held every year from 1876 until 1884. In 1878, what became known as the "Niagara Creed" was put forth: a fourteen point statement of faith for what was to be considered "true Christianity". This was adapted from the original Nicene Creed, which many Christians hold to be their defining criteria of faith.

In the Niagara Creed, it was felt that Christianity needed to be simplified, in order to appeal to the theologically unsophisticated masses, in the hope of winning more converts.

The fourteen point creed of the Niagara Bible conference of 1878, on what is to be accepted in order to be a "true Christian", is as follows:

1. The verbal, plenary inspiration of the Scriptures in the original manuscripts.
2. The Trinity.
3. The Creation of Man, the Fall into sin, and total depravity.
4. The universal transmission of spiritual death from Adam.
5. The necessity of the new birth.
6. Redemption by the blood of Christ.
7. Salvation by faith alone in Christ.
8. The assurance of salvation.
9. The centrality of Jesus Christ in the Scriptures.
10. The constitution of the true church by genuine believers.
11. The personality of the Holy Spirit.
12. The believer's call to a holy life.
13. The immediate passing of the souls of believers to be with Christ at death.
14. The premillennial Second Coming of Christ.[16]

Capitalist Christianity

With their distrust of older traditions, and focus on reforming Christianity for a new American age, these new Protestants looked to capitalism and marketing for ideas on how to win converts.

Bolstered by a new popular belief that the acquisition of wealth and societal success should be considered a sign of God's grace towards the individual (the Prosperity Doctrine), these reformed Christians looked not towards the Church for role models, but to rich Christian businessmen. This was the beginning of fundamentalism, which has for many observers, due to its presence on TV and in politics, become the loudest and most visible form of Christianity, despite being such a wild departure from orthodoxy, its devotees much fewer in number than Catholicism.

The term "fundamentalism" comes from a set of ninety essays published between 1910 and 1915, called "The Fundamentals". It was then republished in 1917 by the Bible Institute of Los Angeles as a four volume set, and distributed widely.

These manuals explaining how to be a modern Christian were funded by several successful American businessmen including the founder of

---

[16] https://wweologycentral.net/blog/the-niagara-creed/.

Lyman Oil, Lyman Stewart, and the founder of Quaker Oats, Henry Parsons Crowell.

"The Fundamentals" defended mainstream Protestant beliefs and attacked nuanced critique, liberal theology, Catholicism, socialism, modernism, atheism, Christian Science, Mormonism, Spiritualism, and evolutionary theory.

Fundamentalism's pivotal moment lies in Henry Parsons Crowell's company, Quaker Oats, which was the world's first packaged grocery brand. Despite the name, it had no affiliation with the Quaker sect, and merely appropriated their image. Quakers hold to a doctrine of good health, and Crowell thought that this association would help convince the public that they were buying a healthy breakfast food.

The marketing concept of putting cereal in a box with graphics on the front was a breakthrough. Previously, customers would buy oats scooped and bagged by a grocer from a barrel. From week to week, the oats might be sourced from different farms, and thus the quality varied. If, however, the oats were combined from regular sources into a homogenous product of consistent quality, and put in a box with a reassuring picture and logo, the people would begin to trust the brand.

Quaker Oats in its original packaging from the 1890s.

This transferral of faith from the barrel to the brand works just like psychological conditioning, and can be easily compared to the sigil magic discussed in Chapter 11. Images can carry great power of persuasion. Now the logo and Quaker image could be put in newspapers, magazines, and on posters, separately from the oats, allowing for many more modes of advertising, making Quaker Oats a recognisable favourite.

The Quaker Oats approach was wildly successful, and made Henry Parsons Crowell a rich man. As a man of faith, he reasoned that if the approach could work well for cereal then it could also be applied to evangelism. He pridefully reasoned that as a marketer, he could do a better job spreading God's Word than the clergy. First though, the message needed to be honed. The traditional Protestant Christian message was to be reduced to a more manageable and simplified formula: The Fundamentals (Silliman, 2015).

As the fundamentalist message spread, gradually their churches shifted from being community-based to being service-based. This gave rise to the twentieth century TV evangelist. Gospel showbiz with rock concerts in churches, sound systems, light shows, and larger than life ecstatic preachers followed. The flock became consumers, looking from church to church asking, "What can this church do for me?" "What services does it provide?" Fundamentalism became big business, with hotlines, credit card donations, and of course, tax exemption.

It is this familiar type of "capitalist" religion that antitheists (and traditionalists) are most prone to react to. It soon became not just big business, but big politics. Many toes are trod upon especially when fundamentalism, and its Bible literalism, gets its paws on education, with its science-denying "Young Earth" creationism, homophobia, and anti-abortion stance. In the secular backlash, often other religions get tarred with the same brush, as if they are all on the same team.

As a further development, Islam, influenced by American Christian fundamentalism, also developed its own fundamentalist movement. This can be seen most dramatically with Daesh, aka Islamic State (I'm personally not keen on the term ISIS as this is the rightful name of the unaffiliated Babylonian goddess as well as being a common female given name). Just as Christian fundamentalism is a modern development, Daesh recruits through glossy magazines, social media, and smart phones, with a radically altered and simplified departure from Islamic tradition.

Beware of modern movements that try to claim an ancient authority!

CHAPTER 17

Religion's suspicion of magic: the witch trials

Biblical magic

Christianity has had a similarly complex relationship with magic, as it has had with natural philosophy and science.

Much has been made by puritans and pagans alike of the following phrase in the Bible:

Thou shalt not suffer a witch [kashaph] to live (Exodus 22:18).

The precise meaning of the Hebrew word *kashaph*, here translated as "witch", and in some other modern versions, "sorceress", is uncertain. In the Septuagint it was translated as *pharmakeia*, meaning "pharmacy", and on this basis, Reginald Scot, a sixteenth century sceptic and opponent to the persecution of witches who wrote *Discoverie of Witchcraft*, claimed that "witch" was an incorrect translation, and that the term referred to poisoners.

There are many verses in the Bible forbidding divination and sorcery. At the same time, there are also many acts of magic done in the name of God. From Jesus we have: walking on water, restoring the voice of mutes, exorcising demons, resurrecting the dead, controlling the weather, feeding the multitudes from a meal for one, making a coin appear in a fish's mouth in order to pay a tax, as well as curing blindness, paralysis, wounds, leprosy, and dropsy (oedema).

There are early depictions of Jesus from the third and fourth century holding a wand to perform his miracles. Perhaps at the time they were happy to view him as a benevolent sorcerer?

Jesus with wand (Ingram, 2007).

In his book *Jesus the Magician* (1978), Morton Smith makes the case that Jesus drew from a long tradition of magicians, especially the Old Testament prophet Elijah, and his successor Elisha. Before Jesus, Elijah also controlled the weather, multiplied food, and raised the dead.

Aaron, the brother and right-hand man to Moses, also performed magical feats in the Old Testament, including turning a stick into a snake, which is a magic trick that is still sometimes performed today (Brier, 1998).

It seems the only difference between a godly miracle and forbidden sorcery in the Bible is whether the power comes from Yahweh or from another source: an individual, Satan, a demon, or another rival deity.

Christianity still engages in magic through its rituals, and through the stories of miracles wrought by prophets, saints, and faith healers.

Invocations of God, angels, and saints, exorcisms, transubstantiation, transmutation, and other rituals are all magic under my working definition (see Chapter 3). All of these are a deep part of the Christian, especially Catholic, tradition, not to mention the speaking in tongues, snake handling, laying on of hands, and other forms of magic practised by some of the churches in the charismatic movement.

All of this shows that Christianity's relationship with magic is highly contextual. Some types of magic are venerated, others merely tolerated, and certain types are considered acts of evil. So why did Christianity begin to perform witch trials? Was there a great Witch Holocaust as some pagans suggest? In this chapter, we will explore some of the history, what happened, and why.

Who were the witches?

The word "witch" has many contexts, but in the context of Western witch trials, it has always meant someone who is in league with Satan. More specifically, someone in direct opposition to God's righteousness, who draws powers from Satan to harm people or their property. There have always been some types of magic that were tolerated by Christians, and other types that were distrusted. Divination, healing, herbalism, and some benevolent types of charm or protection magic, while often distrusted, have not been capital crimes or heresies by themselves. Occasionally, however, these acts of magic have contributed to evidence in witch trials.

During the nineteenth and twentieth centuries, a legend called "the witch cult hypothesis" began to develop. This idea, started by several folklorists, was that witchcraft represented a uniform, organised pagan religion practised throughout Europe, where a god called Danus, and later Diana, was worshipped. Despite the lack of evidence for a widespread ritualised witch religion, this idea captured the imaginations of many writers and thinkers. Later, it was adapted by certain feminists into a goddess-worshiping spirituality, offering a counterpart to "patriarchal" Christianity. The narrative of a feminine religion being persecuted by the masculine church was, and is, an attractive narrative for some feminist ideologies. Women were certainly persecuted for heresies by the Catholic and Protestant churches after all; the only problem is that there has never been any evidence for a uniform "witch cult".

Professor and historian Keith Wrightson (2009), who teaches at Yale, explains medieval witchcraft as: "A body of beliefs and practices regarding supernatural power which stood outside the world of formal religion, which helped people cope with their anxieties and insecurities."

Witchcraft in Europe was never a religion in or of itself. Instead, it was a complex and uncollected assortment of local beliefs and practices. During the Middle Ages and the Renaissance, magic was certainly a part of daily village life in many areas. In these times, there were usually no effective doctors or hospitals in the modern sense, and these roles were instead filled by magicians and practitioners of folk medicine. Common people would consult herbalists, who would often use spells or charms to supplement their treatments. Many of these separate regional traditions live on today for those who care to learn them.

The idea of a witch cult hit the mainstream in 1929, when folklorist Margaret Murray was commissioned to write the entry on "witchcraft" for the *Encyclopaedia Britannica*. She supplied an article that continued to be reprinted until 1969, which became many people's introduction to the concept of witchcraft. Murray used the opportunity to summarise a hypothesis she had put forth in her book *The Witch-Cult in Western Europe: A Study in Anthropology* (1921). Murray was a very interesting and contradictory figure. On the one hand she was a renowned and respected Egyptologist of University College London, and on the other, an eccentric author of pseudo-history. As a

Margaret Murray,
1863–1963.

member and eventual president of the Folklore Society, she was in high standing, regarded as a rational sceptic in most subjects. Her unusual ideas about witches, however, developed into three increasingly unusual books, which were controversial to other folklorists. This was except for one Gerald Gardiner, who took her baton and ran a mile, adapting Murray's historical hypotheses into an occult system for magic (Simpson, 1994). This culminated with Gardiner creating his own religion, Wicca, in the 1950s, which he claimed to be a survival of Murray's hypothesised European witch cult. The word "wicca" is a masculine Anglo-Saxon word for "witch". The feminine equivalent is "wicce", and unlike the common modern pronunciation, both these Old English words had the "ch" sound of "witch". This also goes to show that the original concept of a witch was used for both men and women.

European witch trials through history

Before the ninth century, there were no authorised Christian witch trials in Europe or England. On the contrary, the Church often held the stance that witchcraft is best dismissed as superstition. In 785 CE, the Germanic Council of Paderborn outlawed the *belief* in witches, and this stance was later reinforced by the Holy Roman Emperor Charlemagne, who would go on to unify most of Western Europe for the first time since the Romans. A similar sentiment can be found in the Canon Episcopi, part of medieval Christian law, written around 900 CE, which described black magic as unreal delusions put in the mind by the devil. Witches were not considered heretics, just deceived and foolish people.

Likewise, in the Orthodox Christian Church of the Byzantine Empire, belief in witchcraft was widely regarded as "deisidaimonia" (superstition). In the ninth and tenth centuries, it was the *belief* in witches that was considered a heresy, rather than the condition of being a witch. If magic is your enemy, then why persecute people as witches directly, when it is easier to dispel the very belief in witches as superstition?

In the thirteenth century, the Roman Catholic Inquisition conducted several witch trials, but these were part of a much larger push to punish various types of heresy, of which belief in witchcraft was merely one. Witches were generally not considered a priority in these trials. Inquisitorial courts later became involved in more vicious witch hunts during the fifteenth century.

Even then, not all of the Inquisitional courts acknowledged the existence of witchcraft. By 1610, as the result of a controversial and disorderly witch hunt, the ruling council of the Spanish Inquisition (Suprema) gave an "edict of grace", during which confessing witches were to go unpunished. After this, the Inquisition did not bother witches again, though they still fervently prosecuted heretics.

So for the vast majority of cases and contrary to popular belief, it was not the Catholic Inquisitions that conducted witch trials. As cruel as they were in punishing heretics, we will have to look elsewhere to find the truly violent witch trials of the Middle Ages and Renaissance.

The fear of witches really picked up steam with the Protestant Reformation and the Catholic backlash.

Martin Luther himself made statements which reveal a deep fear of witches and black magic. In reference to the previously mentioned Bible passage in Exodus 22:18, "Thou shalt not suffer a witch to live," he said that witches could steal milk merely by thinking of a cow. In 1538, after a furore about witches who were suspected of poisoning chicken eggs or poisoning milk and butter with magic spells, Luther wrote: "One should show no mercy to these [women]; I would burn them myself, for we read in the Law that the priests were the ones to begin the stoning of criminals" (Karant-Nunn, 1994).

Not all of the fear of witches (or heretics for that matter) came from Church authorities. Medieval churches were also governmental bodies, and sometimes had to submit to public opinion, or, in the worst cases, hysteria, in order to keep the peace.

There were times when prosecution of witches was deemed necessary to appease fanatics and restore order. Because religion was so heavily tied to government in the past, it can become nearly impossible to discern, in particular cases, whether it was politics or religion that was the primary drive for prosecution. It has become popular to blame religion in its entirety, and to believe we are beyond such things. Despite this, public shaming is still common through phenomena such as "cancel culture": mass moral outrage in the age of social media. This is perhaps comparable, albeit not equivalent, to witch hysteria, as thankfully fewer burnings at the stake come to pass.

In the late sixteenth century, King James I of England and VI of Scotland, renowned for his commissioning of the King James Bible (1604), became obsessed with witchcraft after a visit to Denmark, where

several public witch trials had occurred.
He later took part in the North Berwick
witch trials in Scotland, which ran for
two years, and implicated more than
seventy people. This was the first major
witch trial in Scotland, and his experience resulted in James writing the book
Demonologie (1597), in which he discussed necromancy, black magic, divination with evil spirits, witchcraft, demons,
and vampires. The book sought to per-
suade the reader of the reality of devil
worship, by using historic witch trials,
confessions, and the Bible as source evidence. James I had been raised a Protestant, and he shared Martin Luther's fear
of black magic.

King James VI of Scotland,
I of England 1566–1625.

His interest was short-lived, however. After 1599, James started to
become more sceptical of witches and witch trials. In an excerpt from
a letter, he congratulated his son Henry for taking the role of a sceptic
in a trial:

> "The discovery of yon little counterfeit wench.I pray God ye may
> be my heir in such discoveries ... most miracles now-a-days prove
> but illusions, and ye may see by this how wary judges should be in
> trusting accusations." (Akrigg, 1984)

If you are starting to feel that historical witch trials have been a bit
exaggerated and were really not so bad after all ... hold your horses.
The worst is still to come. As we will see, the Germans in particular
developed quite a hysteria for witches, which led to some very grisly
outcomes.

The period following the Protestant Revolution in Germany was
by far the worst time in history for the prosecution and execution of
witches, starting with the witch trials of Trier from 1581 to 1593, where
368 people from twenty-two local villages were burned alive, and
plenty more were incarcerated. In an attempt to prove his loyalty to
the Catholic Jesuits, the Archbishop of Trier, Johan Von Schöneburg,

ordered a purge of Protestants, Jews, and witches. Very few of those who were accused of witchcraft were ever released, and almost all of the accused confessed under torture. Oddly for a witch trial, almost a third of the victims were either from the nobility, or held governmental positions, and the prosecutions were almost certainly a political backlash. At the time in southern Germany, Catholics were trying to reconquer lands that had been seized previously by the Protestants. This was the violent era of the Thirty Years War.

Later, in 1603–1606, a witch trial in Fulda, Germany took the lives of around 250 people. This was also a politically fuelled Catholic counter-reformation action, led by the Prince-Abbot of the Fulda Monastery, Balthasar von Dernbach.

In 1626–1631, the Würzberg Trials took place, with 900 estimated deaths of men, women, and children in the entire principality. Julius Echter von Mespelbrunn, Prince-Bishop of Würzburg, and his nephew and successor Philipp Adolf von Ehrenberg, were in charge of the pogrom. Again the Catholic reconquest of parts of Germany taken previously by Protestants was the fuel for the fire. This witch hunt craze generated a hysteria that echoed in Bamberg around the same time, and until 1680, when around 1000 people were executed, under the judgement of Prince-Bishop of Bamberg Neytard von Thüngen. The catalyst for these events was a night frost that destroyed the crops.

Hammer of the witches

A lot of the fervour of the Renaissance witch trials can be blamed on a very popular book by the name of *Malleus Maleficarum*, which means "hammer of the 'evil-doers'" (feminine), but is most often translated as "Hammer of the Witches". As I have mentioned previously, the word witch was originally used for both men and women, and the tendency to imagine witches as being female is a later development. While the majority of the victims of witch trials were women, the more extreme they became, the more likely men and children were also to be among the victims.

The *Malleus Maleficarum* was written by a Catholic clergyman, Heinrich Kramer, and first published in 1486. It was a bestseller behind only the Bible for the next 200 years. Although the book was discredited, by groups including the faculty of the University of Cologne, for being inconsistent with Catholic doctrine and proposing unethical and illegal procedures, it became a powerful textbook for those concerned with ridding the world of satanic witches, as well as those who used it to give a pragmatic excuse for ridding themselves of political dissenters and other undesirables.

The *Malleus Maleficarum* stated that sorcery was heresy, and prescribed inquisitorial practices for secular courts, in order to prosecute and execute witches. Recommended procedures to obtain confessions included torture. For those found guilty, the punishment was death. At that time, it was typical to burn heretics alive at the stake. So witches, perceived as heretics by some Christians, were to meet the same fate.

Salem

The most famous and well documented witch trial in history was that

MANUAL SORT LABEL   10/27/232:47   uary 1692 and

WAVE# :   30331837837   su......... .rary to the "pop

TRUC......ure" reputation of this trial, only nineteen of the accused were executed, mainly by hanging. Although a very small witch trial by historical standards, much of the trial documentation survives, making it an excellent case study for the mentality and causes of witch hysteria.

This chapter has been a mere summary of historical witch trials. I have addressed some of the complexity, and the ways in which witch trials have been framed by different ideologies, from Neo-Pagans, to medieval Catholics and Protestants and spiritual feminists. What ought to be clear is that Christianity has had many evolving views towards witches from the more lenient to the more bloodthirsty. Witch trials have been at times misogynistic, and at other times equally brutal to males. There have been folk beliefs all through history that can be termed "witchcraft" in a general sense, but there has never been any evidence for a highly organised, widely spread, or cross-cultural witch religion. The witch movements that one sees today are mostly modern, and as long as they are understood to be modern, all power to them. Perhaps this even frees a prospective witch towards a more pragmatic approach to their magic.

CHAPTER 18

The cycle of creativity and inspiration

I would like to take the time here to explore an alchemical concept that I think is fundamental to the way we experience reality. We perceive the world and it suggests itself to us and affects us as concepts. We can then take those concepts, alter them, and use them in turn to change aspects of the physical world.

Solvé et Coagula

In alchemy, there is an important adage: "Solvé et Coagula". Solvé is the old root for the word "solve", as in to solve a puzzle. It means "to release", and implies taking something fixed or physical and releasing its form so that it becomes ethereal, spiritual, or conceptual. It's sometimes translated as "dissolve".

Coagula has the same root as the word "coagulate" and means "to bind". To alchemists it is to take something ethereal, spiritual, or inspirational and solidify it into something either physical like an object, or communicable to others, such as the act of speaking a concept out loud, or like I am doing here: writing it out. These terms have a similar meaning to the concepts of "analysis" and "synthesis" in philosophy. Analysis is when we break a concept into its component parts in order to better understand the details, and synthesis is to bring together related concepts into a "meta-concept" in order to explain a larger pattern.

I have found these terms very useful for explaining the cycle of creativity from inspiration (solvé) to expression (coagula). For example, you might go and see a violin performance. As you observe the performance, the thoughts of the violinist are transmuted into sound through the manipulation of the violin strings. Alchemically speaking, the violinist's thoughts have been "coagulated". That is to say, they are brought from the private subjective space of the violinist's mind (their soul) into a shared "intersubjective" space, where we share experiences. The audience then takes those sounds and processes (solves) them to recreate the music in their own private minds.

Once the music is "solved" by the audience member, it can then "inspire" them. Inspiration originally meant "to take in the spirit of". As human beings, we love to emulate and repeat things we find inspiring. We also often get ideas, thoughts, and pieces of music trapped in our heads, and as we explored in Chapter 9, ideas and spirits live in an overlapping realm, or category. The audience members might feel inspired to go home and practise a musical instrument themselves, thus re-coagulating part of what they have solved. Such is the cycle of inspiration (solvé) and manifestation (coagula).

The human creative spirit is such that ideas can easily be combined, or recontextualised. When we have the urge to emulate a great violin performance, we don't always translate that urge with the aim of literally playing an instrument ourselves. A piece of music can inspire a painting, a short story can be inspired by that painting, and a film can be inspired by that short story ... So ideas can quickly propagate and diversify.

Some might write about the performance, some might emulate the violinist's wardrobe, hoping that some of their creative energy will be transferred, and as we are highly suggestible, that little ritual might actually work if it helps boost someone's confidence. This interaction between ideas, imagination, and behaviour is complex, rich, and fascinating, and accounts for a lot of the effects of real magic.

All social interactions are a myriad of smaller "Solvé et Coagula" cycles. Ideas are not objects, but objects are frequently formed by ideas. Anything that has been built, or made, by human action embodies the process of coagula.

The concept of Solvé et Coagula descends from ancient Jewish lore, going back at least as far as the book of Genesis. Therein, the realm of the mind, ideas, meaning, and spiritual experience is considered "the heavens". Its opposite is the shared space between minds where we communicate and interact with matter, which is termed "the earth". Note that these concepts are quite different from how we typically regard the earth as a mere object on which we live. Hence in Genesis: "In the beginning God created 'the heavens' [solvé] and 'the earth' [coagula]" (Pageau, 2018). In the former is thought, conceptual space, and creative potential, and in the latter, the world was laid out as we perceive and interact with it.

Without communication (coagula), an idea cannot reproduce itself and will be lost. This book here is an example of coagula, and is my attempt to manifest my ideas to be "solved" by the reader, in order that they may start their own creative cycle.

Performer and audience

Most great performers understand on some level that they must observe their audience, and make at least some gesture or acknowledgement in order to let the audience know they too are part of the performance. At this point, there is a feedback loop from the performer to the audience, and back. Part of what a performance is, is a ritual journey through conceptual space where the audience is allowed on board as passengers. Often great performance art happens when the performer is taking an apparent social or emotional "risk" that the audience feels through their empathy. This could be a great singer singing a sad song that comes close to "cracking" their voice, or a stunt person or acrobat taking a bodily risk that triggers our fear response.

Transferral of experience

The end goal of an effective musical performance is, in truth, not the creation of sound. It is the act of creating an experience in the listener. I consider musical performance to be a true act of magic. It is a manipulation of the perception of the audience in accordance with the will of the performer. The same can be said for oratory. People don't perceive the speech as sounds, they perceive it as meaning. Likewise with acting.

We don't "see" facial muscles and bodies moving, we see emotions, and glean the character's inner experiences. With good acting, the actor disappears, and we see only the character. This can happen even when the character is a different age, gender, or race than the actor. One of my favourite examples of this is the song "Postcard from a Hooker in Minneapolis" by Tom Waits. Tom Waits is renowned for having the most gravelly voice in all of popular music. A voice like his could hardly be more masculine, and there is an initial feeling of comedy with the opening line: "Charlie I'm pregnant, and living on Ninth Street."

Despite this, his lyrics and performance soon transcend his voice, and by the end we have forgotten his masculinity entirely, having been taken through a heart-wrenching story of female tragedy.

Thus the performance leaves behind the sound of his vocals and becomes pure meaning. A transferral of experience. We *feel* the song more than we *hear* it.

How to have a novel idea

I have another interpretation of Solvé et Coagula that can be applied to having ideas. I use this method whenever I have a creative block, and it has served me well.

How is it possible to have a novel idea? I suggest there are three primary ways:

1. **Synthesis.** This is the act of putting together two or more old ideas that haven't been combined before. For an example from cooking we have the concept of "chicken vindaloo on rice", and the concept of "spaghetti bolognese". Therefore, I see no reason why there couldn't be chicken vindaloo on spaghetti, or rice bolognese! (One common effect of this type of synthesis is to upset prickly people, which can be used for comedic effect. Try it at your next dinner party.)

2. **Removal.** Take an idea consisting of parts, and remove a fundamental part (analysis). For example, The White Stripes was a rock band consisting of only a singing guitarist and a drummer. This was the so-called "power trio" instrumentation of guitar/bass/drums, with the bass player removed. The removal of the bass player threw their music into an exciting new context, even though the guitar playing or drumming in itself was not significantly outside the norm for a rock band.

Another example would be the unicycle compared with the bicycle. The mere removal of one wheel creates a vehicle that, while harder to master and less energy efficient, is significantly more manoeuvrable. As my friend Sugra, probably the most well known unicyclist in New Zealand, has explained to me: unicycles are, unlike a bicycle, able to travel in a squiggly path, or spin on a spot. The single wheel offers a whole new range of manoeuvrability. In both examples, the removal of a fundamental component creates new attributes and meaning, different from the parent form.

3. **Discovery.** This is the hardest one, as it requires founding a new concept or "logos": that is, a boundary that allows us to recognise a concept, action, or thing separate from that which surrounds it. Occasionally, we can discover something from nature, harness it, and treat it as a new idea. For example, people did not create the phenomenon of electricity, they discovered it. Once the methods of turning kinetic or solar energy into electricity were discovered, we gained a new concept that could now be added or subtracted from other concepts. Take, for example, the electric guitar, which is a synthesis of the acoustic guitar and electricity.

Since our perception is both a "pattern-recognition machine" and a "prediction-machine", one way to have new ideas is to pump "noise" into a system. This can produce perceptions of patterns from randomness (pareidolia). Magical practices such as scrying in a black mirror, or the psychological Rorschach blot-test, take advantage of our natural tendency to arrange random information into patterns.

Engaging with randomness or "sortition", as it is usually referred to by magicians, is an easy way to use discovery in order to have new ideas. I believe that this helps explain what is going on with various forms of divination, from tarot to reading tea leaves. Most forms of divination that I have come across involve some form of sortition, that is, a randomisation, such as the shuffling of cards or the settling of tea leaves at the bottom of a cup. The fortune teller then uses their creativity to notice patterns, either via the shape of the tea leaves, or narrative patterns between the meanings of the tarot cards. This "discovery from noise" is also a big part of the experience behind psychedelic drugs, and the art inspired by them. It can also be used in music, theatre, and film to create other-worldly experiences.

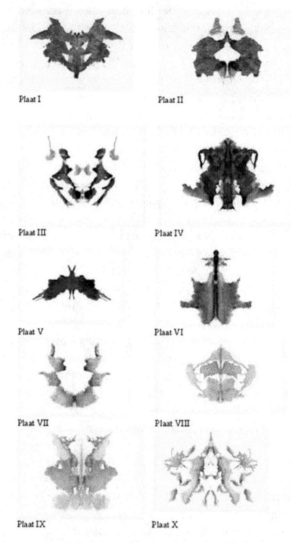

Plaat I

Plaat II

Plaat III

Plaat IV

Plaat V

Plaat VI

Plaat VII

Plaat VIII

Plaat IX

Plaat X

The psychoanalyst Hermann Rorschach's
(1884–1922) original ten inkblot images.

Human culture is like a huge soup of Solvé et Coagula loops. This
cycle of creativity underpins so much of the magical experience, and
is therefore a great conceptual starting point for understanding magic.

CHAPTER 19

Ladder cosmologies

Maps of perception

In order to affect human perception for our magical purposes, it would be useful to have a clearer idea of how our perception is structured, and the types of experiences we can have. In this chapter, I will first outline what I mean by my term "ladder cosmologies" and explain why I think they are useful to a pragmatic magician. Then we will explore two traditions, both ladder cosmologies that have been used for magic, compare them, and relate them to other possible alternatives. These two systems are the sephiroth, or "tree of life", from Kabbalah, and the chakra system used in Hinduism, tantra, and yoga, as well as in Eastern-influenced Western traditions, such as Theosophy.

I will only summarise these systems in the next few chapters, as they are both very complex. Our perception is a rich landscape, and even if the reader initially just grasps the magnitude of trying to map it, that is enough to begin with. Much like walking in a cathedral, the awe of such complex architecture is immediate, even though fully comprehending each artistic detail could take months.

There will be those who are drawn towards the details, and there will be those who are happy to admire the larger picture from afar.

Either way, by framing the systems quickly here I hope to present a snapshot for something that I find is generally missing from discussion in modern Western culture.

Some of you will enjoy my summaries of the sephiroth and the chakras, while others might skim those chapters and come back to them later. For those of you who are new to both Western and Eastern magical traditions, it might at first be hard to understand how influential these systems have been, and still are. However, after a short exploration of magic, you will find one of these two systems, and some that have been influenced by them, popping up again and again like our proverbial red Toyota Corolla from Chapter 1.

An alternative to monism and dualism

Before we get into details, I'd first like to address why we in the modern Western world are no longer in the habit of using perceptual maps. As philosophers, we have become unstuck from the magical traditions of the past. In an effort to become more certain in our knowledge, we began to mistrust our first-person experience, because it is never completely measurable. As magic takes place in the subjective and intersubjective (shared experience) space rather than the objective, measurable space, it is not so important for magicians to define reality from a single observation point, as is required for scientific testing.

Post-Enlightenment philosophers usually try to explain reality from either a physicalist viewpoint, where matter is the most real, or an idealist one, where ideas or "spirit" are the most real. Both of these are types of "monism", which is the idea that all of reality can be explained from a single concept. In the physicalist explanation, the smallest parts of matter, particles, hold the properties that can explain everything else. The opposite point of view is idealism. Idealists presume that everything condenses from ideas, spirit, or a kind of "world mind". This is usually explained as God's, or the universe's, mind. To the idealist, an interconnected whole is the origin of everything that penetrates down to the smallest individual details.

A third view, that tried to have it both ways, is dualism. Rene Descartes, of "cogito ergo sum" fame, proposed that non-physical mind and physical matter are separate, yet equally real. As we only have our senses, our pattern recognition, and our reason to discern what is really going on, we might never experience reality directly, in any pure sense.

It's not even clear to us, given our current advances in quantum physics, that reality can be separated from the act of perceiving it! Indeed, idealists often propose that to experience reality is to create it.

As we only have our experiences and our perception to work with, holding to an objective reality without first understanding what it means to perceive it, seems to me to be building the top of a house before one has built the foundations.

Our perception is capable of a spectrum of experiences, from fine details, all the way up to deep interconnectedness, and everything in between. For this reason, I propose that our perception of reality is more usefully laid out in a spectrum or as a ladder of different experiences, rather than a single type of experience. Every different point on the perceptual ladder is real, yet is limited by the fact that we can only pay conscious attention to one thing at a time. Therefore, we are not able to see the whole, and all the details it contains, simultaneously.

The ladder from earth to the heavens

There are numerous traditional systems that map human perception. Many have become partly or mostly lost to time, but two very old traditional systems which are still in use, are the sephiroth, from Kabbalah, and the chakra system, from yoga.

In both these systems, the most "material" experiences are at the bottom, and the most "abstract" at the top. If one kicks a rock hard with one's bare feet, then no matter how much one believes in mind-over-matter, one can expect sore toes in return.

Pain is a pervasive part of our perceptual reality, no matter how inconvenient it is. For this reason, pragmatically speaking, pain must be considered real, or we are prone to experience more of it than we would like. On the other hand, it is clear that matter arranges itself in ways that can be understood with numbers, geometric shapes, and other mathematical concepts that have no physical reality in themselves. This is the plane of concepts. At the most abstract level, it is possible to have a transcendental experience of being "one with everything", as the cliché goes, where one doesn't feel like an individual anymore. Perhaps not everybody has experienced this, but it has been such a common experience throughout time that it seems reasonable to assume that almost everybody is capable of this experience. Furthermore, different types of concepts arise at different levels of thinking. A specific tree is as real as

Image of Jacob's Ladder from the Luther Bible of 1534.

all of the trees of that species, which are as real as the general concept of trees, which is as real as the concept of plants, which is as real as the concept of life, etc. The fact that we have difficulty deciding which one of these should be "most" real, is not reality's problem. It's a symptom of the human condition that we are unable to see reality laid out all at once in a pattern that makes sense of everything.

I call these systems, where reality is explained from top to bottom, "ladder cosmologies". In traditional systems of meditation, often the goal of the meditator is to learn how to manipulate one's conscious state in order to climb up the ladder from the everyday experiences to the more rare abstract (spiritual) experiences. Both the sephiroth and the chakra systems have been used for this purpose.

CHAPTER 20

The Kabbalist cosmology

Kabbalah is a mystical tradition that arose out of Judaism. It went on to be incorporated into Christian, Persian, and Islamic thinking, before becoming a core system of thought behind alchemy and "proto-science". It has hugely influenced Western philosophy and was used as the primary cosmology of the Golden Dawn, the most influential nineteenth-century occult society. In the Golden Dawn writings, it was also associated with and combined with tarot, as these systems share a similar numerology.

The three veils

At the top of the Kabbalist cosmology is the concept of a void of endless potential called Ein Soph. This is a state in which nothing is differentiated, and nothing can be said to exist. This is the precursor to existence. It is the universe's tendency to spring into action and create itself, similar in concept to the state proposed by science before the Big Bang occurred. Ein Soph is the quality that the universe had before matter and time came into existence. It is also very similar to the Hindu concept of Brahman, an unchanging realm of pure potentiality from which all of reality emanates. Ein Soph is the Kabbalistic concept of God: that from

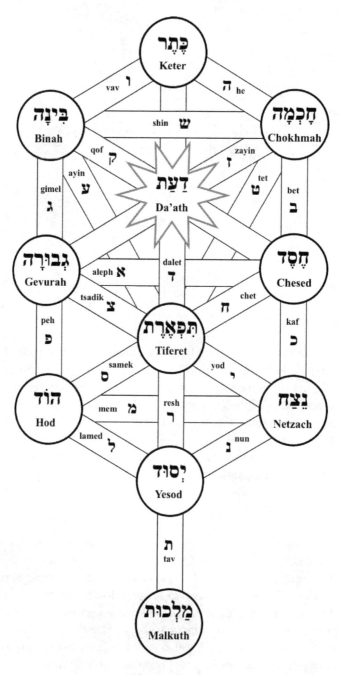

The sephiroth.

which everything we experience springs forth, yet itself a state that is unknowable to us, and which we cannot directly experience, because it precedes existence. It can also be understood as the universe's "creative force". When scientists try to create a state of vacuum, by sucking all the matter out of the inside of a container, we would expect there to be nothing inside. Instead, measurable points of energy pop in and out of existence where there should be nothing: a phenomenon known as "zero point energy". I like to think of this as an indication of a universe that can't help but constantly create itself.

Ein Soph has three aspects known as the "three veils", as they are beyond our perception. These seek to describe what happens before creation. These can be seen at the top of the diagram on the previous page.

- Ein: *Nothing*
- Ein Soph: *No End*
- Ein Soph Aur: *Limitless Light*

This is an attempt to explain a type of infinity. It is nothing (Ein) as there is yet no boundary that can be drawn between things. It has no end (Ein Soph), as there is no line at which one can say that everything is contained. There is limitless light because there are infinite points within and infinite possible connections, and therefore no way to locate or differentiate anything from anything else.

The soul, and angels

Here I must necessarily relate some spiritual concepts: "soul" and "angels". For our purposes, "soul" can well enough be interchanged with the word "mind". A soul certainly has some connotations beyond the mind, such as being that which can transcend the death of the body, but if you find that to be a stumbling block, "mind" will do well enough to start with. Second is the concept of "angels" (*malakh* in Hebrew). In Western culture, angels have unfortunately become thoroughly mixed up with many other ideas about beings and spirits which have little to do with the angels of the Old Testament. In Kabbalah, angels are not winged people, nor are they the souls of the dead. They are more like "living information". Powers that transmit universal concepts to us, and which can be harnessed through ritual, meditation, and prayer.

In the *Sefer Yetzirah, The Book of Creation in Theory and Practice* by Aryeh Kaplan (1997), it is explained that:

> We have already spoken of the teaching that there are angels created with every word of God. Elsewhere we find that angels are created every day, with a new troop being made every morning. On the other hand, there are many angels who are known by name, such as Gabriel and Michael, who have permanent existence. These are obviously a second type of angel … In discussing this, the Kabbalists arrive at a significant conclusion. They state that there are two basic kinds of angels: permanent angels and temporary angels …

We can see here that angels are something more akin to spiritual flows of information, like codified units of meaning that are sent back and forth between the spiritual plane and the experiential plane. Some are attached to universal truths, while others serve short-lived missions. They are not like spiritual versions of human beings with human free will, but more like "spiritual telegrams", or the spiritual version of the packets of ones and zeros that are sent as digital code from computer to computer over the internet. Elsewhere, it is described that lesser angels are temporarily created with every prayer, like arrows of intent. Both the words "angel", and the Hebrew "malakh", mean "messenger", and it seems that originally the emphasis was on the message, like a letter being sent in the mail, and less on a kind of being who behaves like a spiritual mailman, who has a life after work and plays golf on the weekend.

The four worlds

The Hebrew tetragramaton from the Bible YHVH (often pronounced "Yahweh"), as well as being a name for God, is thought, in Kabbalah, to stand for four conceptual worlds, as follows:

- **Atziluth:** Y. The archetypal world of highest abstractions.
- **Briah:** H. The creative world of ideas and intuition, generalised core-aspects, and universal forces. It's here that the archangels dwell, which are spiritual transmitters of universal energy, or information. It is the realm of "neshamah", the intellectual part of our soul, or mind, which is that which we use to comprehend abstract ideas.

- **Yetzirah:** V. The formative world. Related to the art of design, it is akin to the blueprints from which one creates a piece of architecture. It is the realm of "types", where things can be categorised. It is the dwelling place of the lower angels, which are transmitters of conceptual information, and specified spiritual energies. It is the dwelling place of our "ruach", which is the emotional/intuitive part of our soul or mind. And finally, it is the space where we use our "mind's eye", or the parts of our imagination that correlate with our senses. It's where we visualise things and make sense of experiences, such as music.
- **Assiah:** H. This is the manifest world, which we interact with and communicate in. It's the realm of shared experience as well as the plane of matter. Here is the residing place of "nepesh", which is part of the human soul which can be found alike in animals and other earthly beings.

To understand these four "worlds", one can use an example of a car.

Assiah would be a specific red Toyota Corolla that you can use to drive around. Yetzirah would be the concept of all Toyota Corollas, as a type of car which you can recognise while driving around, or read about in car magazines. Briah would be the concept of cars and automobiles in general, and Atziluth would be the concept of travel: the need from which we developed cars in the first place.

The three pillars

The sephiroth are laid out in three columns. These are the three vertical aspects of the diagram on page 180. On the left column downwards from the top are Binah, Gevurah, Hod. On the middle column: Keter, Da'ath, Tiferet, Yesod, and Malkuth. On the right column: Chokhmah, Chesed, and Netzach. The right column represents Mercy, and the left represents Severity. These two are often related to Boaz and Jachin, the two symbolic pillars that stood at the front of King Solomon's temple. They represented his powers as a judge, to mete out mercy on one hand or punishment on the other. This same symbolism is often still seen in the two pillars at the front of many modern courthouses, and also appears in several of the cards in the Rider-Waite tarot, as well as in the lodges of the Freemasons. Another connotation of the two pillars is that of "flow" on the right, and "containment" on the left. This concept of containment or restriction is similar to the idea of "logos", a term we inherited from the ancient Greek philosopher Heraclitus, and which is used in several places in the Bible, sometimes translated misleadingly as "the Word". John 1:1 says "In the beginning was the Word [logos]." That is, before there could be anything, there had to be a boundary that can be drawn around something, in order that it may be differenti- ated from other things. Heraclitus is famous for saying, "You cannot step in the same river twice." The water that makes a flowing river is constantly changing, yet the concept of a river, its "logos", remains. In Kabbalah, the concept of the river would be "higher", which is to say, more abstract than, the water you could collect in a bucket.

To understand the concepts of "flow" and "containment", the right and left pillars in Kabbalah, we can continue with the river metaphor. The flow is the movement of the water, without which the river would run dry. The containment is the river bed and banks that direct and contain the water.

The central pillar is Mildness. It represents the mixing of the other two pillars. The universe must have an amount of flow and an amount of containment in order to be habitable, and human beings must have an amount of freedom and an amount of discipline in order to go about their lives.

Too much flow is often represented biblically as a flood. That which washes all differentiation away. A person dropped in the middle of the ocean has no clear sense of direction, no floating object or foothold with which to steady themselves, and no clear understanding of distance. They are in a state of too much "flow". Yet, a state without flow has no motivation, no movement, no energy, and no decisions to be made, and therefore cannot contain life.

In Kabbalah, the right pillar of flow and mercy is considered mascu- line, and the left of containment and severity is considered feminine. The central pillar is the outcome of the coming together of these attributes. The pillars also represent the right side of the brain and its associative thinking, and the left side with its logical thinking and categorisation. In Western culture, logic is usually presented as masculine and intu- ition as feminine, but in Jewish lore this is the other way around. The associative/intuitive is the male aspect, and the rational/logical is the feminine aspect.

The central pillar is the balancing, decision making, and productive powers of the mind, which rely on the right mixture between right and left.

The sephiroth

The sephiroth are a series of nodes that represent attributes of reality. They relate both to the way we think in our minds and also the ways our environment appears to us. There are paths from one sephirah to another, and each of these paths is ascribed one of the letters of the Hebrew alphabet. In traditional Kabbalah, these twenty-two letters can be chanted in meditation, allowing a connection to the particular path. Later, we will see something similar in the chakra system, in which each of the fifty letters of the Sanskrit alphabet are also chanted as mantras.

Sephiroth are sometimes described as garments that God wears in order to relate to creation. They present in the universe as we observe it, and also in man, who is considered a microcosm to the universe's macrocosm.

As Kabbalah describes the sephiroth as emanations of God from the most abstract to the most physical. We will start at the top of the ladder. The "God's eye" point of view. (For those of you who are agnostic or atheist, remember that this "God" is the universe's "creativity", a concept that does not necessarily require belief from us.)

As we continue, you may want to refer back now and again to the diagram of the ten sephiroth at the beginning of this chapter.

The first sephirah describes a transcendental state just beyond the mind.

Keter: *Crown*
Keter can be thought of as "pure will", or "God's desire". In the Zohar, one of the primary Kabbalistic texts dating back to the thirteenth century, it is described as "the most hidden of all hidden things". Keter stands for those abstract concepts which are beyond the mind's comprehension. It is visualised during meditations as being above the head. Keter has no differentiated content, but contains the potential for all content. It stands for the type of experience where one realises one can't know any more. It is the gulf at the edge of what is knowable. Keter is as close as we get to consciously experiencing Ein Soph, the primordial void of endless potential from which everything emanates. Keter can be related to pure consciousness.

As a king is the highest ranking person in a kingdom, and symbolised as the "head" of state, Keter is like the concept of monarchy, which is more abstract that the king, and which the king serves as his higher authority above his station as a human being. The king is subservient to "the Crown".

The next three sephiroth are personal aspects. They are "in" the mind, and therefore only appear to the individual, remaining hidden from others.

Chokhmah: *Wisdom*
This is the experience of intuitive insight, especially that which flashes across the consciousness. It is the node where the super-conscious interfaces with the conscious. It stands for the ability to look at an aspect of existence and uncover its underlying form or pattern. The word Chokhmah itself may be broken into two words, "Chokh" ("potential") and "Mah" ("what is"). Thus, Chokhmah means "the potential of what is". Chokhmah is the associative mind that we would nowadays think of as the right side of the brain. It is the feeling of being in "the zone" when creating art, playing sports in a team, writing, or playing music. In psychology, these types of experiences are referred to as "flow states". Chokhmah is also the state of "transcendence" in meditation. As the final state of consciousness that can be fully felt or experienced, Chokhmah is sometimes referred to as the "Abba", or supernal father: that which seeds all of our experience.

Binah: *Understanding*
Binah is the understanding that comes from thinking things through. It is described poetically as the womb which gives shape to the spirit of God. It stands for the part of the mind responsible for deductive reasoning, which we associate with the left side of the brain. As Chokhmah is inspiration, Binah is creative limitation and control. It is the state of mind where we understand an idea in relation to other ideas. It is described as the supernal mother or "Imma": that which gives form to the seed of thought. Too much Binah in an individual is over-analysis.

Da'ath: *Knowledge*
This is the state of meditation or consciousness where one fully understands the rest of the sephiroth as a complete working system in flow. It can therefore be compared with the state of enlightenment that is the goal of many forms of meditation. For this reason, it is not always considered a true sephirah, but that which happens when all

the sephiroth combine. It is here that decisions are made by relating between Chokhmah and Binah. It is the decisive mind that balances the right and the left sides of the brain. It is a state of clear decision making and it corresponds to the point where the spine meets the skull.

The next seven sephiroth are visible in the world through form, action, and behaviour.

Chesed: Often translated as "kindness", this might be better understood as "intimacy", or the crossing of boundaries. It has also been described as "flow", in the sense that water has no boundary until it is contained. As intimacy, it is love between people, and God's love and mercy to man. Chesed can be found in the act of charity and our ability to be sociable. Too much Chesed is like a flooding river which escapes the boundary of its banks. In Jewish morality, too much Chesed is also associated with promiscuity and hedonism. A feedbacking electric guitar at a rock concert is Chesed, where the signal becomes saturated, and causes a chain reaction, like a flood, which is difficult to control. While flow is necessary for existence, and controlled flow equals power, flow without boundaries is destructive.

Gevurah: *Discipline. Judgement. Limitation.*
Gevurah is that which guards against unfettered flow. It is containment. That which allows things to maintain their shape, and the strength that holds them. It is God's judgemental might. It is associated with absolute adherence to the letter of the law, and the strict meting out of justice. It is the might to confront one's enemies, and to push back against threat. It is the will to withhold kindness to those who are deemed unworthy because they might misuse that kindness. Gevurah must work in balance with Chesed, as too much Gevurah is restraining and cruel. It is metaphorically the left arm and hand to Chesed, which is the right arm and hand. Both forces are of action. In the moral sense, Gervurah is discipline.

Tiferet: *Beauty*
This sephirah looks at the recipient, Malkuth, and decides how much Gevurah, containment, to use, in order that the right amount of Chesed, flow, comes through the system. In music, it is Tiferet that allows the performer to relate to an audience, and how much

Chesed and Gevurah they should balance in order to entertain. In relation to each other, Chesed is the emotion and excitement behind a performance, and Gevurah is the structure and restraint. Tiferet can be understood as a lower emanation of Keter and as a higher emanation of Yesod and Malkuth. Tiferet acts as a central body, much like the sun in our solar system, whereas Keter could be seen as the less visible centre of all creation, the great attractor. Tiferet is the only sephirah connected to all the other sephiroth. The reason Tiferet is "beauty" is that it is in balance, and all beautiful things suggest a balance. In meditation, it can be associated with the heart, and the emotions that we relate to the heart.

Netzach: *Victory*

This is the sephirah of perseverance. While sprinting would be a Chesed activity, marathon running is a Netzach activity. To be able to run a marathon, one must apply some limit in order to ration one's energy. Netzach is where we find the power to overcome obstacles and limitations. It is associated with emotion and passion, music and dancing. It is the patience to complete a long-term goal. It is also associated with leadership: the ability to rally others to action. The next sephirah, Hod, represents the community which the leader calls to action.

The upper sephiroth deal with God's will or the higher parts of the soul, while Netzach and Hod are that which is closest to man. Netzach and Hod are where we consider how to act, so our will can become manifest.

Hod: *Splendour*

Hod is focus, staying on task, and keeping form. It is self-discipline. Connected to Gevurah, Tiphereth, Netzach, and Yesod. Hod and Netzach are associated to the feet in the sense of walking or stand-ing, offering the means for activity. The feet take a person to the place where they would act. Associated with the Jewish prayer and the act of submission on which prayer is a meditation, Hod is the state of focused attention necessary for meditation. It is the place where our unconscious desires, which come from Netzach, are given symbolic form. These can then manifest unconsciously through Yesod, into physical action in Malkuth. The rabbi Zalman Shachter-Shalomi said, "Hod is like doing your dirty laundry." It is a force that breaks down spiritual energy into differentiated forms. It is associated with the learning and rituals that engage the intellect, activities that we would now associate with the "left brain". According to the occultist Dion Fortune, when one does magic through symbols, images, or idols, one is channelling the magic through Hod.

Yesod: *Foundation. Connection.*
Yesod is that which connects the physical world and the "inter-subjective" space where we communicate, to the other sephiroth, which are all in different parts of the spiritual/conceptual plane. It is the foundation and transmitter between the higher sephiroth and the manifest plane below. A good communicator conveys their meaning through Yesod, where they decide how to best relate to the recipient, Malkuth. Associated with the sexual organs, Yesod is the masculine aspect which transmits the creative forces of the other sephiroth into the feminine Malkuth below. As Yesod communicates between the upper sephiroth and Malkuth, it can be compared with the Holy Spirit in the Catholic Trinity. Dion Fortune says that Yesod, when meditated on, gives an understanding of life force. As it is the sephirah of communication, it can be associated with public relations, advertising, public speaking, and propaganda.

Malkuth: *Kingdom. The Recipient.*
Malkuth is the physical world of matter, from our body and immediate surroundings, to the stars. It is also the place where we can have shared experiences. It is likened to the anus and the feet, which, whether sitting or standing connect one to the Earth. Malkuth gives tangible form to the other sephiroth. It is the receiving physical plane Assiah. It serves as the opposite pole to Keter, which is divine will. The interaction between Keter and Malkuth can be seen to reflect the alchemical adage "as above so below" (from the Emerald Tablet), which is related to my earlier description of "Solvé et Coagula" in Chapter 18. It receives the creative forces of the other sephiroth, and manifests them. It is the foundation and transmitter between the higher sephiroth and the physical plane below.

In the spiritual space of the other sephiroth, concepts are separate. Only in Malkuth can they truly come together. Without physical space, concepts cannot be manifest. This can be related to the printed word which, though physical, can give access to the most abstract and intangible concepts and feelings.

The sequence of the sephiroth

The sephiroth can be understood as a system as follows:

If one is to first have an idea, and then act that idea out in the world, the initial spark will start in Keter. Though the thought has its precursor in Keter, it won't be conscious until it appears, as an inspiration, in Chokhmah. This inspiration will then be reasoned, shaped, and moulded in relation to other thoughts in Binah. This, idea could then be relayed to a group of people through Chesed. Then once those people have received the message, a plan emerges in Gevurah, and the group of people begin work to see the idea through. To complete the task, the message in Chesed and the plan in Gevurah must be balanced. Too much talk will prevent things from getting finished, while too little explanation can cause the plan to fail. In Netzach is found the emotional endurance to finish the job. In Hod, the focus and method is found to keep the group on task until the job is complete. In Yesod, the finished product is presented to others, and in Malkuth the message is received.

With the description of the sephiroth, and the previous example, one now ought to be able to understand how a ladder cosmology might function, and from that we can now begin to imagine ways it might be used. The sephiroth can function as a map to help us better understand conscious states in ourselves and others. The sephiroth is, of course, only one example; one which has been foundational to Western magic and philosophy. Now we will take a quick look at the chakra system which evolved from descriptions in Vedic texts, and which is foundational to Eastern magical systems including yoga, and tantra.

CHAPTER 21

The chakras

Chakra means "wheel" in Sanskrit. Cha comes from the word "chalana", meaning movement, and Kra comes from "KarOti", meaning "doing". So a chakra is something that enables movement. In yoga meditation, the chakras are conceptualised as nodes of prana, which is the life force or vital principle. Prana, like the word "spirit", is associated with the breath. It can be compared with the Hebrew term "ruach", which is "God's breath", a spiritual force that sustains all living things. Prana is thought to accumulate at the different chakras, and through meditation one can gain control over this flow, and therefore have access to all the different conscious states which are mapped out by the chakras.

The chakras are conceptualised as parts of the "subtle body" (sūkshmaśarīra) that symbolise the conscious states which can be accessed through meditation. The subtle body is thought to be in the first layer of the spiritual realm, which is closest to the physical. Hopefully by now, the reader has a clear idea about the nature of the spiritual realm, but if one is still squeamish about the term, understand that for my purposes, it correlates to the world of thought, form, and ideas.

Kundalini

Kundalini is a Sanskrit term meaning 'coiled snake'. It is a way to comprehend how consciousness can "rise" through various stages while meditating, or during the various conscious states that we find ourselves in during the day.

As one increases in skill in yoga meditation, it is said that the kundalini, a normally dormant energy, rises up like an uncoiling snake to access each chakra. After much practice, some meditators are said to be able to reach the highest chakra, Sahasrara, which causes a state of consciousness associated with enlightenment, and a deep connection to Brahman, the interconnected, undifferentiated source of everything. Brahman is a term for the same type of experience that the Kabbalists refer to as "Ein Soph". An undifferentiated void of endless potential out of which the universe emanates. In this state, there is not yet any matter or time. However much we may seek a true state of nothingness, little bits of "something" can't help but spring into existence.

While Western yoga often only teaches the concept of the rising kundalini, originally in the Sanskrit writings there is a balancing upper kundalini, which descends. In this older system, the goal was not only to learn how to transcend the physical plane in order to gain an experience of pure spirit, but also to learn to bring the upper kundalini energy down to affirm it in the physical plane. With meditative breath exercises, each inhalation was visualised with a descending kundalini, which can be associated with the feeling of one's diaphragm descending as the lungs fill. Each exhalation in turn was related to a retraction of the upper kundalini and a rising of the lower kundalini. I prefer this older, more traditional conception, as it grants as much importance to the physical as it does to the spirit, balancing the system out. Perhaps the westernised yoga that only discusses the upwards kundalini helps explain why many New Age yoga practitioners appear to have their "head in the clouds". Remember that it's just as important to keep your "feet on the ground", lest we lose the ability to relate to the rest of the world around us!

The chakras in the East and the West

The chakras are first mentioned in Buddhist tantric texts around the eighth century, including the *Hevajra Tantra* and *Caryāgiti*. These earliest systems mention only four chakras, but this developed into more complex systems later.

The chakra system seems to have first appeared in the West in the 1880s, mostly through the occult books of Helena Blavatsky (the founder of Theosophy), the writings of Henry Steel Olcott, and Sir John Woodroffe's (aka Arthur Avalon) book *The Serpent Power*.

The chakra system that Western yogis follow comes from a 1577 Sanskrit text written by Pūrṇānanda Yati, called the Ṣaṭcakranirūpaṇa or "Explanation of the Six Chakras". It was the sixth chapter of a longer work, and was first translated into English in 1918. There had been an earlier, related, seven chakra system in a thirteenth century text called Śāradā-tilaka, but this is largely unknown in the English-speaking world.

The chakra system later underwent several adaptations such as the association with seven different colours in Charles W. Leadbeater's 1927 book *The Chakras*, and the associations of each chakra with a nerve plexus in the body (added by Baman Das Basu, an Indian army physician). Originally in the Vedic writings, the chakras were not thought to have a physical presence, being nodes in the *subtle* body. To complicate matters, some of these later Western adaptations have influenced modern Indian thinkers and gurus, especially when the chakras are taught in English (Leland, 2016).

There is a different rainbow colour system that was added in the 1930s by Roland Hunt, who wrote a book called *The Seven Keys to Colour Healing*. This and other colour codes are now common with the modern teaching of chakra systems but are not found in older systems (Leland, 2016).

In India and other nations with Hindu and Buddhist roots, there are numerous variations on the chakra tradition containing five, six, seven, fourteen, and as many as forty-nine chakras (Baghel & Pradhan, 2015).

For my purposes, I will explore the seven chakra system, as this is the one most accessible to English speakers. An exploration of the traditional Indian chakra systems, let alone Tibetan systems, could fill a library, and is therefore not feasible for us in a single chapter. So I will summarise that which is most common to the English-speaking world, albeit including the Sanskrit terms and mantras which are fundamental, but unfortunately left out in most Western chakra teachings. These will help us to understand the original purpose of the chakras for the traditional Vedic yogis, and also help us to relate them to the sephiroth from Kabbalah.

As one of the most common applications of the chakra system is to elevate one's consciousness towards more abstract experiences during yoga, they are usually explained from the bottom of the ladder up, as the beginning meditator will at first engage the lower chakras. Being able to reach each consecutive conscious state associated with each rising chakra is considered an achievement for the yogi. However, as I wish to compare the chakras with the sephiroth described in the previous chapter, I will start at the top and work downwards. This corresponds to the downwards kundalini, a force (prana) like our emanations in the sephiroth, which is vitally important to traditional Eastern yoga.

The chakra system

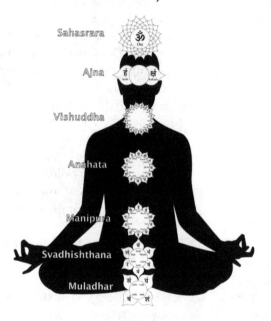

The nadis

Whilst the chakra system looks at first like a simpler system than the sephiroth, due to its arrangement in a single column, the nadi system in yoga adds left/right/centre concepts onto the chakras that correlate to the three pillars we have discussed in the sephiroth. The three nadis from the left to the right are, Ida, Shushumna, and Pingala.

Ida is the left side, which is associated with the moon and the feminine. The word Ida means "comfort" in Sanskrit. It courses, in the male, from the left testicle to the left nostril, like a river, and is sometimes compared to the holy river Ganges.

Pingala is associated with the sun, and is masculine. The word Pingala means "orange" in Sanskrit. It courses in the male from the right testicle to the right nostril, and is compared to the holy Indian river Yamuna.

As with left and right in the sephiroth, the Ida and Pingala nadis are often seen as referring to the two hemispheres of the brain. Pingala is the extroverted aspect, and it corresponds to the left hemisphere. Ida is the introverted aspect, and it refers to the right hemisphere. The feminine Ida nadi controls all the mental processes, while masculine Pingala controls all the vital processes. Just like the three pillars in the sephiroth, this may at first feel backwards to our modern association of "female as intuitive" and "male as rational", but it just goes to show how different philosophies change over time, and differ from culture to culture. I personally enjoy the fresh perspective that this apparent reversal grants me.

The central nadi is Shushumna, which, like the middle pillar in the sephiroth, denotes balance and connects all the chakras.

The chakras summarised

Every chakra is assigned a location in the body where the three nadis are thought to cross. Each chakra has as its symbol a lotus bud, which is thought to blossom as one gains access to the particular chakra through meditation. Each lotus has a number of petals which are different for each chakra, and each petal of the lower six chakras, totalling fifty, has a symbolic meaning and is assigned a letter of the Sanskrit alphabet. These letters can also be spoken as syllables, and chanted in succession as a mantra. Each of these letters was considered a power from which the universe is constructed, and they were to be meditated upon one by one, then released or "dissolved". With each release, one was thought to transcend that aspect of the world, allowing one to become closer to the Godhead. This same concept is found in older Kabbalist traditions, with the chanting of the twenty-two letters of the Hebrew alphabet, each of which corresponds to a path between two sephiroth.

Sahasrara: Crown

Sahasrara means "thousand petalled". Often referred to as a thousand-petalled lotus, it is said to be the most subtle chakra in the system, relating to pure consciousness. It is from this chakra, like Keter, that all the other chakras emanate. When a yogi is able to raise his or her kundalini (energy of consciousness) up to this point, the state of "Nirvikalpa Samādhi" is experienced. This describes a state without self-consciousness, where the knower and act of knowing become dissolved.

This is the most abstract of all obtainable experiences in yoga. It is a state where all distinctions are broken down, and one's awareness is expanded beyond what can be explained in words. Here one achieves a vantage point where the mind is fully comprehended, and is above the usual states of mental function. It is the transcendent state of "ego-death", which is often discussed in the psychedelic community with the consumption of entheogens or psychedelic drugs.

When compared with the sephiroth, this chakra appears to be something conceptually a little lower than Keter. It incorporates that which is explained as Da'ath and is the last state of consciousness that can be fully comprehended. This contrasts slightly with Keter, which is just beyond what is knowable to humankind, and therefore cannot be comprehended. I consider Sahasrara the final, most abstracted experience a person can have, and Keter to be a state which is just beyond the reach of human beings.

Sahasrara is associated with a feeling of ecstasy. Some Kabbalists also associate Keter with a feeling of "delight".

As with Keter, Sahasrara is located just above the head.

Traditionally, Sahasrara was not considered a true chakra, but as the higher source from which the chakras emanate. It serves as the exit point for the rising kundalini energy as it leaves the lower self and gains access to interconnection with a higher self undifferentiated from other things: Brahman. This is why it is "thousand petalled", meaning it contains uncountable parts, that can no longer be differentiated. Unlike the lower six chakras, these petals are not understood through the Sanskrit letters, as they are no longer communicable through words, and can only be directly experienced.

Ajna: Third eye, brow

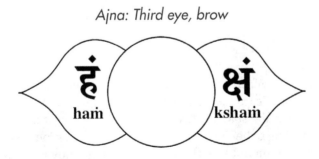

Ajna represents the subconscious mind. Its symbol is a two petalled lotus. Ajna translates as "authority" or "command", or "perceive". It is considered the "third eye" of intuition and intellect, and it is associated with the brain and mind.

Consciousness that is centred at this chakra involves introspection. Opening the "third eye" means integrating the right and left sides of the brain, bringing together the intuition where ideas usually spark, with the judgement and discrimination of rational thinking, thereby separating out the useful from the non-useful. This appears to combine the concepts of both Chokhmah and Binah when compared to the sephiroth. The third eye is also often conceived of as a gate through which psychic phenomena can be experienced, such as out-of-body experiences or clairvoyance.

Vishuddha: Throat

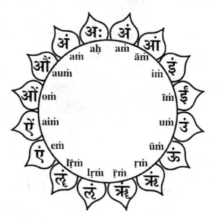

Vishuddha means "especially pure". Its symbol is a sixteen-petalled lotus. The Vishuddha chakra is known as the purification centre. This is compared to the physical throat, which accepts that which can provide nutrition or cause us sickness; food or poison. In its most abstract form, it is associated with higher discrimination, creativity, and self-expression. It is believed that when Vishuddha is closed, a person undergoes decay and death. When it is open, negative experiences are transformed into wisdom and learning. The success and failure in one's life are said to depend upon the state of this chakra, and whether it is polluted or clean. The feeling of being guilty is given as the most prominent reason that this chakra might block the kundalini energy moving upwards as one meditates. It is associated with the sense of hearing, as well as the action of speaking.

Meditation upon this chakra is said to bring about various "siddhis" or occult powers; visions of the past, present, and future, as well as freedom from disease and old age.

This aligns in some of its aspects with Chesed and Gevurrah. These two forces together are where creativity, discernment, and self-expression begin to manifest towards our shared experience.

Anahata: Heart

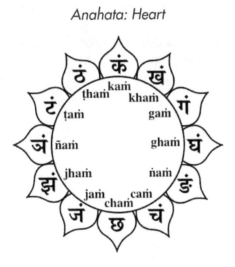

Anahata means the sound produced without touching two parts, or "unstruck", the idea of sympathetic resonance. When two objects, such as stringed instruments, are tuned to the same note, the plucking of one can cause the vibration of the other, even when the two objects are not in contact. The name of this chakra signifies the new awareness that appears when we are able to look at the different and, apparently, contradictory experiences of life with a state of openness and detachment.

At the level of Anahata appears the possibility to integrate opposing forces towards an effect (characterised by sound, in this case), without the two forces being confronted. Inside the symbol of the Anahata chakra, there is a smoky region at the intersection of two triangles, creating a shatkona. The shatkona is a symbol used in Hinduism, representing the union of male and female. Specifically, it is meant to represent a combining of Purusha (the Supreme Being) and Prakriti (Nature).

Anahata is symbolised by a lotus with twelve petals. In Anahata one makes decisions, or follows one's heart, based on one's "higher" self, not the unfulfilled emotions and desires that are considered to be of a "lower" nature. Meditation on this chakra is said to bring about the following abilities: becoming a great speaker, charm towards lovers, the ability to control the senses of others, and the power to leave and enter the body at will. It is also the chakra of creativity and art.

Anahata serves as a junction between our body, mind, emotions, and spirit. It is the bridge point between the upper chakras, which have more to do with our spiritual nature, and the lower chakras, which are more connected to the physical.

This aligns with the sephirah Tiferet.

The lower three chakras have to do with the physical world.

Manipura

Manipura is located at the navel. It means "City of Jewels". This is the chakra of digestion and metabolism. It is symbolised by a ten-petalled lotus. Manipura is associated with sight and action, and is considered the centre of willpower. When this chakra is energised and in balance, one has the quality of being assertive. If unregulated, however, it can lead to preoccupation with controlling others on one side, or becoming overly submissive on the other. Successful integration at this level gives one the quality of being assertive and cooperative, without being aggressive or weakly passive. It is similar to Hod and Netzach in Kabbalah: ambition, focus and planning.

Svadhishthana

Meaning: Where your self is established. This chakra is located at the genitalia, and connected to the sense of taste. Svadhishthana is symbolised by a six-petalled lotus. Svadhishthana is often associated with pleasure, sense of oneself, relationships, sensuality, and procreation. It is thought to be blocked by guilt and regret. Svadhishthana is associated with the unconscious and with emotion. It is closely related to Muladhara, where the different Samskaras (according to yoga, these are dispositions that we are born with that, like imprints, affect who we will become) lie dormant, and Svadhishthana is where these Samskaras find expression. It aligns with the sephirah Yesod.

Svadhishthana contains unconscious desires, especially sexual desire, with an emphasis on pleasure seeking.

Muladhara

Meaning: Root-flux. Located at the base of the spine. Often referred to as the root chakra, it is associated with smell, control over speech, and work and physical health. Muladhara is symbolised by a four-petalled lotus. It is similar to the sephirah Malkuth, though it appears to contain aspects of Yesod as well. Muladhara is the plane where karma is expressed, in the same way as Malkuth is the plane where spiritual concepts manifest in Kabbalah.

Muladhara is located at the base of the spine, and encompasses the first three vertebrae, the bladder, and the colon. The most primitive responses to life-threatening situations involve energy at this point. As such, it is associated with the basic fear of being attacked or injured. From the other side, it is also related to attacking, being aggressive, and searching out prey. One who has an unregulated focus of energy at this chakra is constantly afraid of being injured, or has a strong tendency to hurt and injure others. A balance at this first chakra grants one stability, as one has conquered the tendency of seeing the world in black-and-white terms.

Though often associated nowadays with curing illnesses and improving health, the chakras were not originally for this purpose. Instead, meditating on the chakras was intended to improve the yogi's understanding of their true nature, that allows one relief from the attachments to human wants and physical reality, and to show a spiritual reality that was considered free of Maya (illusion, deception, or magic trickery) and therefore more "real".

CHAPTER 22

The sephiroth and chakras compared

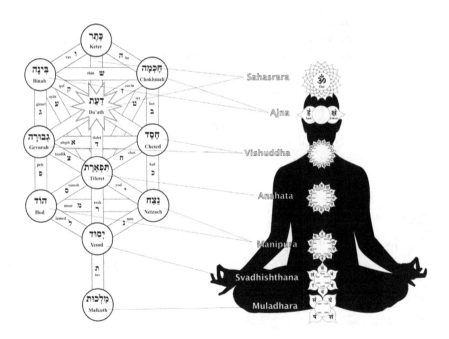

Mapping the human body

The chakra system is almost always mapped onto the body, though the chakras themselves are properly understood to be part of the "subtle body", where the "lower" parts of the spiritual realm, or if you like, the realm of ideas and mind, interface with the physical body. Focused meditation at these points is supposed give one an awareness of the balance of physical and spiritual aspects of ourselves.

The sephiroth can be mapped onto the body, but most of the time this is understood to be only a metaphor. Instead only Malkuth is said to be on the physical plane, and even then I have found in Kabbalist writings that it also corresponds to a realm of shared experience, which is not always strictly physical. All the other sephiroth are considered to be different aspects of the spiritual plane. Chakras are linked to physical health, while the sephiroth are more often applied to spiritual and mental health.

A stacked and fractal system

The ten sephiroth, as a full system, are said to be repeated again in each of the four worlds; Atziluth (the archetypal world), Briah (the creative world), Yetzirah (the formative world), and Assiah (the manifest world). The Malkuth of Atziluth connects to the Keter of Briah, etc. So each sephiroth system stacks on top of another in a chain, until it is repeated four times.

To complicate matters more, the sephiroth are considered fractal in nature, with each of the ten sephiroth residing again in each individual sephirah. This fractal cosmology has no comparison in the chakra system, and from what I have found so far, is unique to Kabbalah.

Channelling prana

The chakras each have branches to distribute prana throughout the body; these are said to be 360 in number, and have no comparison in the sephiroth.

The Hebrew and Sanskrit alphabets as mantras

As well as the ten sephiroth (not including Da'ath), there are twenty-two connecting paths, each marked by a Hebrew letter.

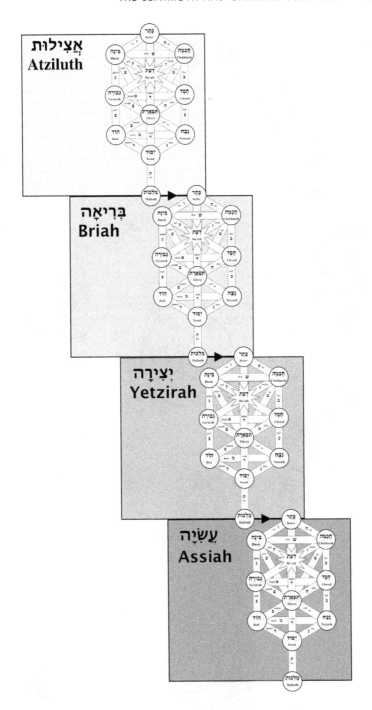

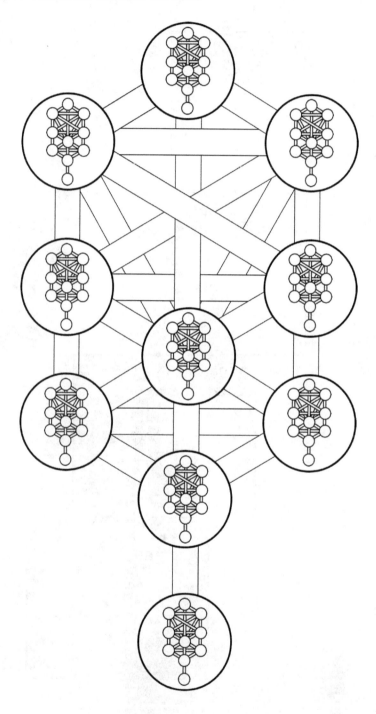

Each path is the equilibrium between two sephiroth. These add up to thirty-two paths, if each sephirah is also considered a path. This complex interlinking is unique, though it has a parallel in the older conceptions of the chakra system, especially from around the sixteenth century, which link the fifty letters of the Sanskrit alphabet to the petals on each of the lower six chakra lotus symbols. These six are considered to be the true chakras, with Sahasrara being a transcendent aspect achieved as one leaves the chakras and gains a transcendent connection with the godhead. Each of the petals has a syllable, connected to each letter of the alphabet, which can be chanted as a mantra. Each of these allows access to a specific aspect of power that anchors one to reality. In the sephiroth, chanting the thirty-two paths was sometimes associated with manifestation magic, such as the creation of a Golem (an artificial life form). In comparison, the goal in the chakra system was to be released from each manifesting power, so that one could reach one's higher self (Atman).

On my diagrams, I have included these letters with transliterations, so that the reader can get a feel for this idea, though we will not go into further detail in this book.

The elements

In pre-Western chakra systems, as well as the petals, each chakra was associated with one of the elements: earth, water, fire, wind, and space, and each chakra had a specific Hindu deity or deities connected to it. They are usually from low to high: Ganesh, Brahmā, Vishnu, Rudra, Īśvara, Sadāśiva, and Bhairava. These are distributed differently, depending on the number of chakras. There is some suggestion in texts that the elements could be shifted between chakras by the yogi for different results (Wallis, 2016).

Later versions of the sephiroth, especially those used in alchemical magic and the version adapted by the Golden Dawn, use the four classical elements of fire, water, earth, and air. To my knowledge, this incorporation of the elements is not such a big focus in the older Jewish Kabbalah.

Focal points for meditation

Both the sephiroth and the chakras show states of consciousness that can be accessed through meditation. However, the sephiroth is not just for representing modes of consciousness, but also constitutes a moral map, and a cosmology for understanding how the world takes form, both in the macrocosm of the universe and in the human propensity to create through procreation, art, performance, teaching, and all forms of knowledge.

The chakra system is highly experiential in nature. At each point the yogi was to understand something about reality. The sephiroth can be treated in a similar fashion.

Other ladder cosmologies

There appear to be no other cosmologies quite as complex as the sephiroth or the chakra system in Western education. Certain parallels can be drawn perhaps to Maslow's Hierarchy of Needs, which is a much more simple attempt to outline what must be taken care of before a human can "self actualise", or reach their potential. It might also make sense to compare Freud's superego, ego, and id as a much simpler explanation of those parts of the mind that can cause mental illness when out of balance, as well as sub-personalities from which our human drives can emerge. This idea of different drives coming from different aspects of the psyche is one of the traditional uses of the chakra system.

An attempt was made by Timothy Leary, which was later expanded on by Robert Anton Wilson, to align states of consciousness with evolutionary stages in their "Eight Circuit Model of Consciousness". Although I admire the attempt, I don't find their model particularly compelling, and I feel it has not dated well with ongoing scientific discoveries. It seems overly reliant on Leary's own personal drug-taking experiments rather than any research into common experience or benefitting from the refinement by many practitioners over time that is offered by older traditions.

There are other systems that I suspect may have been used as ladder cosmologies, but I have not found enough evidence of this usage to allow me to fully describe them here. One of these is Yggdrasil: the Norse mythological "World Tree". Yggdrasil has nine positions, or "worlds", and each is home to different types of deities. These realms and corresponding deities might correspond to types of consciousness and the types of experiences and spirits that one might meet at each junction. So little information remains, however, about how Norse religious rituals and magic (*galdr* and *seiðr*) were done that, unless we discover more Norse writings, I must leave this tantalising idea as a mere hypothesis. It suggests something that can be tried by magicians, but not something we can be scholarly about.

Lastly, the Catholic hierarchy of angels known as "choirs", were also used to comprehend different spiritual aspects of God's creation, similar to, and possibly inspired by the sephiroth. This idea goes back at least as far as Pseudo-Dionysius the Areopagite in the fifth or sixth century in his book *De Coelesti Hierarchia* (On the Celestial Hierarchy). Angels and angel hierarchies went on to become a central part of Western magic during the Renaissance. The previously mentioned Elizabethan magician John Dee, who conjured up the British Empire, was particularly central to the continued practice of angelic magic.

The Italian Catholic scholar Marsilio Ficino summarised the angelic order thus:

- Seraphim speculate on the order and providence of God.
- Cherubim speculate on the essence and form of God.
- Thrones also speculate, though some descend to works.
- Dominions, like architects, design what the rest execute.
- Virtues execute, and move the heavens, and concur for the working of miracles as God's instruments.
- Powers watch that the order of divine governance is not interrupted, and some of them descend to human things.
- Principalities care for public affairs, nations, princes, magistrates.
- Archangels direct the divine cult and look after sacred things.
- Angels look after smaller affairs, and take charge of individuals as their guardian angels. (Ficino, 1474)

Using ladder cosmologies for magic

Both the chakras and the sephiroth, as traditions, show that there is a lot going on with human perception through the sheer variety of conscious states that they outline. Much like the spectrum of the rainbow that we traditionally divide into seven colours, perhaps the practical use doesn't come from the exact number of labels we assign so much as the importance of mapping them in the first place. If one is to pursue results that involve achieving a variety of conscious states in oneself and others, it would do well to have a map. The map is not the territory itself, but that doesn't mean that maps aren't vital for navigation.

Likewise, while it might be a fulfilling magical experiment to come up with a fresh perceptual map for one's own magical experiments, the chakras and sephiroth show us that a working cosmology of consciousness is no simple task, and might even benefit from the several centuries of refinement that both these traditions have had. The failure of so many other attempts to catch on, including Leary's Eight Circuit Path, is probably evidence for this.

Perhaps not everyone would be convinced, but to me the study of these older systems, and the complexity of their refinements over the centuries, show how far the comparatively young study of psychology needs to come in order to properly map conscious or perceptual states. There is plenty of scope in the future for scientific testing that is guided by these older systems, and perhaps this is something we will see more of down the line.

If you are taken by the idea, I would suggest learning either the chakra system or the sephiroth and seeing if it has an effect on how you go about in the world. Both have been used extensively for magical purposes. The chakra system has been used by numerous schools of yoga, for purposes ranging from stress management, to personal fulfilment, and to lucid dreaming, to spirit contact, and astral travel, and the sephiroth is foundational to many of the modern Western magical traditions that descend from it, including the Golden Dawn and Aleister Crowley's Thelema, both of which offer ample published instruction on how to make one's start with ritual magic.

CHAPTER 23

Magic and morality

In previous chapters we have examined magic as a tool for personal empowerment, but now I have a small problem. It is possible that up to this point, I might have inadvertently encouraged some very bad behaviour. Given my descriptions of magic, is there anything preventing us from using magic to lie, cheat, steal, curse our enemies, charm new lovers, deceive people out of their hard-earned cash, or otherwise behave in a self-serving manner? Is there anything inherently moral about magic?

While I have, until now, purposely been exploring magic as a morally neutral concept throughout this book, I will now discuss several reasons why I think it's a bad idea to use magic to harm or cheat people.

Our perception, as previously discussed, is a constant process. A feedback loop between what we observe in the world and how we behave. The world clearly affects our behaviour, but as I have explained with Red Toyota Corolla syndrome (the Baader-Meinhof effect), how we behave also changes the way we see the world. It is self evident that if you walk around in the world looking for enemies, you increase your chances of getting into altercations, and if you look for friends, you will make more efforts to get along with people, eventuating in more friendships.

As a junior wizard under the Wizard of New Zealand, I have spent a lot of time walking the streets engaging people on numerous topics, most of all magic. Often, my costume is mentioned and people enjoy taking photos of the old Wizard and me. When questioned about magic, I often use the costume as an example.

"Why are you in costume?" they ask.

I reply: "Everyone is in costume. My wizard costume acts as an 'open sign'. It shows people that I am available to come and talk to (or ask for photos). In my wizard costume, I 'appear'. In contrast, most people are dressed to make them blend in, or 'disappear'."

This is especially the case for people who dress to be identified as a member of a subculture. I have found these people tend to only interact with other people who are wearing similar clothes. What you wear, and how you present yourself, affects your "reality tunnel". It changes how you feel, and this affects your role and identity in the moment. It also changes how people respond to you and whether they notice you in the first place, and this, of course, changes how you feel. This all becomes a cycle of intention and interaction (Solvé et Coagula). One which can take some effort to interrupt or control.

There is no way around this: *All power wielded changes the wielder first, and those who the wielder intends to affect second.*

For this reason, it is difficult to curse another person without also becoming more paranoid yourself. In succeeding with a curse, after all, you are proving to yourself that such curses are effective, and if they are effective on someone else, then why not on you? It is difficult to carry a weapon around with you without priming yourself for a fight. The reverse is also true. Giving pleasure usually feels good. Giving a gift that is appreciated feels like its own small gift. Those who know they can hurt others have the burden of knowing that others can hurt them.

In some conceptions of karma, it is thought that what you do with your intentions now will have an impact on how well your life will go in the future. It is often thought that there is a delay between the action and the repercussions. In my mind, however, the most important and interesting repercussions are instant. One's perception becomes primed by the deed, and that in turn changes the way we see the world in terms of opportunity or threat. The spy or conman that deceives others must live in fear of being discovered. The fighter must live in fear of being defeated, whereas the attentive lover opens themselves up to being loved in return.

Do not practice magic if you are afraid of being changed, for the very first thing that will happen is that you *will* be changed. This is unavoidable. Indeed, being afraid of being changed will already change you! Instead, opening oneself up to being changed must be the initial intention behind *all* magic.

If wisdom is knowledge well applied, then I think the wizard (Anglo-Saxon for "wise one") is an appropriate archetype for one who uses magic well, and for positive change. The term "warlock" is Anglo-Saxon for "oath-breaker". Therefore, I reserve the term warlock for those who use magic to deceive for personal gain or from self-destructive urges at others' expense. In comparison, the term witch is completely neutral and serves as a good placeholder for the middle ground.

This is also why I think that magic which is directed at others is best applied directly in the open, rather than behind the safety of closed doors. A wizard ought to take responsibility for their actions. They should be able to explain their intentions, and should have self-belief enough to confidently answer to criticism. To hide behind closed doors in order to escape criticism or judgement is to attempt to practise magic without being changed oneself. Much of the power of magic becomes diluted by this self-inhibition, or worse, it becomes accidentally self-directed.

Most of the spells cast under these conditions will only affect the spell-caster. Without feedback from other people, the spell-caster risks self-delusion and solipsism. People often talk about magic as if it is a dangerous and reckless act. However, the most common thing that goes wrong in magic by far is self-delusion. The pragmatic magician must measure their prowess by the affects they can produce, not by how hard they wish it to be so.

Another issue that has been raised to me is this. If magic is to be in accordance with the will of the magician, then which will? Why not the self-destructive will? Why not the resentful will? Why not the impulsive will? This is no simple question. Many of our desires, constructive or destructive, are pre-rational, and some are subconscious. As discussed earlier in Chapter 5 with the experiments of the neuroscientist, Antonio Damasio, emotions often precede rationality, and emotional decision making is many times quicker and easier than considered, rationalised, decision making.

As I discussed in Chapter 6, Carl Jung's concept of the "shadow" discusses how we all live with unconscious wills, and that if not properly integrated, these unconscious wills can become self-destructive.

As people, we generally prefer to think of ourselves as good or well intentioned. Yet all of us have the capability of causing harm, and certainly at least on occasion, a drive to wish harm on others, even if only in the imagination.

To address our destructive drive, we seem to be presented with two options: to push the drive away and ignore it, or to seek to understand and address it. The first method will work initially, but may falter in times of stress. The human mind is perverse in the sense that asking it to ignore something often produces the opposite effect. At best, the ignored issues will be pushed into the "shadow", where they might present in unconscious ways.

These can be bad dreams, or projections that we put on others who become the scapegoats for our own inner unpleasant feelings. To address one's own destructive side takes bravery, and rarely starts as a pleasant exercise. Usually it is initially outright painful. Hopefully the outcome is a kind of peace treaty with the destructive drive, so that one neither has to suppress those thoughts, nor act upon them, but rather observe them in a detached way.

We can see this when people feel challenged. They can become stubborn, defiant, or defensive. Some popular life coaches suggest that the goal is to stop feeling at all, and become detached from one's ego. I think this can sometimes just push the problem elsewhere. A magician ought to have enough of an ego to be aware of their own desires. They should own the responsibility of making their desires manifest, or diffusing them, and be responsible for the outcome, even when it is failure or unpleasantness. Egos are a necessity. Without an ego, "I did this," there can be no responsibility.

One needs to be aware where a drive is coming from. For instance, where someone has been wronged by another, and it has caused an upset ego, then one ought to realise that to act out of revenge is to continue the destruction. A vengeful drive that is acted out in this way can easily be redirected back at the vigilante. It is better to acknowledge harm done and to act in a way so as to reduce the harm, or stop it from happening again. If the original wrong was unintentional, then calmly making the wrongdoer aware ought to be more constructive than doing an equal or greater harm in retaliation.

In magic, because the first to be changed is the magician, this is even more important. The human psyche is complex to the point where parts of it are capable of attacking each other. Putting magic into this equation can compound the complication.

If you do something negative over and over, you will keep experiencing repercussions for as many times as it takes for you to realise what is happening and change your behaviour.

If you are going to engage in magic, it is best to be very certain of what you want, to believe that it is a reasonable thing to want, and to believe that receiving it will relieve the want.

If, for instance, one lives in the tropics and is sick of feeling too hot, the answer is to move to a temperate climate, not to shift to the Antarctic, where one will start to dream about shifting back to the tropics.

I hope those of you who are already magicians, and those of you who intend to become magicians, will factor this in to your approach. Best of luck and will in your magical endeavours.

CHAPTER 24

Superstition

Hopefully I have made my point in previous chapters that magic need not be reliant on belief in order to function. Personally, I find the most interesting magic to be that which works on people regardless of what they believe to be true. Nevertheless, because it is so often brought up in the discussion of magic, and because it is a common tactic of dismissal by those who distrust the word "magic", I will now discuss superstition, its relation to belief, and how it relates to the way magic works.

Here, I will define superstition as a type of magic which requires belief to function. That is, on some level the affected party must accept that the magic has the power to affect them. As such, purely superstitious magic ought not to work on those who don't believe. This seems simple enough at first, yet the nature of belief is not so simple to pin down. It is possible to believe in something partially. Emotional or intuitive beliefs can appear in a person at the same time as opposing rational disbeliefs. People can have habits that they continue long after they have lost faith in the effectiveness of those behaviours. As I have previously outlined, most people behave in ways that don't always align with their stated beliefs.

Superstition can play strongly on this duality of belief. Warlocks, and other deceivers, can sometimes find the best targets among those who announce their disbelief the hardest, as these people often pay less attention to their emotions and intuitions. Cognitive dissonance and its ability to overload the brain can be used to make a person more suggestible, a method often used by cult leaders. Effective superstitions play on the subconscious.

Our rational mind usually has trouble controlling our emotions, and, as we have discovered in Chapter 5, the emotions are normally vital to decision making. For this reason, often the easiest way to combat a destructive superstition is to use a *benevolent* superstition. This is sometimes referred to as "apotropaic magic". Whether or not curses can function according to some kind of paranormal action, it is nevertheless clear that a huge part of their effectiveness is psychological in nature. The ability to turn parts of someone's mind against themselves is dangerous enough, even without any paranormal forces that might be at play. Therefore, psychological defences, such as benevolent superstition, can be very effective. Apotropaic magic includes such well-known examples as "touching wood", or "crossing the fingers" for protection from bad luck, and hand gestures or amulets to ward off the "evil eye". These have something in common with grounding exercises, which are in general use in psychotherapy as well as in the occult, where they are called "banishing rituals". These can serve to remove unwanted thoughts of the kind that have been associated with chattering demons and other spirits (Chapter 8). It's not clear to me why magic, or superstitious ritual, would be inferior to the thought exercises of cognitive behavioural therapy, or similar modalities. If it's "all in the mind", as mainstream counselling techniques suggest, then a good game of pretend, even a psychodrama such as an exorcism, ought to work on similar lines to a thought exercise. For bang for buck, I'd even be willing to put my money on the exorcism!

Two types of thinking

In his book *Thinking Fast and Slow* (2013), Daniel Kahneman proposes that we can classify thinking into two systems. System one is a fast, energy-efficient mode that consists of our instincts, habits, and skills. System two is a logical, calculating, and deliberative mode that engages when we try to solve more complex problems, such as learning something new.

Daniel Kahneman.

He gives the following frameworks for the two categories of thinking:

System one: Fast, automatic, frequent, emotional, stereotypic, unconscious.
Examples (in order of complexity) of things System one can do:

- Determine that an object is at a greater distance than another
- Localise the source of a specific sound
- Complete the phrase "war and ..."
- Display disgust when seeing a gruesome image
- Solve $2 + 2 = ?$
- Read text on a billboard
- Drive a car on an empty road
- Think of a good chess move (if you're a chess master)
- Understand simple sentences
- Associate the description "quiet and structured person with an eye for details" with a specific job.

System two: Slow, effortful, infrequent, logical, calculating, conscious.
Examples of things System two can do:

- Prepare yourself for the start of a sprint
- Direct your attention towards the clowns at the circus

- Direct your attention towards someone at a loud party
- Look for the woman with the grey hair
- Try to recognise a sound
- Sustain a faster than normal walking rate
- Determine the appropriateness of a particular behavior in a social setting
- Count the number of A's in a certain text
- Give someone your telephone number
- Park into a tight parking space
- Determine the price/quality ratio of two washing machines
- Determine the validity of a complex logical reasoning
- Solve 17×24.

These two categories of thinking can help explain why we are prone to certain cognitive biases, logical fallacies, and superstitions. As each system can function separately, we will often have both systems running at the same time, sometimes in a conversational manner.

For instance, if one is in minor car accident after a black cat has crossed one's path, System one might regard the cat as being responsible for the event at the same time as System two is reaching for a more logical alternative.

System one compares things with patterns that one already understands, and tends to engage heuristics (mental shortcuts). I will give two examples of these that can have an effect on superstitious thinking:

- *The Availability Heuristic:* The easier it is to recall the consequences of something, the greater we perceive these consequences to be. While this can sometimes be a beneficial mode of thinking, the ease of recalling something does not necessarily correlate to the probability of it happening. The reverse can also be true; likely risks are not always easily predicted until they have become familiar.
- *The Overconfidence Effect:* We often have undue confidence in what our mind believes it knows. People often overestimate how much they understand about the world, and underestimate the role of chance. This is related to the "certainty of hindsight". When an event is understood after it has occurred, it can create a false confidence in predicting that event again. This is especially at play with mental illnesses, such as post-traumatic stress disorder, especially when the PTSD is a result of a rare occurrence. The sufferer can end up taking great efforts to avoid the event happening again, or spend an undue

amount of time worrying in mental preparation, even when a repeat occurrence is improbable, for example being struck by lightning.

In creating a narrative for past events, we will often try to shoehorn an occurrence in the present to fit the story in order to overcome the cognitive dissonance caused by not having an explanation. This is especially potent in the case of trying to prevent bad luck, and can be the impetus for all kinds of superstitions and paranoid thinking. Once one has a story with which to order events, one's attention will often be redirected towards future events that can be made to fit that story. This can then become a belief system, such as "the law of returns", or "bad karma", or a conspiracy theory.

As discussed in Chapter 1, one's attention has a powerful effect on one's perception, and that in turn affects one's opportunities to act. This concept can also become a powerful self-fulfilling prophesy. Purposefully redirecting this tendency towards positive results, and away from negativity, is a great place to start when it comes to self-directed magic.

It might seem that the end goal of using the System one and two categorisation would be to attempt to move beyond System one type thinking and to practise more of System two type thinking. That, however would be a misunderstanding of Dr Kahneman's message, and could become a recipe for exhaustion. System one is not only unavoidable, but is also our *dominant* mode of thinking. Instead the goal ought to be to use System two to understand System one and then to have System two redirect System one towards pragmatic results. It is more efficient to doctor one's magical thinking in order to achieve one's goals than it is to try the impossible task of removing magical thinking altogether.

"We, many of us, have a sense, which I believe is erroneous, that when we have a thought that just came naturally, there is reasoning behind it" (Daniel Kahneman, 2013).

Kahneman explains a type of circular relationship between System one and two. Often we have a quick associative idea using System one, and then, because we don't question it, System two ends up endorsing that idea. Because reasoned thinking can be exhausting, System two is usually very lazy, only reasoning something if it's clear that there is something going on that would require it. Put simply, if we attribute too much value to our intuitive ideas then System two will only ever be engaged to support them. This is Kahneman's suggestion as to why superstitions are so pervasive, even if we "ought to know better".

He goes on to explain that, contrary to the popular conception that our brain forms models of reality, it is really more like a prediction machine. One that is forever separated from fully comprehending reality. This explains, in part, why we tend to only be able to see patterns that we recognise, with unfamiliar potential patterns often being "invisible", or at least disregarded (inverse Red Toyota Corolla syndrome).

Perhaps because of this, some superstitious people really are seeing something happen that other people can't, but are unable to fully explain it in terms that their more rational friends can accept.

For pragmatic magicians, System one can be purposely engaged when magical experiences are desired, and System two ought to be engaged later, when testing the truth claims of a magical idea.

The sometimes contrary nature of the two systems is not always something that needs to be fixed. As long as one is aware what is going on.

> One argument that has been made to bridge the gap between belief and action is that superstitious actions are rational strategies for hedging one's bets (Vyse, 1997). If the cost of action is cheap and the reward one seeks is great, then it may make sense to perform superstitious acts even if one does not believe that the action will have its intended outcome. (Risen, 2016)

Superstition can be a tool

Being uncertain often feels unpleasant, causing stress and sometimes cyclic thinking as one scrabbles for an unavailable answer. Superstitions engage associative thinking that can be retooled in order to create a useful fiction (Chapter 4). Because System one thinking can believe in something despite System two's protests, it is also possible for System two to purposefully create a belief to quieten System one. This can work even while System two understands the belief to be a fiction. There is scope here for using magical rituals for self-suggestion to relieve stress.

Superstition as a term is usually used to point to an unorthodox mode of thinking, from the point of view of an orthodox mode of thinking. It was used historically by the ancient Romans to point to the inadequacy of early Christian thinking, then later by Christianity to point to the inadequacy of pagan thinking, and then later still by Enlightenment thinkers to point out the inadequacy of the overly religious. As such, it is often a reference to other factors deemed unworthy, such as the foreignness of a certain culture or the differing etiquette of a lower social class. Where one comes up against people using the word "superstition" in a conversation, it is often enough to dispel their argument to point out that it is a mere dismissal. If a so-called superstition can be shown to produce controllable real-world results (pragmatism), then that ought to be enough to address the concern that it is "misguided". Otherwise, the accusation of superstition is probably in "bad faith", revealing a prejudice rather than a rational concern.

Unlike scientific results, acts of magic, including superstitions, do not have to involve rational explanations, they simply have to work. Superstitions tend to arise in people where they have to face uncertainty. Particularly the endless searching for the solution to a problem that is unsolvable due to unknown factors. Superstitions, used tactfully, can help silence this type of cyclic thinking which might otherwise cause interference or stress. This approach can have a beneficial effect, as long as one engages the superstition purposefully and within certain bounds. As soon as a credible, more rational explanation comes along, the superstition ought to be dropped. While these kinds of mind-hacks are possible, one ought not to underestimate the amount of practice it takes to wrangle System one.

Jane Risen, associate professor of behavioral science at the University of Chicago, has studied the effects of stress on our tendency towards superstition:

> Padgett and Jorgenson (1982) found that superstition was more common in Germany during periods of economic threat and Keinan (1994) demonstrated that Israelis who were living under conditions of high stress (those living in cities that suffered missile attacks during the Gulf War) reported a higher frequency of magical thinking than Israelis who were living in similar cities that had not suffered attacks. Furthermore, experiments that randomly assign participants to feel a lack of control find that they report more superstitious beliefs (Whitson & Galinsky, 2008). (Risen, 2016)

What's more, a person's irrational beliefs, likes and dislikes, can produce surprising physical effects:

Research has also shown that people are less accurate throwing darts at a picture of someone they like (e.g., a baby) than at someone they do not like (e.g., Hitler), even though the dart cannot cause harm to the actual individual and even when participants are provided financial incentives for accuracy. (Risen, 2016)

It seems that the effects of our beliefs are harder to pin down that a lot of people think!

A visitor once came to the home of Nobel Prize-winning physicist Niels Bohr and, having noticed a horseshoe hung above the entrance, asked incredulously if the professor believed horseshoes brought good luck. "No," Bohr replied, "but I am told that they bring luck even to those who do not believe in them."

While this oft-repeated anecdote may be mere folklore (no one apparently remembers the written source), it outlines a potential use case. What if Niels Bohr used his horseshoe to quiet a noisy System one belief? Perhaps the horseshoe served as a reminder to leave System one, as much as possible, at the entrance to his home so that he could get on with his physics work using System two, undisturbed by irrationalities, once inside.

This kind of "don't tempt fate" joke could work within a small effort; having the horseshoe causes a large effect: peace of mind, and more work done.

The superstition experiment

A 2010 experiment at the University of Cologne, published by the Association of Psychological Science, found that simple "good luck" superstitions can improve people's performance during tests of skill (Damisch et al., 2010).

Several experiments were conducted on university students as follows:

- Twenty-eight students were given ten attempts to putt a golf ball into a hole at a distance of one metre. Those who were told they had been given a lucky ball scored higher with a mean of 6.42 successes, than the neutral ball, which gave a mean of only 4.75.

- Fifty-one students were timed in solving a transparent puzzle cube where the player was to tilt the object in order to get small balls in place. Those who were told that the tester was "pressing their thumbs" for good luck (the German equivalent to crossing one's fingers) scored higher. Participants in the superstition-activated condition solved the task faster, with a mean of 191.5 seconds over the first control group, who scored a mean of 319.7 seconds. (A second control group scored a mean of 342.3 seconds.)
- Thirty-one students were asked to bring a lucky charm to an experiment. During the experiment, they were asked several questions about their lucky charm. Then the lucky charm was taken to a different room "to be photographed". Some of the students then had their charm returned before they were timed to find as many German words as they could from a string of letters: D, S, E, T, N, R, I, and E. The other group took the test without their lucky charm. Those who were in possession of the charm scored higher, with a mean of 45.84 words, while those who didn't have their charm scored a mean of 30.56.

The study concluded that a "good luck" superstition can have a positive effect on performance, and that this was caused by increasing the self-confidence of the participants.

Curses

If the benevolent use of a superstition can be considered a "blessing", then the malevolent use would be a "curse": that is, manipulating the beliefs of System one for the purpose of causing harm to an opponent.

Examples of this are grave curses that can be found on tombstones in many cultures, to prevent disinterment by robbers attempting to steal treasures that were buried with the dead. This was done, for example by ethnic Greeks who were among the victims in the "Armenian Genocide" by the Ottoman Turks (1915–17). These curse spells can be seen as a magical equivalent to modern trespass laws. In cultures and times where magic, as a faith-based construct, was more respected than law (another faith-based construct), curses would be used instead of, or alongside, the law.

In cases of trespass or the breaking of social morals, the criminal would be cursed by fear of supernatural punishment. This could work even in the absence of real spirits, if the accursed believed strongly that something terrible would befall them. The results would be psychosomatic illness, or a high enough level of stress to cause a mental breakdown.

If the entire community around them believed in the curse, then the accursed could be banished. That is, cut off from their home, shelter, and supply of food. In some communities with limited resources and dangerous neighbours this could be a death sentence. Note that in such cases, it didn't matter if the accursed believed in the curse, as long as it was enforced, exactly like a law, by their community. (Something which I also discussed in Chapter 9.)

As I outlined in Chapter 17, curses were sometimes the only recourse for the disadvantaged when they felt they were wronged. Such was sometimes the case for homeless people in the Middle Ages, where the fear of witchcraft was rife. When times were tough and charity was hard to come by, a disadvantaged person could use the fear of a curse in order to extort alms from the community. This, of course, was dangerous where communities were prone to punishing witches.

Breaking superstitions to dispel stress

When people have become possessed by superstitious fear, one possible approach to relieve them is through the irreverent breaking of superstition. This can be dangerous if not done thoroughly, as it can lead to reinforcing the fear, so it is best to break as many superstitions as possible at the same time, starting with many that the person *doesn't believe in*. If someone feels they have been given the evil eye, try smashing a mirror while under a ladder, in the presence of a black cat, while shouting the number thirteen and finish with being given the evil eye! Hopefully all the curses will cancel each other out, and the absurdity and accompanying laughter will lift the spirits and remove the fear. In this way, one curse is more dangerous than several, and humour and absurdity are useful tools for the pragmatic magician.

CHAPTER 25

Smart people traps

The glass bead game

The only way to learn the rules of this Game of games is to take the usual prescribed course, which requires many years; and none of the initiates could ever possibly have any interest in making these rules easier to learn.

—*The Glass Bead Game* (Hermann Hesse, 1943)

In his classic book, *The Glass Bead Game* (*Das Glasperlenspiel*, 1943), Hermann Hesse describes an institution of elite monk-like intellectuals called the Castellians. This all-male society has devoted itself entirely to playing a nearly infinitely complex game which seeks to perfectly harmonise all human wisdom, from the sciences, music, and literature, to philosophy. Set in the distant future, the Castellians are obsessed with the forgone "creative ages", which they believe will never be surpassed, so they forgo creating anything new. Instead, they dedicate themselves to analysing and connecting the ideas of the past through public ceremonial games which last for days or weeks, and in which they hope to eventually unify the pattern of all human wisdom in a perfect game. Players are trained from boyhood, and have to give up marriage,

Hermann Hesse, 1877–1962.

business, and their social positions in the outside world in order to devote their lives to the game.

The main character of the book, Joseph Knecht (German for "servant"), rises through the ranks as a promising young student, becoming a master player, and then achieving the highest office as "Magister Ludi" ("master of the game"), a similar position to that of the pope in the Catholic Church. Shortly after obtaining his office, however, Knecht suffers disillusionment due to a number of connected life experiences he has had with institutions and people in the outside world, and resigns his position. This shocks the Castellians, putting the authority of the game in question.

This book was intended by Hermann Hesse firstly to portray a Utopia to fulfil a heartfelt wish for a world of order, removed from superficiality, and secondly as a self-aggrandising critique, to purge himself of such a futile concept. A perfect order is something that has been sought by intellectuals throughout our history, from Pythagoras to the alchemists such as Isaac Newton and the early physicists, and it is something that has, despite its allure, never been achieved.

The history of magic is also especially full of individuals, and societies, who have attempted to discover such a perfect order, as well as sly charlatans who exploit the promise of a "key to all wisdom" to such dreamers. For this reason I have coined the term, "*Smart People Traps*".

As Smart Person Traps often utilise jargon as one of their many snares, let's refer to them from now on as *SPTs*.

SPTs are a type of spell that may involve debates, games, pranks, conspiracy theories, self-improvement schemes, academic departments, hobby groups, and subcultures that trap intelligent people, first by appealing to them as a special elite group, then by being endlessly fascinating, amusing, or simply obtuse, all *without providing any real-world practical value.*

The snare of fascination

A good SPT needs to take advantage of the very intelligence that normally immunises the smart person against regular tricks or scams. Just as less intelligent people tend to prefer easier tasks, intelligent people prefer intellectually stimulating tasks. Therefore, a good SPT needs an exclusive high bar of entry.

With a higher degree of curiosity than their average IQ cohorts, smart people also tend to be contrarians. As smart people crave novelty, theories and systems that run counter to common consensus offer the richest soil for new fascinating facts and concepts.

Put simply, defending a controversial proposition is harder than defending the status quo, and therefore it provides more intellectual status to the smart person. Unlike regular people, smart people also love to have their beliefs tested, as this gives them the opportunity to "flex" their intelligence.

less smart than they are, are very often just people of average intelligence who are trying to appear smart. This is why the truly smart are so often *contrarians*.

Occasionally, particularly ironic smart people enjoy the challenge of defending a proposition that primarily attracts stupid people. An example of this is the "moon landing conspiracy". There exist on the internet and in books some very detailed defences of the idea that the 1969 moon landing was faked, despite the existence of a lot of footage, witnesses, a huge NASA infrastructure, and other evidence.

It is important to note that a smart defence of a stupid theory is not an SPT for the defender, so much as it is an SPT for anyone who takes the time to debate them!

SPTs can also appeal to the ego. A "because-I-said-so" style defence that's buried in jargon and academic parlance will, often, be taken for a proper argument, simply because people can't be bothered going to the effort of dissecting it. Smart people, being often just as lazy as everyone else, will sometimes see the jargon they recognise and mistake such an argument, like the Trojan Horse, as one from their own team.

Normally, smart people pride themselves on their special ability to debunk scams. For something to be a real SPT, the intelligence of the target must be the very liability that causes them to fall for the trap. Indeed, people of low to average intelligence are immune to Smart People Traps, and are usually repelled by them. Often they will write such things off as being "a waste of time", and while this is often a tactic to preserve their own ego in the face of something they don't understand, in the case of SPTs they are, of course, completely correct.

To spot an SPT, one needs to look for its effect. If the enormous amount of work put in, in order to participate in the trap, delivers almost no practical value, or none at all, then you have an SPT. If something looks like a trap at first, but starts to return dividends over time, then it is not an SPT. SPTs can appear in layers, and arguing about whether something is or isn't an SPT can sometimes be its own SPT.

Because the world mostly consists of average and below-average people, any pursuit that is only understandable by extremely smart people can cut those smart people off from communicating with everyone else. Even if an idea is so amazing that it could fix the world if only everyone would believe in it, it will become futile if almost everyone is not intelligent enough to understand it.

An example of this is Plato's idea of a rule of philosopher kings (from his utopian dialogue *Republic*). In order to achieve a type of government in which philosophers hold all the power, they have to expend a great deal of effort winning over regular Joes and Josephines. This would take up so much of their time, in fact, that they would effectively be reduced back down to the level of regular politicians, who must rely on unsophisticated sophistry.

The complexity bias

We seek rich, satisfying lives, and richness goes along with complexity. Our favorite songs, stories, games, and books are rich, satisfying, and complex. We need complexity even while we crave simplicity … Some complexity is desirable. When things are too simple, they are also viewed as dull and uneventful. Psychologists have demonstrated that people prefer a middle level of complexity: too simple and we are bored, too complex and we are confused. Moreover, the ideal level of complexity is a moving target, because the more expert we become at any subject, the more complexity we prefer. This holds true whether the subject is music or art, detective stories or historical novels, hobbies or movies. (Norman, 2016)

Complexity bias is a logical fallacy wherein people will frequently give more credence to a complex explanation than a simple one. It can lead people away from simpler tasks and solutions towards those that take more time and effort and have more opportunities for failure. Sometimes simpler methods with be met with incredulity: "That will never work."

This tendency was tested for a paper called "Sensible Reasoning in Two Tasks: Rule Discovery and Hypothesis Evaluation" (Farris & Revlin, 1989).

The subjects were given a set of three numbers: 2, 4, 6 and told that these conformed to a mathematical rule. They were then asked to say their own three numbers, and were told whether their guess confirmed to the rule or not. This was repeated until they either discovered the rule, or quit the game.

The subjects gave all sorts of answers, but the true answer proved very hard to guess. In the end, it was revealed that the rule was "any three numbers in ascending order". All the participants assumed that the rule must be much more complex than this, so none won the game. The problem turned out to be so hard to solve precisely, because the rule was much simpler than expected.

Donald A. Norman suggests that not only do we often expect complexity, but that we frequently get more enjoyment out of something that is complex than simple. He uses the example of coffee and tea, both of which can be as simple as a single ingredient steeped in hot water and filtered:

> Coffee and tea start off as simple beans or leaves, which must be dried or roasted, ground and infused with water to produce the end result. In principle, it should be easy to make a cup of coffee or tea. Simply let the ground beans or tea leaves [steep] in hot water for a while, then separate the grounds and tea leaves from the brew and drink. But to the coffee or tea connoisseur, the quest for the perfect taste is longstanding. What beans? What tea leaves? What temperature water and for how long? And what is the proper ratio of water to leaves or coffee?
>
> The quest for the perfect coffee or tea maker has been around as long as the drinks themselves. Tea ceremonies are particularly complex, sometimes requiring years of study to master the intricacies. For both tea and coffee, there has been a continuing battle between those who seek convenience and those who seek perfection. (Norman, 2016)

For many of us, there is real enjoyment in making simple tasks complicated.

As smart people are capable of keeping track of information at a higher degree of complexity than other people, there are certain activities, games, and discussions that only interest smart people, and I argue, many of these have little to no practical value.

So let's look at a couple of the more innocuous and amusing SPTs, before we get into the even more bizarre world of magical SPTs.

The world's most detailed computer game

One of the most overt and amusing examples of an SPT is a computer game called Dwarf Fortress. Dwarf Fortress is a simulated-world game first released in 2006, where the initial aim is to take care of a group of dwarves and build them a fortress for their needs. When loading it up one is met with a retro ASCII text layout and menus that lull one into a false sense of simplicity. Despite its ridiculously primitive graphics, the level of detail in the game is nearly indescribable.

Looking initially like a distant ancestor of Sim City, this false sense of security is first set in doubt when confronted with screen after screen and menu after menu of options, which delve into almost every conceivable detail of the generated fantasy world. Before one can construct the fortress or improve it, the player must mine for resources, which involves digging through layer upon layer of rock and soil strata. Over 200 varieties of minerals, each with its own qualities, are modelled in the game, and each of these has its own function.

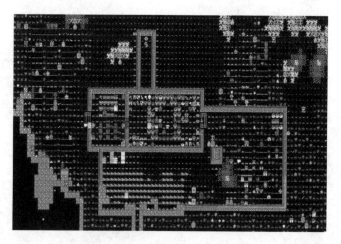

Dwarf Fortress during gameplay.

Every possible characteristic of each dwarf character is modelled, from their personal thoughts and personality traits, to their trainable skills and their ever-changing relationships with the other dwarves and creatures.

Each has its own favourite foods and drinks, all of which are highly important to the mechanics of the game. Fail to brew and deliver a variety of drinks, from mead to mushroom-wine, to each character based on their individual preferences, and the characters might just become belligerent, eventually causing a coup that can topple their dwarf society.

Combat entails detailing the very anatomy of every dwarf and the various monsters, such as goblins and dragons, that threaten the fortress. This includes not only statistics of damage to arms, legs, torso etc., but also a model of their nervous systems!

Constructing a sandwich to feed a dwarf character entails collecting or farming each ingredient individually, then processing these according to the job prescriptions of each character and assembling them in a kitchen, which the dwarves have to build from materials they have gathered in the landscape.

The dwarves get happiness bonuses if the tunnels that they mine through the many-layered earth are properly smoothed, or even etched into intricate patterns. They become grief stricken if a beloved pet or family member passes away. Random events, such as cases of dwarf vampirism, sudden stampeding elephants, or dwarf-eating carp, can put the fortress into crisis mode.

In the Reddit forum where fans can discuss the game, one player warns another, "Be careful not to get any butterflies stuck in the hinges of your front door." Apparently this small detail can cause the dwarves to become dangerously trapped inside the fortress, much like the obsessive players of Dwarf Fortress who have become addicted to the game! Much of the gameplay is recorded into history menus which can easily out-span a novel in the sheer amount of text and detail.

There is no way to win Dwarf Fortress, so most games eventually end in the destruction of the fortress. The motto of the game among the online community of players has become: "Losing is fun" (Davis, 2020; Urquhart, 2019).

Despite this complexity, nay because of it, Dwarf Fortress has become a cult classic since its inception in 2006, with more than 100,000 subscribers on its Reddit forum alone.

Even with its already staggering level of detail, the game is, at the time of the publishing of this book, still under construction! Future versions promise even more detail, such as a fully functional magic system and complex military campaigns.

As one can imagine, the learning curve for the game is immense, discouraging all but the most dedicated players, who earn no credit for their efforts outside their own small dedicated community. Perhaps the one claim to mainstream success that Dwarf Fortress has, is that it was once name-dropped as a major influence of Minecraft, one of the world's most popular computer games since its 2011 inception, and one that went on to earn its creator, Markus "Notch" Persson, millions.

Unlike many SPTs, Dwarf Fortress doesn't hide the fact that it's an enormous time-hole. It wears its complexity on its sleeve. Many people start playing it out of a sense of ironic humour and curiosity, and many of these go on to be aficionados. To quote Hermann Hesse once again, this time from his novel *Steppenwolf* (1927): "ENTRANCE NOT FOR EVERYBODY. FOR MADMEN ONLY!"

Obscurantism in academia

There are many natural scientists, and especially physicists, who continue to reject the notion that the disciplines concerned with social and cultural criticism can have anything to contribute, except perhaps peripherally, to their research. Still less are they receptive to the idea that the very foundations of their worldview must be revised or rebuilt in the light of such criticism. Rather, they cling to the dogma imposed by the long post-Enlightenment hegemony over the Western intellectual outlook, which can be summarized briefly as follows; that there exists an external world, whose properties are independent of any individual human being and indeed of humanity as a whole; that these properties are encoded in "eternal" physical laws; and that human beings can obtain reliable, albeit imperfect and tentative, knowledge of these laws by hewing to the "objective" procedures and epistemological strictures prescribed by the (so-called) scientific method. (Sokal, 1996)

So begins the controversial paper that caused the "Sokal Affair". In 1996, Alan Sokal, a disgruntled physics professor, angry about postmodern critiques of science in academia, submitted a fabricated paper arguing that quantum gravity is a mere social and linguistic construct. He undertook the stunt in order to learn if *Social Text*, an academic journal of postmodern cultural studies, would: "publish an article liberally salted with nonsense if: (a) it sounded good, and, (b) it flattered the editors' ideological preconceptions".

Sokal's parody, which was cloaked in postmodern jargon, was published in the journal, causing a huge scandal in academia and beyond.

Sokal explained his reason for the stunt as follows:

> In short, my concern over the spread of subjectivist thinking is both intellectual and political. Intellectually, the problem with such doctrines is that they are false (when not simply meaningless). There is a real world; its properties are not merely social constructions; facts and evidence do matter. What sane person would contend otherwise? And yet, much contemporary academic theorising consists precisely of attempts to blur these obvious truths—the utter absurdity of it all being concealed through obscure and pretentious language.

The Sokal paper is a benchmark for the type of nonsense that can serve as an SPT. My favourite part of the prank is that Sokal didn't bother at all to write it under a pseudonym, but used his own name and job title:

> Alan D. Sokal
> Department of Physics
> New York University

Though nearly unreadable, there are nevertheless some hilarious tongue-in-cheek nuggets in the paper, such as:

> But all this is only a first step: the fundamental goal of any emancipatory movement must be to demystify and democratize the production of scientific knowledge, to break down the artificial barriers that separate "scientists" from "the public."

One of the reasons that Sokal's paper was able to sneak in alongside "genuine" or, at least, "earnest" papers, is that academic philosophy has long been plagued by obscurantism.

Alan Sokal.

Perhaps starting as an unwillingness to simplify complex arguments, or worse, an unwillingness to be understood by the "lower classes", many philosophers make no attempt to be readable. Much like occult societies, many philosophers seek to only be read by the initiated. Those readers who do not make it all the way through such papers can then be blamed for not being smart enough to understand them. Those who can make meaning from these walls of jargon-filled text, flowery language, and neologisms often feel personally validated by the difficulty of the task. If the same arguments were presented instead in simple terms, then there would be no bragging rights and, therefore, often the less comprehensible papers and books are the most highly valued. In response to students who complained that his lectures were obscure, the Neo-Freudian postmodernist philosopher Jacques Lacan (1901–81) said in 1988:

> I can see that for today, the attention you give to straightforward
> things is somewhat wavering. We are confronted by this singular
> contradiction—I don't know if it should be called dialectical—that
> the less you understand, the better you listen. For I often say very
> difficult things to you, and see you hanging on every word, and I
> learn later that some of you didn't understand.

It seems that for every student who was willing to admit they were confused, there were many more who stayed silent in fear of being found out.

Lacan, in his 1973 seminar "Encore", said that his writings were not to be understood. Instead, they would affect a meaning in the reader, like that induced by mystical texts. As we can see, sometimes there is not much difference in effect between certain philosophy books, and the, often cryptic, tomes of the occult. Intelligent people are as much at the mercy of their pride as anyone else, and this is only more so when smart people are in competition with each other.

The Dr Fox effect

The flair and confidence with which a lecturer performs is often a better predictor of how highly their audience will rate them than the actual content of their lecture. This tendency was tested at a continuing-education conference for psychological professionals in the early 1970s at Lake Tahoe. A speaker named Dr Myron L. Fox gave a lecture entitled *Mathematical Game Theory and Its Application to Physician Education*[17] to an enrapt audience. Much like the Sokal paper, the lecture was, in fact, deliberate nonsense full of neologisms, contradictory statements, and non sequiturs. The lecturer was not the holder of a real doctorate, but a fairly prominent TV actor called Michael Fox, who had been trained to give the lecture only the day before. Despite having a role as Captain Ritter on the extremely popular TV sitcom, *Hogan's Heroes*, and a role on the Batman TV show as Inspector Basch, nobody recognised him or noticed that he was an imposter.

"Dr Fox" (actor Michael Fox).

[17] More can be read about the Dr Fox stunt at: https://weirdexperiments.com/.

In truth, the stunt was part of a psychological study in which the researchers were trying to test their hypothesis that students rated their teachers more for their personality than their command of a subject or the content of their teaching.

A speech devoid of content was created, and performed by the actor who had no prior knowledge of the subject. Michael Fox was encouraged to adopt a lively manner, convey warmth to the audience, and to intersperse the nonsense with humour.

The lecture was given three times to separate small audiences of both professionals and students. Fifty-five graduate students, psychiatrists, psychologists, and educators produced overwhelmingly positive feedback for the lecture.

The three men behind the stunt were: John E. Ware, assistant professor of medical education and health care planning at Southern Illinois School of Medicine, Donald H. Naftulin, associate professor and director of the division of continuing education in psychiatry at the University of Southern California School of Medicine, and Frank A. Donnelly, an instructor in psychology at the University of Southern California (see Naftulin et al., 1973).

Later, Naftulin revealed the satire to the surprised audience. John Ware remembers that the next morning at the conference, a physician from Oregon was showing slides of how he sets up his practice: "Someone got up and said: 'It's a fake, you are just showing us a bunch of your old home slides.' It was embarrassing because this was real."

A journalist later wrote in the *Los Angeles Times*: "There are implications in this study, though, that even its instigators have not perceived. If an actor makes a better teacher, why not a better congressman, or even a better President?" (Schneider 2011).

Ten years after the hoax, Ronald Reagan, previously an actor, was elected to the White House.

Examples from the occult

Many occult books throughout history are nearly impenetrable in their writing, or are obscure in their origins. Often, their readers revel in this mystery, which contributes to their appeal.

The very word "occult" comes from a Latin root meaning "hidden". This can refer to the hidden nature of something. For instance, many people can drive a car, though most people don't fully understand the mechanics that allow a car to work, and therefore this aspect of the car is "occult" knowledge to them. The other context of "occult", however, is that which is purposely hidden, to be revealed only through decoding, or that which contains secrets that are only revealed to the initiated.

Sometimes the occult nature of a text only comes about due to a change in context. Most of the Bible for instance, was not intended to be cryptic or occult, but the symbolism has become "occult" to most people over time, due to lost contexts. Often, the answers to these works can be found with enough study. Matthieu Pageau's book *The Language of Creation* (2018) for instance, does a great job of uncovering the original symbolism in the book of Genesis, and despite Pageau's strong intellect, is an easy read.

Many of the occult aspects of the Bible are layers built on top of the original meaning by later interpretations. Sometimes this has come about via an attempt to shoehorn biblical lore into later political or social struggles.

Other times, ancient texts were occult from the beginning; such is clearly the case with the book of Revelation. While the original reasons for encoding the messages in this writing have almost certainly disappeared with the passing of time, this doesn't stop some people from continuing to scan its pages for prophecies of things yet to come.

Another "occult" or hidden aspect in Western magic is the influence of initiatory secret societies, such as the Freemasons. Freemasonry appears to have emerged out of the medieval guild system, where its initiation and "occult" nature, as a secret society, started as a way to protect trade secrets. In other cases, such as with Renaissance alchemical texts, the cryptic nature of the writing was an attempt to avoid persecution where alchemy was forbidden by law, due not only to its incorporation of magic, deemed unchristian by Church authorities, but also due to fear that the transmutation of substances into gold might topple economies via inflation.

Despite all these more pragmatic concerns, the occult has always enjoyed a romantic mystique, and often by design. This has unfortunately allowed Enlightenment thinkers, and other detractors, who can't be bothered trying to uncover the hidden meaning of these texts, to write the whole enterprise off as superstitious nonsense or "woo".

Crowley's Book of the Law

One such figure who wore his mystery like a fashion accessory, and who was deeply influenced by both Revelation and Freemasonry was, of course, Aleister Crowley.

When I read the writings of Aleister Crowley, I always feel a strong whiff of a practical joke. Yet Crowley has numerous dedicated followers among modern magicians, including his loyal Thelemites, who practise the religion he founded. intelligentsia, and while many of these types of books seek to trap those who are not so great at critical thinking, Crowley, and especially *The Book of the Law* seem to attract an intelligent occult audience.

Aleister Crowley 1874–1947, dressed for a Golden Dawn ritual.

Never mind that Aiwass might be an in-joke for "I was", as in "I was Aleister Crowley". Crowley insisted that Aiwass was both a being of superior intelligence to human beings, and an incarnation of "The Fool" from the tarot deck; the archetypical know-nothing who nevertheless can achieve great things, being ignorant of his own limitations.

> In his absolute innocence and ignorance he (Aiwass) is The Fool; he is the Saviour, being the Son who shall trample on the crocodiles and tigers, and avenge his father Osiris. Thus we see him as the Great Fool of Celtic legend, the Pure Fool of Act I of Parsifal, and, generally speaking, the insane person whose words have always been taken for oracles. (Crowley & Marlow, 1996)

Is Aiwass the archetypical fool because we, like fools, are being duped? Or is there magical understanding hidden in the joke itself? Is it nonsense disguised as wisdom, or is it wisdom disguised as nonsense disguised as wisdom? Many have argued over Crowley's true intentions with *The Book of the Law*. Either way, he knew full well, even in the case that he was channelling a real entity, that he was messing with the reader. These questions about Crowley's intentions are unanswerable, and a lot of the book is indecipherable.

It is in *The Book of the Law* where Crowley's most famous motto is written:

"There is no law beyond 'Do what thou wilt'. Love is the law, love under will."

This became the centrepiece of his entire magical outlook, and the central motto of the religion he founded, Thelema.

> I was still obsessed by the idea that secrecy was necessary to a magical document, that publication would destroy its importance. I determined, in a mood which I can only describe as a fit of ill temper, to publish The Book of the Law, and then get rid of it for ever. (Crowley, 1909)

The Book of the Law itself is a syncretic hodge-podge of stream-of-consciousness, containing terms and names from Egyptian mythology, and some that sound Egyptian but don't appear anywhere else, either cobbled together out of parts of previous gods, or invented wholesale. While, as with all good SPTs, it contains many meaningful sounding nuggets, it's not clear to anybody what it's about exactly. Borrowing

Crowley's mystique, there are of course some occultists who claim to know what it all means, if only you become initiated into their circle.

So that you can make up your own mind, here are the opening lines:

1. Had! The manifestation of Nuit.
2. The unveiling of the company of heaven.
3. Every man and every woman is a star.
4. Every number is infinite; there is no difference.
5. Help me, o warrior lord of Thebes, in my unveiling before the Children of Men!
6. Be thou Hadit, my secret centre, my heart & my tongue!
7. Behold! It is revealed by the minister of Hoor-paar-kraat.
8. The Khabs is in the Khu, not the Khu in the Khabs.
9. Worship then the Khabs, and behold my light shed over you!
10. Let my servants be few & secret: they shall rule the many & the known.
11. These are fools that men adore; both their Gods & their men are fools.
12. Come forth, o children, under the stars, & take your fill of love!
13. I am above you and in you. My ecstasy is in yours. My joy is to see your joy.

All of this isn't to undermine Crowley's achievement of being one of the primary magicians who updated magic for the modern Western world. As an expert attention seeker, his obscurantism has only served to propel him into prominence.

Due to the Enlightenment, magic had, prior to Crowley, become denigrated as fantasy or superstition by mainstream-educated society.

Crowley remains one of the main figures who reframed magic as an act of will, the practice of altered states of consciousness and a manipulation of human psychology. This refined vision has had enormous impact, not only for future magical systems such as Chaos Magic, but also for the self-help industry which gained popularity in the 1950s, the counter culture movement of the late 1960s, and various influential cults like Scientology (whose founder, L. Ron Hubbard, was a former Thelemite). Having said all this, much of Crowley's work, *The Book of the Law* included, serves, for many readers, as a Smart Person Trap.

The Golem ritual

Although I consider much of the Kabbalah to be a genuine attempt to explain some very difficult aspects of human perception and the way reality appears to us, it is also a tradition that, due to its nearly total unwillingness to simplify anything, is a perfect hiding place for SPTs. The magical aspects of the Kabbalah frequently involve chanting Hebrew phrases and letters, all of which have an inbuilt numerology (gematria) due to the fact that the Hebrew alphabet also serves as their original number system. As you can imagine, the implications of this are that meanings of words, including their numerical values, get complicated fast.

One way to protect a magical ritual from ever being debunked is to make it too difficult to correctly perform. As pragmatists we ought to be wary of jumping through too many hoops without a reward. One such ritual that I find particularly amusing are the following Kabbalistic instructions on how to create a Golem, a clay servant that is brought to life by magical words:

> For each letter, one must go through the entire sequence of 221 (or 231) Gates. Each such sequence contains 442 letters, and therefore, in completing all 22 letters of the alphabet, one will have made use of 4862 letters. Each of these letters will have been pronounced with the five primary vowels and the four letters of the Tetragrammaton, a total of twenty pronunciations for each letter. This means that the entire exercise makes use of 97,240 pronunciations. Assuming that one can pronounce four syllables a second, it would take approximately seven hours to complete this entire process ...
>
> An initiate should not do it alone, but should always be accompanied by one or two colleagues.
>
> The Golem must be made of virgin soil, taken from a place where no man has ever dug. The soil must be kneaded with pure spring water, taken directly from the ground. If this water is placed in any kind of vessel it can no longer be used. The people making the Golem must purify themselves totally before engaging in this activity, both physically and spiritually. While making the Golem they must wear clean white vestments.
>
> These authors also stress that one must not make any mistake or error in pronunciation. They do not say what must be done if one

errs, but from other sources, it would appear at the very least, one would have to begin the array from the beginning. (Kaplan, 1997)

It's not clear that anyone has ever attempted this arduous task, but it seems that if they did and the Golem failed to come to life, it would be easy to blame the failure on making a mistake when there are 97,240 chances to get the chant wrong! Or, if not that, perhaps the failure can be blamed on using the wrong soil. Indeed, it's nearly impossible to verify that one has the correct soil that no man has ever dug! Or perhaps the ritualists failed to purify themselves, as there are no clear instructions on how one is to perfect the purification! In any case, this is hardly a spell designed with practicality in mind.

One way to create interest in a work is to surround it with a dramatic magical mystery. By the same token, a way to avoid all criticism is to obscure one's work in an impenetrable cryptic code, or ritual, that promises, much like the emperor's new clothes, to only reveal itself to the most worthy. Hopefully, this is warning enough to not get involved in magical SPTs.

The danger of becoming trapped by magic

Pragmatic magic is in the doing, not in the details. If we are to apply pragmatism correctly, it doesn't matter how much knowledge one can recite, how dense the spell book, or how flowery one's language is; a real magician must be measured by their results. In many cases, the true magic of many a spell book is not so much in its use to the practitioner as its propensity to trap a reader in a mystique that ensures a lucrative return for the publisher. I implore you to avoid such spells, unless of course you are the writer of the spell book.

How to lever a Smart Person Trap into a tool

As we read about in the first chapter, what you pay attention to determines what you can get done. As our minds are both pattern recognition systems and prediction systems, one way to get new ideas is to pump nonsense into the system. Especially the type of nonsense that appears to mean something, that you can never quite put your finger on.

This is why very creative, intelligent people can sometimes break out of a Smart Person Trap, as long as they never got that deeply into it in the first place.

Rabbi Loew and Golem by Mikoláš Aleš, 1899.

So Dwarf Fortress, an exercise in obsessive detail and ridiculously complex game mechanics, became Minecraft, a game that has had massively wide appeal, because it focused on only a few unique and valuable aspects of the original's gameplay.

Likewise, the people who did the most with the magic of Crowley and his *Book of the Law* were not those magical orders and armchair magicians who tried to decode every cryptic line, but those who took the gist of it, and applied that to art and music. David Bowie, and Jimmy Page of Led Zeppelin, were, for instance, particularly taken by Crowley and had a lot to do with his increase in popularity in the 1970s. This, in turn fed their own stardom.

Likewise, perhaps the biggest direct influence of John Dee and Edward Kelly's Enochian magic has been on horror movies and Anton Lavey's Church of Satan, none of whom appear to have understood a word of it.

This is both the beauty and the danger of a Smart Person Trap: if you are smart enough to understand it, you are too smart to use it!

With this, I bid you Adieu. Best of luck on your new magical journey. May it bear you fruit and positivity, and allow you many fascinating conversations and relationships. Hopefully with some of the people whom you now understand much better having read this book.

Ari Freeman
2021

If you would like to follow my work please join my mailing list:
http://eepurl.com/hH7wg9

Subscribe to my YouTube channel: **Pragmatic Magical Thinking**

Or send me an email: arifreeman@gmail.com

REFERENCES

Bibliography

Akrigg, G. P. V. (Ed.) (1984). *Letters of King James VI & I.* Berkeley & Los Angeles, CA: University of California.

Arrington, R. L. (1982). Advertising and behaviour control. *Journal of Business Ethics, 1*: Berlin: Reidel1, 3–12.

Atmanspacher, H. (2020). The status of exceptional experiences in the Pauli–Jung conjecture. London: Routledge. https://doi.org/10.4324/9780367855659-7

Baghel, S., & Pradhan, M. (2015). *Psychological Significance of the Chakras.* Jhansi, India: Bundelkhand University.

Bateson, G. (1972). *Steps to an Ecology of Mind: Collected Essays in Anthropology, Psychiatry, Evolution, and Epistemology.* San Francisco: Chandler.

Besant, A., & Leadbeater, C.W. (1901). *Thought-Forms.* London: The Theosophical Publishing House.

Beavan, V., Read, J., & Cartwright, C. (2011). The prevalence of voice-hearers in the general population: A literature review. *Journal of Mental Health, 20*(3): 281–292. https://doi.org/10.3109/09638237.2011.562262

Brown, D. (2007). *Tricks of the Mind.* London: Channel 4 Books.

Campbell, J. (1949). *The Hero with a Thousand Faces.* New York: Pantheon.

Campbell, J., & Moyers, W. (1988). *The Power of Myth.* New York: Doubleday.

247

Carroll, L. (1865). *Alice in Wonderland*. New York: Macmillan.

Carroll, P. J. (1987). *Liber Null & Psychonaut: An Introduction to Chaos Magic*. Newburyport, MA: Weiser (p. 164).

Cicero (55BCE). *De Oratore*.

Clarke, A. C. (1962). *Profiles of the Future: An Inquiry into the Limits of the Possible*. London.

Crowley, A. (1909). *Liber AL vel Legis, Book of the Law*. Newburyport, MA: Weiser. Reissue edition, 1987.

Crowley, A., & Marlow, L. (1996). *The Law Is for All: The authorized popular commentary of liber al vel legis sub figura Ccxx, the Book of the Law*. Los Angeles, CA: New Falcon.

Damisch, L., Stoberock, B., & Mussweiler, T. (2010). Keep your fingers crossed! *Psychological Science, 21*(7): 1014–1020. https://doi.org/10.1177/0956797610372631

Dawkins, R. (1976). *The Selfish Gene*. Oxford University Press (pp. 192, 199).

Dawkins, R. (2006). *The God Delusion*. Boston, MA: Mariner.

Donald, M. (2002). *A Mind So Rare: The Evolution of Human Consciousness*. New York: W. W. Norton (pp. 51–55).

Draper, J. W. (1874). *History of the Conflict between Religion and Science*. New York: D. Appleton (pp. vii, xi).

Farris, H. H., & Revlin, R. (1989). Sensible reasoning in two tasks: Rule discovery and hypothesis evaluation. *Memory & Cognition , 17*(2): 221–232.

Fernyhough, C. (2016). *The Voices Within: The History and Science of How We Talk to Ourselves*. London: Profile.

Feyerabend, P. (1975). *Against Method*. London: New Left Books.

Ficino, M. (1474). *De Christiana religione* (p. 119).

Galbraith, J. K. (1958). *The Affluent Society*. London: Penguin (p. 496).

Gamow, G. (1985). *Thirty Years that Shook Physics*. Mineola, NY: Dover.

Goddard, N. (2012). *Core Psychiatry (3rd edn.)*. Amsterdam, the Netherlands: Elsevier Health Sciences. https://doi.org/10.1016/B978-0-7020-3397-1.00005-7

Godden, D. R., & Badderley, A. D. (1975). Context-dependent memory in two natural environments: On land and underwater. Stirling, UK: University of Stirling.

Graiver, I. (2016). The mind besieged: Demonically-induced obsession in monastic psychology in late antiquity. In: *Muses, Mystics, Madness: The Diagnosis and Celebration of Mental Illness* (pp. 23–33). Oxford: Inter-Disciplinary Press.

Hesse, H. (1927). *Steppenwolf*. B. Creighton (Trans.). Berlin: S. Fischer.

Hesse, H. (1943). *The Glass Bead Game (Das Glasperlenspiel)*. M. Savill (Trans.). New York: Holt, Rinehart and Winston.

Ingram, H. (2007). *Jesus as a Magician and Manipulator of Spirits in the Gospels.* Birmingham, UK: University of Birmingham (Chapter 12).

James, W. (1884). What is an emotion? *Mind, 9*(34): 188–205.

James, W. (1907). *Pragmatism: A New Name for Some Old Ways of Thinking.* Mineola, NY: Dover, 1995.

Jaynes, J. (1976). *Origins of Consciousness in the Breakdown of the Bicameral Mind.* Boston, MA: Mariner (pp. 214, 323, 328).

Johnstone, K. (1979). *Impro: Improvisation and the Theatre.* London: Faber and Faber (p. 165).

Jung, C. G. (1931). *Dream Symbols of the Individuation Process: Notes of C. G. Jung's Seminars on Wolfgang Pauli's Dreams.* Princeton, NJ: Princeton University Press, (illustrated edition, 2019).

Jung, C. G. (1964). *Man and His Symbols.* New York: Doubleday.

Kahneman, D. (2013). *Thinking, Fast and Slow.* New York: Farrar, Straus and Giroux.

Kaplan, A. (1997). Sefer Yetzirah: *The Book of Creation in Theory and Practice (Revised Edition).* Newburyport, MA: Weiser.

Karant-Nunn, S. C. (1994). Neoclericalism and anticlericalism in Saxony 1555–1675. *Journal of Interdisciplinary History, 24*(4): 615–637.

King James VI and I. (1597). *Demonologie.* England.

Kramer, H. (1486). *Malleus Maleficarum.* Innsbruck, Austria: Speyer.

Lacan, J. (1988). *The Seminar of Jacques Lacan: Book II: The Ego in Freud's Theory and the Technique of Psychoanalysis.* J. Forrester (Trans.). New York: W. W. Norton, (p. 114).

Leadbeater, C. W. (1927). *The Chakras.* Wheaton, IL: Anand Gholap Theosophical Institute, 2009.

Leland, K. (2016). *Rainbow Body: A History of the Western Chakra System from Blavatsky to Brennan.* Lake Worth, FL: Ibis.

Lewis, C. S. (1952). *Mere Christianity.* New York: Macmillan.

Longden, E. (2013). Learning from the voices in my head. TED Conferences.

Marik aka Defrates, M. (2000). *Sigils, Servitors and Godforms.* Toronto, Canada: Spiral Nature.

McGaugh, J. L., & Roozendaal, B. (2012). Role of adrenal stress hormones in forming lasting memories in the brain. In: *Current Opinion in Neurobiology, 12*(2). https://doi.org/10.1016/S0959- 4388(02)00306-9 (p. 205)

Miller, R. (1987). *Bare-faced Messiah: The True Story of L. Ron Hubbard* (first American edn.). New York: Henry Holt (p. 184).

Morsella, E., & Poehlman, T. A. (2014). The inevitable contrast: Conscious vs. unconscious processes in action control. *Frontiers*: 194).

Murray, M. (1921). The witch-cult in western Europe: A study in anthropology. Oxford: Clarendon.

Naftulin, D. H., Ware Jr., J. E., & Donnelly, F. A. (1973). The Doctor Fox lecture: A paradigm of educational seduction. *Journal of Medical Education*, 48: 630–635.

Narby, J. (1999). *The Cosmic Serpent: DNA and the Origins of Knowledge*. New York: Orion (pp. 10, 12)

Nadasdy, P. (2007). The gift in the animal: The ontology of hunting and human–animal sociality. *American Ethnologist*. https://doi.org/10.1525/ae.2007.34.1.25

Norman, D. A. (2016). *Living with Complexity*. Cambridge, MA: MIT Press.

Orléan, A. (2004). What is a collective belief? In: *Cognitive Economics: An Interdisciplinary Approach*. New York. Springer. https://doi.org/10.1007/978-3-540-24708-1_12

Pageau, M. (2018). *The Language of Creation: Cosmic Symbolism in Genesis*. CreateSpace Independent Publishing Platform.

Posthumus, D. (2017). All my relatives: Exploring nineteenth-century Lakota ontology and belief. *Ethnohistory*, July: 385. https://doi.org/10.1215/00141801-3870627

Rassool, G. (2020). *Evil Eye, Jinn Possession and Mental Health Issues: An Islamic Perspective*. London: Routledge.

Risen, J. L. (2016). Believing what we do not believe: Acquiescence to superstitious beliefs and other powerful intuitions. *Psychological Review*, 123(2): 182–207.

Sacks, O. (1985). *The Man Who Mistook His Wife for a Hat*. New York: Summit.

Sacks, O. (2012). *Hallucinations*. New York: Pan Macmillan (p. 208).

Simpson, J. (1994). Margaret Murray: Who believed her, and why? *Folklore*, 105(1–2): 89–96. https://doi.org/10.1080/001558 7X.1994.9715877

Smith, M. (1978). *Jesus the Magician*. New York: Harper and Row.

Sokal, A. D. (1996). Transgressing the boundaries: Towards a transformative hermeneutics of quantum gravity. *Social Text*, 46/47: 217–252.

Stangor, C. (2011). *Principles of Social Psychology—1st International Edition*. Victoria, BC, Canada: BC Campus.

Stephens, R., Atkins, J., & Kingston, A. (2009). Swearing as a response to pain. *NeuroReport*, 20: 1056–1060. https://doi.org/10.1097/wnr.0b013e32832e64b1

Symons, J., & Calvo, P. (Eds.) (2009). *The Routledge Companion to Philosophy of Psychology*. London: Routledge/Taylor & Francis (p. 200).

Tero, A., Ito, K., Takagi, S., & Bebber, D. P. (2010). Rules for biologically inspired adaptive network design. *Science*, 327: 439. https://doi.org/10.1126/science.1177894

Tesla, N. (1919). *My Inventions: The Autobiography of Nikola Tesla*. New York: Experimenter Publishing (pp. 3, 4).

Vaihinger, H. (1911). *The Philosophy of "As If": A System of the Theoretical, Practical and Religious Fictions of Mankind. (Die Philosophie des Als Ob).* C. K. Ogden (Trans.). Leipzig, Germany: Reuther & Reichard, 1924.

Veissiere, S. (2015). *Varieties of Tulpa Experiences: The Hypnotic Nature of Human Sociality, Personhood, and Interphenomenality.* Oxford University Press (p. 7)

Vygotsky, L. (1934). *Thinking and Speech.* Cambridge, MA: MIT Press.

Wilson, R. A. (1993). *Reality Is What You Can Get Away With.* Los Angeles, CA: New Falcon.

Films

Bierman, R. (Director) (1989). *Vampires Kiss.* Hemdale Film Corporation, London.

DeGrasse Tyson, N. (Presenter), Druyan, A, & Soter, S. (Writers) (2014, March 9). *Cosmos: A Spacetime Odyssey: Episode 1: Standing Up in the Milky Way.* Cosmos Studios, Santa Fe, NM.

Fleming, S. (Director) (2010). *A Murder of Crows.* Episode 3, Season 29 of *Nature.* CBC.

Moore, A., & Vylenz, DeZ. (Directors) (2003). *The Mindscape of Alan Moore* (Documentary).

Mother Melania (2013). Excerpt from: *Battling Darkness: Hollywood & The Rise of Exorcism.* https://youtube.com/watch?v=IcOpUikRHrk

Web pages

Anon (1979, November 24). New documents show scientologists plotted to have writer jailed. *New York Times.* https://nytimes.com/1979/11/24/archives/new-documents-show-scientologists-plotted-to-have-writer-jailed.html (retrieved October 10, 2022).

Arch Wizard of New Zealand (1997). The imperial British Conservative Party. https://web.archive.org/web/20041011184706/http://www.wizard.gen.nz/Articles/IBC.html (retrieved June 15, 2022).

Brier, R. (1998). The Great Egyptians: Ramses the Great. *TLC Video.* Excerpt: https://www.youtube.com/watch?v=5YuTJlFW_f0&t=523s (retrieved January 11, 2023).

Buskirk, A. (2010, March 11). Atoms, Genes, and Other Useful Fictions. *House of Learning.* https://www.youtube.com/watch?v=TKkgM2eECnA (retrieved January 6, 2023).

Cage, N. (2012). Nicolas Cage reveals "nouveau shamanic" acting technique. https://youtube.com/watch?v=Z1JyukEGjb0 (retrieved January 6, 2023).

Davis, J. (2020). Dwarf fortress is the craziest game you've (probably) never heard of. https://ign.com/articles/2019/03/16/dwarf-fortress-steam-story (retrieved October 10, 2022).

Dennett, D. (2008). The illusion of consciousness. https://youtu.be/fjbWr3ODbAo (retrieved January 6, 2023).

Hauck, D. W. (2019). Alchemy in 3 minutes. https://youtube.com/watch?v=fOedLIGdgt0 (retrieved January 6, 2023).

Hubbard, L. R. (1967). HCO policy letter of 18 October 1967. https://xenu.net/fairgame-e.html (retrieved January 6, 2023).

Kaptchuk, Dr Ted J. (2014). What is a placebo? https://youtube.com/embed/bbu6DolnUfM?autoplay=1&rel=0 (retrieved January 6, 2023).

Kompus, K. (2017). Hearing voices: The science of auditory verbal hallucinations—*Science Weekly* podcast. *The Guardian* https://www.theguardian.com/science/audio/2017/jul/19/hearing-voices-the-science-of-auditory-verbal-hallucinations-science-weekly-podcast (retrieved January 6, 2023).

Luhrmann, T. (2017). When God talks back. Chicago Humanities Festival. https://youtube.com/watch?v=WHtOUBTsItc& (retrieved January 6, 2023).

Madigan, S. (2009). Narrative therapy with children. (retrieved January 6, 2023).

Mastin, L. (2010). The human memory. http://human-memory.net/types_short.html. (retrieved January 6, 2023).

Muhammed, T. (2008). Waswasah – causes and solutions. https://youtube.com/watch?v=TYtNezQU61w& (retrieved January 6, 2023).

Neilson, S. (2016). A mental disease by any other name. Nautilus https://nautil.us/a-mental-disease-by-any-other-name-rp-7111/(retrieved January 6, 2023).

Noë, A. (2012). You are not your brain. *big think*. https://www.youtube.com/watch?v=MoOHWHEJOLU (retrieved January 6, 2023).

Schneider, R. U. (2011). The Legendary Dr Fox Lecture – Footage Found! weirdexperiments.com. https://ruschneider.webs.com/apps/blog/entries/show/8846691-the-legendary-dr-fox-lecture-footage-found- (retrieved January 11, 2023).

Silliman, D. (2015). How a pioneer of branding invented Christian fundamentalism. https://religiondispatches.org/how-marketers-invented-old-time-religion/ (retrieved January 6, 2023).

Te Awekotuku, N., & Waimaire Nikora, L. (2003). Nga taonga o Te Urewera. https://researchcommons.waikato.ac.nz/handle/10289/784 (retrieved January 6, 2023).

Urquhart, E. (2019). The dwarves who built the road to fortnite, in praise of dwarf fortress, an ugly, impossible, beautifully weird game. https://slate.com/technology/2019/06/dwarf-fortress-fortnite-minecraft-strange-play-it.html (retrieved January 6, 2023).

Wallis, C. D. (2016). What is kundalini? https://youtube.com/watch?v=Zwzt9XtSq5Q&t=2s (retrieved January 6, 2023).

Wrightson, K. (2009). Early modern England: Politics, religion, and society under the Tudors and Stuarts. https://oyc.yale.edu/history/hist-251/lecture-14 (retrieved October 10, 2022).

INDEX